Keyboarding & Word Processing Essentials

Microsoft® Word 2010

Susie H. VanHuss, Ph.D.
Distinguished Professor Emeritus
University of South Carolina

Connie M. Forde, Ph.D.
Mississippi State University

Donna L. Woo
Cypress College, California

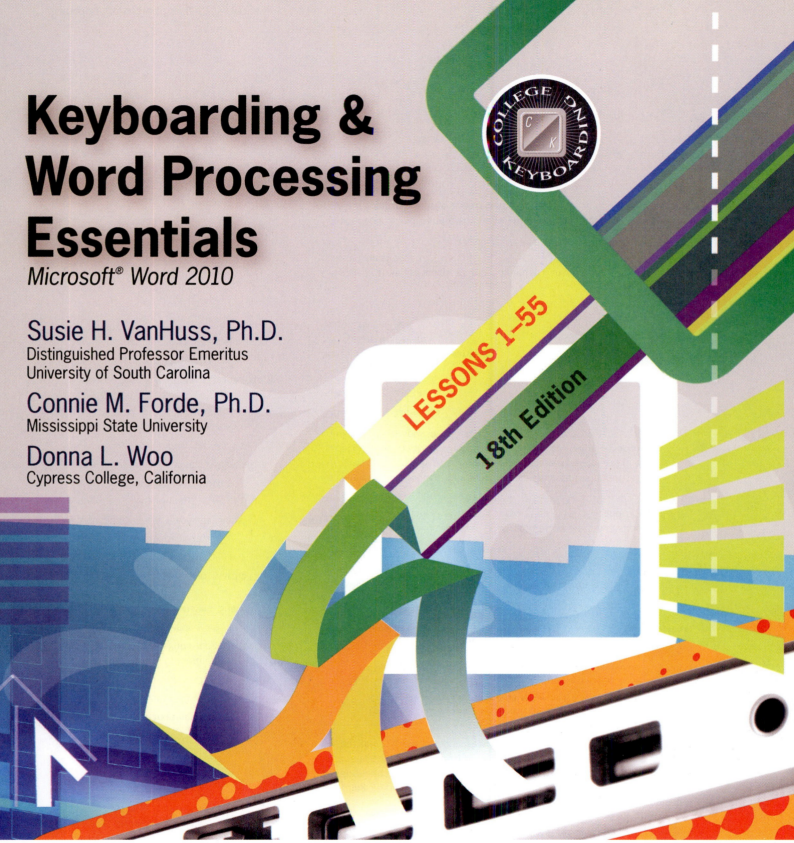

LESSONS 1-55

18th Edition

COLLEGE KEYBOARDING

SOUTH-WESTERN
CENGAGE Learning™

Australia • Brazil • Japan • Korea • Mexico • Singapore • Spain • United Kingdom • United States

D0072552

SOUTH-WESTERN
CENGAGE Learning™

**Keyboarding & Word Processing Essentials,
Lessons 1–55, Eighteenth Edition**
Susie H. VanHuss, Connie M. Forde,
Donna L. Woo

Vice President of Editorial, Business:
 Jack W. Calhoun

Vice President/Editor-in-Chief: Karen
 Schmohe

Vice President/Marketing: Bill Hendee

Sr. Acquisitions Editor: Jane Phelan

Sr. Developmental Editor: Dave Lafferty

Consulting Editors: Catherine Skintik;
 Mary Todd, Todd Publishing Services

Editorial Assistant: Conor Allen

Associate Marketing Manager: Shanna
 Shelton

Sr. Content Project Manager: Martha Conway

Sr. Media Editor: Mike Jackson

Sr. Print Buyer: Charlene Taylor

Production Service: PreMedia Global

Copyeditor: Gary Morris

Sr. Art Director: Tippy McIntosh

Internal Designer: Grannan Design, Ltd.

Cover Designer: Grannan Design, Ltd.

Cover Image: © Markus Dziable, iStock:
 © penfold, iStock; illustration, Grannan
 Design, Ltd.

Sr. Rights Specialist, Photos: Deanna Ettinger

Photo Researcher: Bill Smith Group

Sr. Rights Specialist, Text: Mardell Glinski
 Schultz

For product information and technology assistance, contact us at
Cengage Learning Customer & Sales Support, 1-800-354-9706

For permission to use material from this text or product,
submit all requests online at **www.cengage.com/permissions**
Further permissions questions can be emailed to
permissionrequest@cengage.com

Keyboarding Pro DELUXE 2 illustrations: © Cengage Learning

Key reach images: © Cengage Learning, Cengage Learning/Bill Smith
Group/Sam Kolich

Keyboard images: © Cengage Learning

Microsoft Office screen captures: © Microsoft Corporation. Microsoft is
a registered trademark of Microsoft Corporation in the U.S. and/or other
countries.

The names of all products mentioned herein are used for identification
purposes only and may be trademarks or registered trademarks of their
respective owners. South-Western disclaims any affiliation, association,
connection with, sponsorship, or endorsement by such owners.

ISBN-13: 978-0-538-49538-7

ISBN-10: 0-538-49538-3

South-Western Cengage Learning
5191 Natorp Boulevard
Mason, OH 45040
USA

Cengage Learning products are represented in Canada by
Nelson Education, Ltd.

For your course and learning solutions, visit **www.cengage.com/highered**
Visit our company website at **www.cengage.com**

Printed in the United States of America
2 3 4 5 14 13 12 11

Contents

It Keeps Getting Better

College Keyboarding solutions have a track record of ensuring success, and they just keep getting better. You can rely on the new *18th edition* to provide print and digital solutions for *Microsoft Word 2010* that work for you. **College Keyboarding 18e** builds on its time-tested tradition to train, improve, and assess proficiency in Keyboarding and Word Processing skills, ensuring classroom and workplace success.

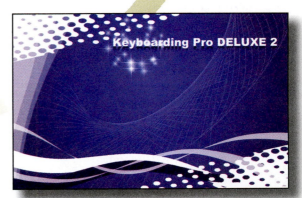

One Series: the Right Number of Lessons

Make your life easier with proven textbooks and software that have the appropriate number of lessons for today's course. Plenty of documents and a strong instructional model combine to build confidence and proficiency in keyboarding, formatting, and word processing skills. The **new 18th edition** merges the strengths of the *Essentials* series and the efficiencies of the *Certified Approach*.

Keyboarding Pro DELUXE 2: Your KEY to Success

NEW! Keyboarding Pro DELUXE 2™ now checks formats as well as keystrokes, helping you build the skills needed to create professional documents and meet the challenges of the digital workplace. It's engaging, interactive, easy to navigate, and provides motivating, instant feedback.

Web Reporter for In-Class or Online Courses

Online courses just got easier with Web Reporter. Students use their browser to send instructors assignments. Instructors can manage their classes, view documents, and utilize the gradebook with ease.

Reliable, Dependable, Easy to Use

Correct techniques, an abundance of crafted drills, and a variety of meaningful routines keep lessons fun and build skill. Both the textbook lessons and software work together to teach the new keys, reinforce proper reaches, emphasize technique, encourage accuracy, and build fluency.

Extra Practice Builds Confidence and Success

An **additional 20 lessons** that emphasize either speed or accuracy challenge you to improve at every level.

Technique Drills provide extra practice to strengthen accuracy and techniques.

Supplementary textbook drills provide reinforcement.

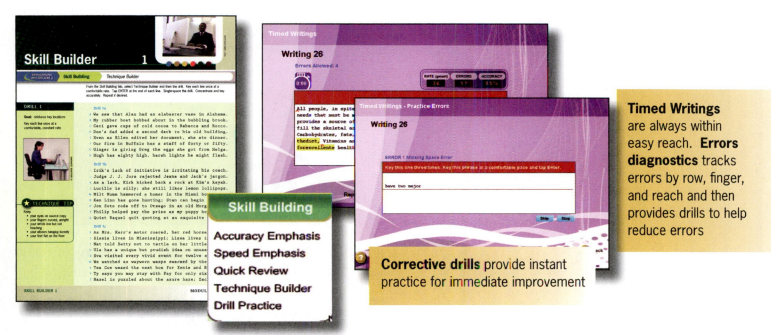

Timed Writings are always within easy reach. **Errors diagnostics** tracks errors by row, finger, and reach and then provides drills to help reduce errors

Corrective drills provide instant practice for immediate improvement

Always Fresh, Always New

The lessons are completely updated with an abundance of new documents and additional practice. *Keyboarding Pro DELUXE 2* is fully integrated with the textbook.

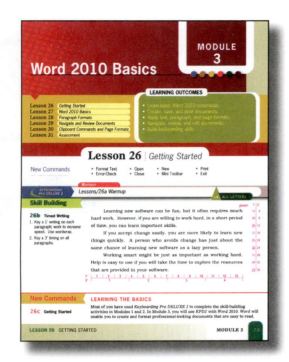

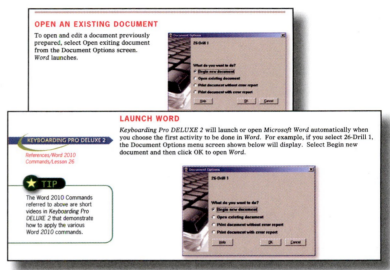

Formats Now Checked

Keyboarding Pro DELUXE 2 now checks formats and keystrokes, including commands such as fonts, alignment, spacing, merge, tables and more.

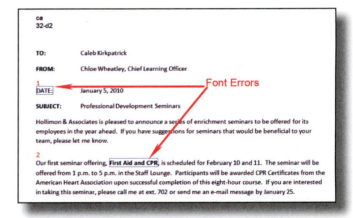

Communication Skills Integrated

Exercises apply the **communication activities** in *Keyboarding Pro DELUXE 2*

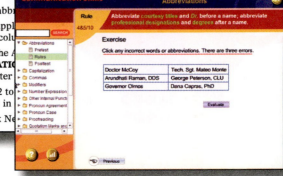

The Path to Learning Microsoft® Word 2010

Follow the highlighted **Path of the Ribbon** (Tab/Group/Command) to learn the relevant steps of new commands. Drills apply each new command; once again, apply the path.

Path introduced here - - - - - - - - →

Path reinforced here - - - - - - - - →

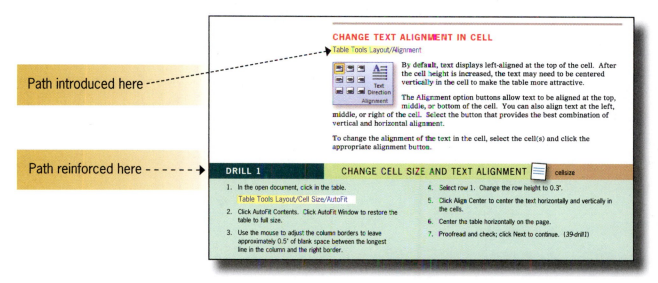

Trouble Shooting helps you along the way by providing tips on difficult portions of the lesson.

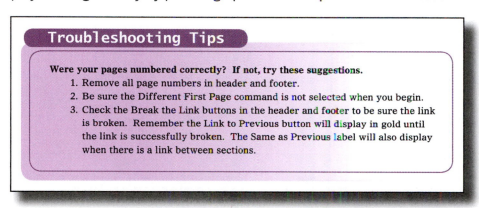

Quick Check solutions let you know you're on the right track.

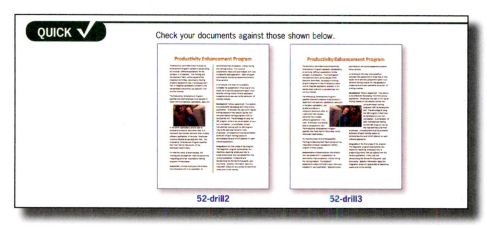

College Keyboarding 18e: It Keeps Getting Better

This comprehensive series now merges the strength of the *Formatting Essentials* series and the efficiencies of the *Certified Approach* in one series. *College Keyboarding 18e* has a new lesson structure: **Lessons 1-55** focus on keyboarding, word processing, and formatting; **Lessons 56-110** move into more advanced word processing commands and provide loads of document formatting reinforcement; the **Complete Course (Lessons 1-120)** adds 10 additional lessons with topics for certification.

Advanced Word Processing, Lessons 56-110, 18e
978-0-538-49540-0

Advanced word processing skills are the focus of this text. Ten modules emphasize memos and letters, advanced reports, mail merge, graphics, meeting documents, medical and legal documents, employment documents with advanced word processing commands. Two comprehensive projects are also included.

Keyboarding and Word Processing, Complete Course, Lessons 1-120, 18e
978-0-538-49647-6

The Complete Course adds 10 additional lessons with topics for certification.

Keyboarding Pro DELUXE 2 Student License Package
978-0-840-05335-0

Keyboarding Pro DELUXE 2 now checks document formats and fully supports Lessons 1-110.

Reviewers

SHARON BREEDING
Bluegrass Community and Technical College, Regency Campus
Lexington, KY

KAREN CARPENTER
West Georgia Technical College–
LaGrange West Campus
LaGrange, GA

MARILYNE CLEEVES
Cuesta College
San Luis Obispo, CA

WENDY CONLEY
Learey Technical Center
Tampa, FL

SHARON COOPER
Sullivan University, Louisville

ALDENE FRICKS
St. Louis Community College at
Meramec

CHRISTINE GREENE
Genesee Community College
Batavia, NY

CORA NEWMAN
Technical College of the Lowcountry
Beaufort, SC

JEANESE RILEY
Savannah Technical College

To Our Teachers and Students,

Thank you for choosing our keyboarding materials. We have designed them to make it easy to teach and learn keyboarding, formatting, and *Word 2010* skills. We hope they meet your needs and wish you much success in developing these valuable career skills.

Your College Keyboarding authors,
Susie VanHuss
Connie Forde
Donna Woo

www.collegekeyboarding.com

Technology Tools Working for You

You are about to tap into the best print and digital tools available for keyboarding and word processing instruction. Quite simply, South-Western provides **Tools that Work**, tools that have prepared thousands of students for success in school and beyond. Following is a brief discussion of the technology tools that accompany *College Keyboarding 18e, Lessons 1–55*:

- *Keyboarding Pro DELUXE 2*
- *Web Reporter*
- Website Resources

KEYBOARDING PRO DELUXE 2

Keyboarding Pro DELUXE 2 is the perfect companion for either online or in-class keyboarding instruction. This all-in-one keyboarding and document processing software will launch either *Microsoft Word 2010* or *Word 2007*; it is compatible with *Window 7, Windows Vista, or Windows XP*. *Keyboarding Pro DELUXE 2* includes 110 lessons focused on

- New key learning
- Keypad lessons and timings
- 20 extra skill building lessons for improving either speed or accuracy
- Timed Writings with error diagnostics
- Drills customized to correct the pattern of errors each student experiences

- Format and keystroke error checking
- Videos of proper keyboarding techniques, *Word 2010* commands and tutorials for using *Keyboarding Pro DELUXE 2*
- Multimedia review of communication skills, and document formats with activities

MAIN MENU

The Main menu includes the primary tabs to use the software and navigation buttons to execute common commands.

Lessons Lessons 1–25 teach the keys and build skill on the keyboard. You'll see demonstrations of correct techniques and practice at least five different types of drills that are fun and keep you motivated. Drills are keyed both from the screen and from the textbook. The number of lessons available on the Lesson Menu depends on the length of your course. A red checkmark appears after the lesson name when it is completed.

Skill Building As soon as you know the alphabetic reaches, use the 20 accuracy or speed lessons to build fluency; see the Skill Building menu below. Speed and accuracy goals are individualized; e.g., in the 1' speed building drill below, each quarter-minute goal is marked in red. Use **Technique Builder** to practice the drills found in Skill Builders 1–5 in the textbook. **Drill Practice** recommends drills to correct the errors you make most frequently on Timed Writings. Review the Error Diagnostic Report for full details.

Timed Writings Easy access to all timings is available from the Timed Writing tab as well as from the lessons. Error diagnostics tracks specific accuracy problems and then provides drills by row, by finger, or type to improve accuracy (Lesson 26 and beyond). Your 3-5 best and last 40 timings are reported on the Timed Writing Report.

References Videos reinforce the *Word 2010* commands that are presented in each lesson. **Communication Skills** reviews 16 common language arts topics; each includes a pretest, posttest, rules, examples, and exercises to check understanding. **Document Formats** illustrate and review common document formats. **Tutorials** teach you to transfer your student record and troubleshoot issues.

Keypad You will learn the numeric keypad by touch and build your skill. Timed writings build skill.

NAVIGATION

The navigation buttons at the bottom of the Main menu execute common commands:

 Help for queries about the software.

 Word Processor for creating documents; it does not launch *Word 2010*.

 Send File for online students to upload files to the Web Reporter for the instructor.

 Web Reporter for viewing comments online from your instructor.

 Logout for quitting the program.

CREATING YOUR STUDENT RECORD

Launch *Keyboarding Pro DELUXE 2*: From the Start menu, select Programs, then South-Western Keyboarding, and click *Keyboarding Pro DELUXE 2* or *Keyboarding Pro 6*.

Create your student record (one time only). The student record reflects your work.

1. Select **New User** from the Login screen.
2. Complete the required fields. Record your security question and answer; keep this information in a safe location.

Non-distance learning class: Select your class from the Class drop down menu. Ignore Class Code. If you are creating the student record on a **flash drive**, see the *User's Guide* for instruction. Subsequently when logging in, select your name from the Log In screen and key your password. If you do not see your name, click the Folder icon; browse to locate your student record.

Distance learning class: Leave the Class field empty. Copy and paste your **Class Code** to the Class Code field.

- Locate the document provided by your instructor with the Class Code.
- Double-click the Class Code to select it. Right-click the Class Code and choose *Copy*.
- Toggle (Alt + Tab) to the New Student dialog box and paste the Class Code in the Class Code field. To paste, right-click in the Class Code field, and choose *Paste*.
- Click OK. The software will issue a **Student ID**.

If you create your student record at school, you will need to download it to your home computer. To download your student record to your home computer, click **Locate Online Student** from the Login screen and copy/paste in your Class Code and Student ID. This is a one-time process. (See *User's Manual*.) Do **not** create a second student record.

3. Transfer your student record if appropriate. See the videos under References.

- To transfer your student record to a flash drive, use the Export command.
- If you are using Web Reporter, select Yes when logging out to upload your work.

COMPLETING DOCUMENTS IN WORD 2010

Beginning in Lesson 26, you will create documents in *Word 2010.* Follow the Standard Procedures when completing documents.

Standard Procedures for *Word* Documents

1. Key and format the document following the textbook directions.

2. Proofread and verify formats. Preview for placement.

3. Check the document when you are completely satisfied. Mistakes will be counted and shown above each paragraph and errors will be highlighted. Formatting error are displayed in blue.

4. Select Display Error List for an explanation of each error.

5. Scroll to the bottom of the screen to view the report of errors, gwam, number of errors, etc. Print if directed by instructor.

6. Click NEXT to move to the next application.

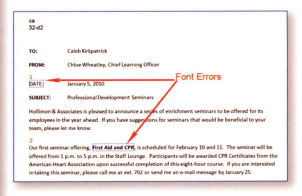

Format errors display in a blue box; errors are numbered.

When you choose a word processing activity, the Document Options dialog box displays:

Begin new document begins a new pass.

Open an existing document opens an activity so that you can can continue to work. Edits are numbered in sequential order (Edit 1, Edit 2, etc.).

Print document prints the document in *Word* format; errors are not marked.

Check existing document checks and displays results.

When selecting a word processing application from the Lesson menu, *Word* launches and the Document Toolbar displays in the upper right corner. **Back** saves the document without checking it. **Check** compares your document to the solution, reports your results, and grades the document if appropriate. NOTE: A document must be 90 percent complete or it will not be checked. When the checked document displays, the Document Toolbar changes: **Error List** identifies the type of mistakes. **Next** takes the user to the next exercise without closing *Word*.

Back Check

Error Next
List

Reports Numerous reports are available from the menu bar. Each report hyperlinks to a specific lesson or document. Instructors can view these same reports in Web Reporter or the Instructor Utility.

Reports Option Help
- Summary Lessons 1-25
- Summary Lessons 26-110
- Skill Building Report...
- Timed Writings...
- Cumulative Error Diagnostic..
- Document and Production Tests
- Performance Graphs ▸
- Grade Book

Web Reporter

Web Reporter is an easy solution for online users to send assignments to the instructor. The relationship with the Web Reporter is established when you create your student record and paste in the Class Code. For best results when using Web Reporter, use a direct connection to the web rather than a wireless connection. To use Web Reporter, you'll need to re-enter various information you added when you created your student record. Log into Web Reporter to view comments from your instructor or grades posted to the various assignments or production tests.

To access Web Reporter, enter your user name, password, security question and answer, and e-mail.

Web Resources www.collegekeyboarding.com

The website has several resources to enrich your experience, give you immediate feedback, and help you master the word processing concepts. From the website, choose *College Keyboarding 18e*, and then *Lessons 1–55*. **Data files**, organized by module, are available for download; simply click on the link, download, and unzip the file. If you are using *Keyboarding Pro DELUXE 2*, these files will open automatically; occasionally you will be directed to insert a file, in which case you will need to access the data files. Flash cards, chapter quizzes, practice quizzes, web links, and more are also provided to increase your engagement and help you master the course. These chapter resources are also available as a *WebTutor Toolbox* for use with Blackboard, Angel, and other learning management systems.

ELECTRONIC MAIL

Electronic mail (or **e-mail**) is a message sent by one computer user to another. E-mail was originally designed as an informal, personal way of communicating. However, it is now used extensively in business. For business use, e-mail should not be casual or informal.

Business writers compose e-mail messages in two ways. First, the writer may compose the entire communication (or message) in the body of the e-mail. Second, the writer may compose a brief e-mail message and then attach electronic documents to it. Distribution of electronic documents via e-mail is a common business practice; these documents include many types of document formats, e.g., memos, letters, reports, contracts, worksheets, and presentations. It is important for the business writer to recognize the importance of attractive and acceptable formats of all documents, including e-mail messages.

Using e-mail requires an e-mail program, an e-mail address, and access to the Internet.

Address e-mail carefully. Key and check the address of the recipient, and always supply a subject line. Also, key the e-mail address of anyone who should receive a copy of the e-mail.

Format the body of an e-mail single-spaced; double-space between paragraphs. Do not indent paragraphs. Limit the use of bold, italics, and uppercase. For business use, avoid abbreviations and emoticons (e.g., BTW for *by the way* or ;- for wink).

Attach electronic documents to an e-mail message using the attachment feature of the e-mail program. The attached file can then be opened and edited by the recipient.

CREATE AN E-MAIL ACCOUNT

If you do not have an e-mail account, several companies provide free e-mail service. The following directions can be used to create a Hotmail account:

1. Use an Internet browser to go to *www.hotmail.com.*
2. If you do not have a Hotmail account, click the Sign up button and key the information to set up your e-mail account.

USE E-MAIL TO SEND A DOCUMENT

The process of sending a document via e-mail is simple. You can create, format, and edit the document in *Word*; when you are ready to send the document, use the Send Using E-mail command and choose to send the document as an attachment. Your e-mail screen opens with the *Word* file as an attachment. The receiver must have *Microsoft Word* on her computer to open your document. If the reader does not have *Word*, or if you do not want the reader to be able to edit your document, you can choose to send the attachment in PDF or XPS format. *Word* will save the document in the PDF or XPS format and then attach a copy to your e-mail.

If you save the document on a web server, such as Sky Drive, you can use the option to Send a Link. This creates an e-mail and places a link to the saved file on the web server; the recipient clicks the link to open the file.

Word provides five options for sending documents you create as an e-mail:

Send as Attachment	An e-mail message is created with a copy of the document as an attachment.
Send a Link	The document must be saved to a web server before this option becomes available. This creates an e-mail message with a link to the document.
Send as PDF	*Word* saves a PDF version of the document and then creates an e-mail with the PDF attachment.
Send as XPS	Saves an XPS version of the document and then creates an e-mail with the XPS attachment. (XPS format is similar to PDF but not as widely used.)
Send as Internet Fax	You must subscribe to an Internet fax service before using this option. *Word* sends the document to that service for faxing.

To use e-mail to send a document:

File/Save & Send/Send Using E-mail

1. Key the document and save it.
2. Follow the path to display options for sending the e-mail, such as Send as Attachment. Select one of the options.
3. Your e-mail program opens a new message, with the document name listed as an attachment and also in the Subject line. If you selected the Send a Link option, the link is displayed in the e-mail message box.
4. Key the address of the person to whom you are sending the e-mail; key your message.
5. Send the e-mail.

Know Your Computer

The numbered parts are found on most computers. The location of some parts will vary.

1. **CPU (Central Processing Unit):** Internal operating unit or "brain" of computer.

2. **CD-ROM drive:** Reads data from and writes data to a CD or DVD.

3. **Monitor:** Displays text and graphics on a screen.

4. **Mouse:** Used to input commands.

5. **Keyboard:** An arrangement of letter, figure, symbol, control, function, and editing keys and a numeric keypad.

KEYBOARD ARRANGEMENT

PHOTOS © 2010 SHUTTERSTOCK.COM. BY PERMISSION.

1. **Alphanumeric keys:** Letters, numbers, and symbols.

2. **Numeric keypad:** Keys at the right side of the keyboard used to enter numeric copy and perform calculations.

3. **Function (F) keys:** Used to execute commands, sometimes with other keys. Commands vary with software.

4. **Arrow keys:** Move insertion point up, down, left, or right.

5. **ESC (Escape):** Closes a software menu or dialog box.

6. **TAB:** Moves the insertion point to a preset position.

7. **CAPS LOCK:** Used to make all capital letters.

8. **SHIFT:** Makes capital letters and symbols shown at tops of number keys.

9. **CTRL (Control):** With other key(s), executes commands. Commands may vary with software.

10. **ALT (Alternate):** With other key(s), executes commands. Commands may vary with software.

11. **Space Bar:** Inserts a space in text.

12. **ENTER (return):** Moves insertion point to margin and down to next line. Also used to execute commands.

13. **DELETE:** Removes text to the right of insertion point.

14. **NUM LOCK:** Activates/deactivates numeric keypad.

15. **INSERT:** Activates insert or typeover.

16. **BACKSPACE:** Deletes text to the left of insertion point.

DEVELOPING KEYBOARDING SKILL

Learning Outcomes

Keyboarding

+ To key the alphabetic and numeric keys by touch.

+ To develop good keyboarding techniques.

+ To key fluently—at least 25 words per minute.

+ To develop reasonable accuracy.

Communication Skills

+ To develop proofreading skills.

+ To apply proofreaders' marks and revise text.

Document 6
Letter

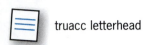 truacc letterhead

1. Key the following transmittal letter for the report to **Ms. Sakakibara**, beginning at approximately 2.5". Supply all necessary letter parts. She provided TruAcc with her business card for contact information at the Midlands Business Partnership.

2. Copy **Mr. Esteban Pinango, Chair of the Board**.

3. Proofread and check; click Next to continue. *(project1-d6)*

> **MIDLANDS BUSINESS PARTNERSHIP**
>
> **MACKENZIE J. SAKAKIBARA**
> **President and CEO**
> 2678 Elmwood Avenue Columbia, SC 29204-1259
> *Telephone* 803-555-0143 *E-mail* mjsakakibara@mbp

The attached report contains our analysis of the Midlands Business Partnership's last annual report and our recommendations for preparing the report for this year. We noted the many strengths of the last report and ways to build on those strengths in this year's report.

A complete summary of the data we collected and our detailed analysis of that data are stored electronically, and we will e-mail the files to you. We think you will be especially pleased to see the comments made in the focus groups. If you have any questions after you review the report and the backup data, please let us know.

Ms. Sakakibara, we thoroughly enjoyed working on this project with you. We would be very happy to prepare a proposal to assist you in preparing next year's annual report if you would like us to do so.

Document 7
Style Guide

1. Review each of the documents you have prepared. Ensure that you have used *Module* document theme and followed all of the standard operating procedures listed at the beginning of Project 1. Preview and proofread each. Print a copy of the documents listed in step 4 below.

2. Prepare a cover sheet using the *Mod* style and use the title **Style Guide** and the subtitle **Model Documents**.

3. Use your name and the current date.

4. For the abstract, key the following:

   This Style Guide includes the following documents: Letters, Memo, Invitation, Table, and Report with Cover Page.

5. Assemble the documents behind the cover page.

6. Check and close. *(project1-d7)*

WARMUP

Warmup

1. Open *Keyboarding Pro*.
2. Go to the Word Processor by clicking the .
3. Key each line twice. Tap ENTER after each group of lines.
4. Close the document by clicking in the upper-right corner.

alphabet 1 Max quietly promised a very big gift for the jazz club next week.
2 Zack worked on five great projects and quickly became the expert.
3 Jack Meyer analyzed the data by answering five complex questions.

figures 4 The invoice dated 9/28/11 was for $17,493.56; it is due 10/24/11.
5 Our dinner on 6/25/11 cost $432.97 plus 18% tip totaling $510.90.
6 The 3 invoices (#49875, #52604, and #137986) totaled $379,912.46.

easy 7 Pam may go with me to town to work for the auditor if he is busy.
8 Jan and six girls may go to the lake to sit on the dock and fish.
9 My neighbor may tutor the eight girls on the theory and problems.

LA **ALL LETTERS**

Timed Writing

1. From the main screen, click the Timed Writings tab.

Timed Writings

2. Choose 3' as the length. Choose *pretest* from the list of writings.
3. Tap TAB to begin. Key from the textbook.
4. Repeat the timing for 3'.
5. Your results will be displayed in the Timed Writing Report, which is available on the menu bar.

	gwam	1'	3'
Most businesses want to be seen as good citizens. Working with		13	4
the arts is one way in which they can give back to the community		26	9
in which they operate. It is easy to support the arts because most		39	13
people believe that a vibrant arts program is key to the quality of		53	18
life for local citizens. Quality of life is a major factor in recruiting		68	23
new employees.		71	24
Most art groups are nonprofits that provide tax benefits to those		13	28
who give to them. A business may give money, services, or products,		27	33
or it may sponsor an event. Sponsoring an event is not the same		40	37
as making a gift. The business receives a public relations benefit		54	42
by having its name linked with the event, whereas a gift may have		67	46
no obvious benefit. Both forms help the arts.		76	49
A business may also support the arts by buying and displaying		13	53
art in its facilities. Some choose to use the art of local artists, while		27	58
others buy high-quality art from well-known artists. The former		40	63
helps to build a good local art community. The latter may bring		53	67
recognition to the business for the quality of its artwork.		66	71

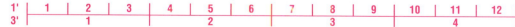

7. Below the last paragraph of the report, insert a Process Arrows SmartArt diagram.

8. Delete the third arrow; you will only use two arrows in this diagram.

9. Key the following information in the shapes:

10. Insert the *Mod* cover page. Key the report title from Document 5 and **Midlands Business Parternership** as the subtitle. Replace the author name near the bottom of the page with **Mark C. Hartman**. Insert the current date in the date field.

11. Key the following abstract:

This report summarizes the objectives, methodology, analysis, conclusions, and recommendations for strengthening the Annual Report of the Midlands Business Partnership.

12. Insert a Continuous section break at the top of the first page of the report.

13. Click in the Header and deselect Different First Page if it is selected. Break the links between the headers for both sections. Go to the footer of Section 2. Break the link between the footers for both sections.

14. Change the page number format to begin with page 1 by going to the footer of Page 1 and clicking Page Number, then Format Page Numbers. Change Starting at to 1. Click Different First Page to suppress the page numbers on the first page of the report. Close the header and footer.

15. Proofread and check; click Next to continue. (*project1-d5*)

Alphabetic Keys

LEARNING OUTCOMES

| Lessons 1–10 | Alphabetic and Basic Punctuation Keys |
| Lessons 11–13 | Review |

- Key the alphabetic keys by touch.
- Key using proper techniques.
- Key at a rate of 14 *gwam* or more.

Lesson 1 | Home Row, Space Bar, Enter, I

1a Home-Row Position and Space Bar

1. *Open Keyboarding Pro* and create your student record.
2. Go to the Word Processor. (The **WP** will appear next to exercises keyed in the Word Processor in Lessons 1–25.)
3. Practice the steps at the right until you can place your hands in home-row position without watching.
4. Key the drills at the bottom of the page several times.
5. Continue to the next page; keep the document on your screen.

HOME-ROW POSITION

1. Drop your hands to your side. Allow your fingers to curve naturally. Maintain this curve as you key.
2. Lightly place your left fingers over the **a s d f** and the right fingers over the **j k l ;**. You will feel a raised element on the *f* and *j* keys, which will help you keep your fingers on the home position. You are now in **home-row position**.

© CENGAGE LEARNING

SPACE BAR AND ENTER

Tap the Space Bar, located at the bottom of the keyboard, with a down-and-in motion of the right thumb to space between words.

Enter Reach with the fourth (little) finger of the right hand to ENTER. Tap it to return the insertion point to the left margin. This action creates a **hard return**. Use a hard return at the end of all drill lines. Quickly return to home position (over ;).

© CENGAGE LEARNING

© CENGAGE LEARNING

Key these lines

a s d f **SPACE** j k l ; **ENTER**
a s d f **SPACE** j k l ; **ENTER**

Document 5
Report with SmartArt Diagram

annual report analysis

1. Note that the report does not conform to the standard operating procedures of TruAcc, Inc.; revise it so that it does.

2. Shrink the title font to fit on one line; apply Heading 2 to second-level headings.

3. Add the initials *mbp* to AutoCorrect and replace with *Midlands Business Partnership* to simplify your work with this client.

4. Find all occurrences of text formatted in italic and replace it with regular text.

5. Insert the footer *Mod Odd Page*. Suppress the footer on the first page.

6. Revise the sections of the report shown below.

~~Information~~ Data Collected for Report Analysis

Several methods of data collection were used. Leaders of the organization were interviewed to determine the objectives they sought to achieve. Public relations and communication professionals employed by TruAcc, Inc. analyzed the last annual report in depth. Consultants conducted ~~three~~ two focus groups: one with stakeholders and one with business community representatives to get their impressions of the last report and ideas of what they would like to see in future reports.

Desired Objectives

The ~~clear~~ consensus of the leaders of the Midlands Business Partnership about the objectives was that the report was designed for ~~three~~ two purposes:

1. To provide stakeholders with information about the accomplishments as well as accurate financial data.

2. To serve as a PR *(write out)* tool with stakeholders, the business community, and the public in general.

Add the following paragraph at the end of the report:

Implementing these recommendations would retain the strengths of the previous report and would improve the areas that were not as effective as they could be. These changes would enhance the public relations aspect of the report significantly.

New Keys

1b Procedures for Learning New Keys

Apply these steps each time you learn a new key.

1. Find the new key on the illustrated keyboard. Then find it on your keyboard.
2. Watch your finger make the reach to the new key a few times. Keep other fingers curved in home position. For an upward reach, straighten the finger slightly; for a downward reach, curve the finger a bit more.
3. Repeat the drill until you can key it fluently.

1c Home Row

1. The Word Processor should be open.
2. Key lines 1–9 once. Tap ENTER once at the end of each line and twice to double-space (DS) between 2-line groups.
3. Keep the document on your screen.

Left Fingers   Right Fingers

Tap Space Bar once.

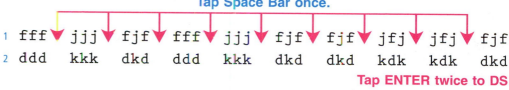

```
1  fff  jjj  fjf  fff  jjj  fjf  fjf  jfj  jfj  fjf
2  ddd  kkk  dkd  ddd  kkk  dkd  dkd  kdk  kdk  dkd
```
Tap ENTER twice to DS
```
3  sss  lll  sls  sss  lll  sls  sls  lsl  lsl  sls
4  aaa  ;;;  a;a  aaa  ;;;  a;s  a;a  ;a;  ;a;  a;a
```
DS
```
5  ff  jj  ff  jj  fj  fj  fj  dd  kk  dd  kk  dk  dk  dk
6  ss  ll  ss  ll  sl  sl  sl  aa  ;;  aa  ;;  a;  a;  a;
```
DS
```
7  f  j  d  k  s  l  a  ;
8  ff  jj  dd  kk  ss  ll  aa  ;;
9  fff  jjj  ddd  kkk  sss  lll  aaa  jjj  ;;;
```

1d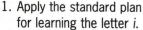

1. Apply the standard plan for learning the letter *i*.
2. Key lines 10–12 in the Word Processor. Keep fingers curved. Repeat until you can key it fluently.
3. Click ⊗ in the upper-right corner of your screen to exit the Word Processor. You will be at the Main menu of *Keyboarding Pro*.

© CENGAGE LEARNING

```
10  i  ik  ik  ik  is  is  id  id  if  if  ill  i  ail  did  kid  lid
11  i  ik  aid  ail  did  kid  lid  lids  kids  ill  aid  did  ilk
12  id  aid  aids  laid  said  ids  lid  skids  kiss  disk  dial
```

Document 3
Draft Invitation

 miguel logo

 invitation

Sarah created a draft invitation and saved it as *invitation* in the data files. Format the invitation as follows:

1. Center-align each line except the *rsvp*, which should be left-aligned.

2. Use a decorative font such as Lucida Calligraphy or Harlow Solid Italic; apply 16-point dark red color; use 2.5 line spacing.

3. Apply the Remove Space After Paragraph command on each line and change orientation to landscape.

4. Use the Insert Picture command to insert the company logo, *miguel logo*, at the top of the invitation. Change the size of the logo to 1" and center it horizontally. Center the invitation vertically on the page.

5. Proofread and check; click Next to continue. (*project1-d3*)

Document 4
Table

 TIP

Center the table horizontally by clicking the Table Move handle to select the table, and then click the Center button.

1. Key the table below. Center-align colum B and right-align column C.

2. Add a column between columns B and C and key the following data: **Unit Cost, $24.50, 65.75, 250.00, 4.25**, and **65.75**. Center the column head and right-align the numbers.

3. Insert a row above the column heads. Merge all cells in the row. Set the row height at 0.5". Key the table title **Pre-Grand Opening Celebration Budget** in 16-point font and bold. Center-align the text vertically and horizontally.

4. Apply Medium Grid 3 – Accent 1 design (same color as document theme). Reapply bold to first row if necessary.

5. Change the row height of rows 2–8 to 0.3". Center the text vertically in the cells.

6. Adjust column widths and center the table horizontally on the page.

7. Proofread and check; click Next to continue. (*project1-d4*)

Description	Quantity/Number	Estimated Cost
Food and beverage	120	$2,940.00
Floral arrangements	4	263.00
Decorations	1	250.00
Party favors	125	531.25
Invitations/mailing	1	65.75
Total Cost		$4,050.00

1e Lesson 1 from Software

Read the information at the right. Then do Lesson 1 from *Keyboarding Pro*.

STANDARD PLAN — for Using *Keyboarding Pro*

1. Select the Lessons tab. Select a lesson from the drop-down list or key the lesson number (Figure 1-1).

2. The first activity is displayed automatically. Follow the directions on screen. Key from the screen. The software will move automatically to the next activity.

Figure 1-1 Lesson Menu

Active Exercise →

← Activity tabs

Figure 1-2 Lesson 1: Learn Home Row and i

3. Key the Textbook Keying activity from the textbook (lines 13–18 below). Click the Stop button to end the activity.

4. Figure 1-3 shows the Lesson Report. A check mark next to the exercise indicates that it is completed.

5. You may print your Lesson Report and view the Performance Graph.

6. From the Main menu, select the Logout button to quit the program. You may choose to transfer your file to another location or send your student record to the Web Reporter.

1f Textbook Keying

1. Key each line once; do not key the numbers. Tap ENTER at the end of each line. Keep your eyes on the book.

2. Click the Stop button to end the activity.

```
13  a  a;  al  ak  aj  s  s;  sl  sk  sj  d  d;  dl  dk  dj
14  j  ja  js  jd  jf  k  ka  ks  kd  kf  l  la  ls  ld  lf
15  a;   sl  a;sl   dkfj   a;sl   dkfj   a;sldkfj  asdf   jk
16  a;   sl  a;sl   dk  fj  dkfj   a;sl   dkfj  fkds;a;   fj
17  f  ff  j  jj  d  dd  k  kk  s  ss  l  ll  a  aa  ;  ;;  fj
18  afj;  a  s  d  f  j  k  l  ;  asdf  jkl;  fdsa  jkl;
```

1g End the Lesson

1. Follow steps 5 and 6 above to print the Lesson Report, send your files to the Web Reporter, and exit the software.

2. Clean up your work area.

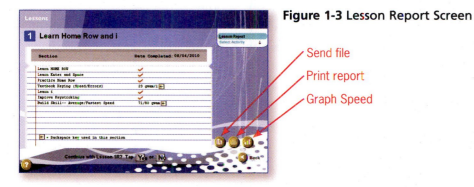

Figure 1-3 Lesson Report Screen

Send file
Print report
Graph Speed

Document 1
Letter

 miguel enterprises

 truacc letterhead

1. Print the data file *miguel enterprises*; this contains the copy and directions for keying the letter.
2. Key the letter beginning at 2.5". Supply all necessary letter parts.
3. Proofread and check; click Next to continue. (*project1-d1*)

Document 2
Memo

 truacc memo

1. Prepare the following memo:
   - Use the information provided below to complete the heading on the memo.
   - Use Find and Replace to locate all instances of *contract* and replace it with *agreement*.
2. Proofread and check; click Next to continue. (*project1-d2*)

To: Senior Executives—Distribution Below | Subject: Miguel Contract

Miguel Enterprises accepted the TruAcc, Inc. proposal to manage the grand opening and marketing of the new Miguel Emporium. Elena Miguel called me today to indicate that she had signed the contract without any modifications whatsoever, and she was having it hand delivered to us today.

Ms. Miguel also requested that our senior staff, as well as the Miguel Enterprises senior account manager, meet with her next Tuesday at 10:30 a.m. in our offices. Please plan to attend this important session, which will take place in the Board Room.

Marlene Delhomme, who is no longer with us, was the account manager responsible for the last two Miguel events. Karl Metze has been assigned as the senior account manager for the Miguel account. Please work with Karl on the proposed plan that we will present at the meeting.

c   Karl Metze

Distribution:
   Haley Edwards
   Jackson Moore
   Lance Davis
   Cristina Kulchar

Lesson 1R | Review

Getting Started

1. Start *Keyboarding Pro.*
2. Select your name and key your password. Click OK.
3. Select Lesson 1R.
4. Key each exercise as directed in the software.

© CENGAGE LEARNING

Fingers curved and upright

1Ra Textbook Keying

1. Key each line once. Tap ENTER twice to double space (DS) between 2-line groups.
2. Try to keep your eyes on the book the entire time you key.
3. Tap ESC or click Stop to end the exercise.

```
1  f  j  fjf  jj  fj  fj  jf  dd  kk  dd  kk  dk  dk  dk
2  s  ;  s;s  ;;  s;  s;  s;  aa  ;;  aa  ;;  a;  a;  a;
```
Tap ENTER twice to DS.
```
3  fj  dk  sl  a;  fjdksla;  jfkdls;a  ;a  ;s  kd  j
4  f  j  fjf  d  k  dkd  s  l  sls  a  ;  fj  dk  sl  a;a
```
DS
```
5  a;  al  ak  aj  s  s;  sl  sk  sj  d  d;  dl  dk  djd
6  ja  js  jd  jf  k  ka  ks  kd  kf  l  la  ls  ld  lfl
```

Skill Building

1Rb Keyboard Review

Key these lines from the software screen as directed.

```
7   f  fa  fad  s  sa  sad  f  fa  fall  fall  l  la  lad  s  sa  sad
8   a  as  ask  a  ad  add  j  ja  jak  f  fa  fall;  ask;  add  jak
9   ik  ki  ki  ik  is  if  id  il  ij  ia  ij  ik  is  if  ji  id  ia
10  is  il  ill  sill  dill  fill  sid  lid  ail  lid  slid  jail
11  if  is  il  kid  kids  ill  kid  if  kids;  if  a  kid  is  ill
12  is  id  if  ai  aid  jaks  lid  sid  sis  did  ail;  if  lids;
13  a  lass;  ask  dad;  lads  ask  dad;  a  fall;  fall  salads
14  as  a  fad;  ask  a  lad;  a  lass;  all  add;  a  kid;  skids
15  as  asks  did  disk  ail  fail  sail  ails  jail  sill  silk
16  ask  dad;  dads  said;  is  disk;  kiss  a  lad;  salad  lid
17  aid  a  lad;  if  a  kid  is;  a  salad  lid;  kiss  sad  dads
18  as  ad  all  ask  jak  lad  fad  kids  ill  kill  fall  disks
```

1Rc End the Lesson

1. From the Main Menu, click the Logout button.
2. If instructed, click Yes to send your record to the Web Reporter.
3. If necessary, click Yes to transfer your student record to another location.
4. Exit the software; clean up your work area.

TruAcc, Inc.

LEARNING OUTCOMES

- Apply keying, formatting, and word processing skills.
- Work independently with few specific instructions.

TruAcc, Inc. (Truthful and Accurate Communications) is a public relations company. You have just been promoted to the position of executive assistant. As an executive assistant, you will prepare documents for TruAcc and two of its clients, applying the formatting and word processing skills you learned in Lessons 26–55. These documents will be used as a Style Guide for all TruAcc employees. Your predecessor, Sarah Vaughn, took an emergency leave, so you will be completing some of the documents that she was not able to finish.

Special instructions for non-*Keyboarding Pro DELUXE 2* users:

Set up a folder named *TruAcc, Inc. Style Guide*. Save each document in this folder as *project1-+document number (project1-d1, project1-d2, project1-d3, etc.).*

Standard operating procedures for the project:

- TruAcc has selected *Module* as the document theme for all communications. *Module* uses *Corbel* heading and body fonts as well as the selected colors for this document theme. Key each document using this theme.

- Unless otherwise instructed, all documents are from Mark C. Hartman, President. Position the title on two lines; do not use a title on internal communications.

- Use data files when they are indicated below the document name.

- Use block letter format with open punctuation and the TruAcc, Inc. letterhead from the data files. Use appropriate opening and closing lines. Key the date at approximately 2.5".

- The data files also contain a TruAcc, Inc. memo form. Use appropriate subject lines if a subject line is not provided.

- TruAcc uses an unbound report format, *Module* theme title and headings, and bullets 114 (❏) on the Wingdings font (row 6 column 3). It also uses the *Mod* cover page with the *Module* document theme.

- Use the date command to add the current date to each document requiring a date.

- Add your reference initials, enclosure notations, and copy notations as appropriate.

- Proofread and check; when you are satisfied with the document, click Next to continue.

★ TIP

Read the standard operating procedures for the project carefully. You will not be reminded to do these steps. Refer to them as needed during the project.

Lesson 2 | E and N

1. Open *Keyboarding Pro.*
2. Locate your student record.
3. Select Lesson 2.

```
1  ff dd ss aa ff dd ss aa jj kk ll ;; fj dk sl a; a;
2  fj dk sl a; fjdksla; a;sldkfj fj dk sl a; fjdksla;
3  aa ss dd ff jj kk ll ;; aa ss dd ff jj kk ll ;; a;
4  if a; as is; kids did; ask a sad lad; if a lass is
```

New Keys

2b E and N

Key each line once; DS between groups.

e Reach *up* with *left second* finger.

n Reach *down* with *right first* finger.

```
e
5  e ed ed led led lea lea ale ale elf elf eke eke ed
6  e el el eel els elk elk lea leak ale kale led jell
7  e ale kale lea leak fee feel lea lead elf self eke

n
8  n nj nj an an and and fan fan and kin din fin land
9  n an fan in fin and land sand din fans sank an sin
10 n in ink sink inn kin skin an and land in din dink

all reaches learned
11 den end fen ken dean dens ales fend fens keen knee
12 if in need; feel ill; as an end; a lad and a lass;
13 and sand; a keen idea; as a sail sank; is in jail;
14 an idea; an end; a lake; a nail; a jade; a dean is
```

2c Textbook Keying
Key each line once; DS between groups.

TECHNIQUE TIP

Keep your eyes on the textbook copy.

```
15 if a lad;
16 is a sad fall
17 if a lass did ask
18 ask a lass; ask a lad
               DS
19 a;sldkfj a;sldkfj a;sldkfj
20 a; sl dk fj fj dk sl a; a;sldkfj
               DS
21 i ik ik if if is is kid skid did lid aid laid said
22 ik kid ail die fie did lie ill ilk silk skill skid
```

Tap ENTER twice to DS

> Reach with little finger; tap Enter key quickly; return finger to home key.

All three sites met the size criteria and are within the cost projections of the Planning Commission. The ~~chart on the next page shows~~ *table shown below details* the comparative costs of the sites when both land and the estimated cost of the infrastructure ~~is~~ *are* considered. *The infrastructure cost estimates for all sites were prepared by J. M. Moore Engineering.*

Site Costs	*center*		
Cost Category	Westlake *center*	Southside *center*	Woodcreek *center*
Land	$2~~7~~**9**0,000	$630,000	$676,000
Infrastructure	175,000	210,000	180,000
Total	$80~~5~~**9**,000	$840**,**000	$856,000

left-align 1st column

Right-align columns with numbers

Other Factors

In addition to the quantitative analysis of the three sites for the theme park, the Committee also did a qualitative analysis of the sites. The Committee *unanimously* agreed that the Southside site was the least desirable from both an access and an aesthetic perspective. Both Westlake and Woodcreek were accessible and desirable. Westlake was given the advantage because of the pond situated on the property. Therefore, the Committee unanimously recommends that the new park be located on the Westlake site.

QUICK ✓

Check your document against the illustrations below.

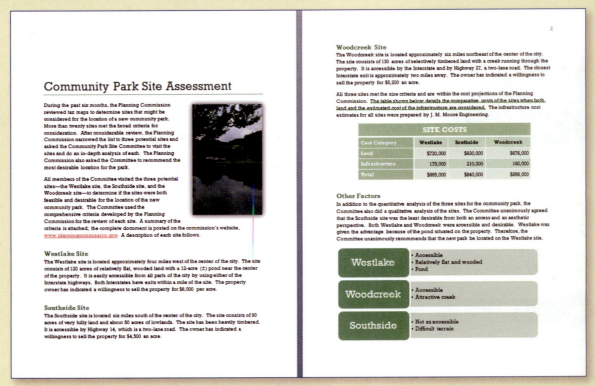

55-d4

Skill Building

2d Reinforcement

Key each line once; concentrate on what you are keying.

23 ik ik ik if is il ik id is if kid did lid aid ails
24 did lid aid; add a line; aid kids; ill kids; id is

n

25 nj nj nj an an and and end den ken in ink sin skin
26 jn din sand land nail sank and dank skin sans sink

e

27 el els elf elk lea lead fee feel sea seal ell jell
28 el eke ale jak lake elf els jaks kale eke els lake

all reaches

29 dine in an inn; fake jade; lend fans; as sand sank
30 in nine inns; if an end; need an idea; seek a fee;
31 if a lad; a jail; is silk; is ill; a dais; did aid
32 adds a line; and safe; asks a lass; sail in a lake

2e End the Lesson

1. If appropriate, send your student record to the Web Reporter.
2. Exit the software; clean up your work area.

© ULTRA.F/JUPITERIMAGES

! WORKPLACE SUCCESS

Keyboarding: The Survival Skill

Keyboarding is a valuable and necessary skill for everyone in this technological world. It is an expected tool for effective communication throughout one's life.

Students who resort to "hunting and pecking" to key their school assignments are constantly searching for the correct letter on the keyboard. Frustration abounds for students who wish to key their research report into the computer, but do not have the touch keyboarding skills required to accomplish the task quickly and proficiently. Students who can key by touch are much more relaxed because they can keep their eyes on the screen and concentrate on text editing and composing.

Some people claim that voice-activated computers will replace the need for keyboarding. Voice activation currently works best in conjunction with keyboarding. The first draft of a document can be inputted using voice; the draft is then edited using the keyboard. Together, this process can greatly speed work performance.

Community Park

~~Report of the~~ Site Assessment

During the past six months, the planning commission reviewed tax maps to determine sites that might be considered for the location of a new theme park. More than 20 [twenty] sites met the broad criteria for consideration. After considerable review, the Planning Commission narrowed the list to three potential sites and asked the Theme Park Site Committee to visit the sites and do an in-depth analysis of each. The Planning Commission also asked the Committee to recommend the most desirable location for the park.

All members of the Committee visited the three potential sites ~~selected~~—the Westlake site, the Southside site, and the Woodcreek site to determine if the sites were both feasible and desirable for the location of the new theme park. The Committee used the comprehensive criteria developed by the Planning Commission for the review of each site. A ~~copy~~ summary of the ~~comprehensive~~ criteria is attached; the complete document is posted on the commission's website, www.planningcommission.gov. A description of each site follows.

Westlake Site

The Westlake site is located approximately 4 [four] miles west of the center of the city. The site consists of 120 acres of relatively flat, wooded land with a 12-acre (±) pond near the center of the property. It is easily accessible from all parts of the city by using either of the Interstate highways. Both Interstates have exits within a mile of the site. The property owner has indicated a willingness to sell the property for $6,000 per acre.

Southside Site

The Southside site is located 6 [six] miles south of the center of the city. The site consists of 90 acres of very hilly land and about 50 acres of lowlands. The site has been heavily timbered. It is accessible by Highway 14, which is a two-lane road. The owner has indicated a willingness to sell the property for $4,500 an acre.

Woodcreek Site

The Woodcreek site is located approximately 6 [six] miles northeast of the center of the city. The site consists of 130 acres of selectively timbered land with a creek running through the property. It is accessible by the Interstate and by Highway 27, a two-lane road. The closest Interstate exit is approximately 2 [two] miles away. The owner has indicated a willingness to sell the property for $5,200 an acre.

Lesson 3 | Review

Key each line at a steady pace; tap and release each key quickly. Key each line again at a faster pace.

© CENGAGE LEARNING

home 1 ad ads lad fad dad as ask fa la lass jak jaks alas

n 2 an fan and land fan flan sans sand sank flank dank

i 3 is id ill dill if aid ail fail did kid ski lid ilk

all 4 ade alas nine else fife ken; jell ink jak inns if;

Skill Building

3b Textbook Keying

Key each line once. DS between groups.

Lines 5–8: Think and key words. Make the space part of the word.

Lines 9–12: Think and key phrases. Do not key the vertical rules separating the phrases.

easy words

5 if is as an ad el and did die eel fin fan elf lens

6 as ask and id kid and ade aid eel feel ilk skis an

7 ail fail aid did ken ale led an flan inn inns alas

8 eel eke nee kneel did kids kale sees lake elf fled

easy phrases   **Tap ENTER twice**

9 el el|id id|is is|eke eke|lee lee|ale ale|jill jak

10 is if|is a|is a|a disk|a disk|did ski|did ski|is a

11 sell a|sell a|sell a sled|fall fad|fall fad|fad is

12 sees a lake|sees a lake|as a deal|sell sled|a sale

3c Technique Practice

Key each line once.

TECHNIQUE TIP

Reach with the little finger; tap Enter key quickly; return finger to home key.

home row: fingers curved and upright

13 jak lad as lass dad sad lads fad fall la ask ad as

14 asks add jaks dads a lass ads flak adds sad as lad

upward reaches: straighten fingers slightly; return quickly to home position

15 fed die led ail kea lei did ale fife silk leak lie

16 sea lid deal sine desk lie ale like life idea jail

double letters: don't hurry when stroking double letters

17 fee jell less add inn seek fall alee lass keel all

18 dill dell see fell eel less all add kiss seen sell

REFERENCES

Gibson, Mark. "Outpatient Costs in the Southeast." *Health Care News*. New Orleans, 2010.

Glenn, Andrew. *Metro Analysis Feasibility Study—Leppard Outpatient Center*. Atlanta, 2010.

Miguel, Isabella. *Hospital Growth Analysis*. Atlanta, 2010.

Page 4

55-d3

Report with Graphics

1. Key the report on the next page, making all edits noted; then follow the remaining directions.

2. Position the title at 2" and apply Title style. Apply Heading 1 style to side headings.

3. Insert page numbers at the top right; do not show on first page.

4. Use Find and Replace to locate all occurrences of *theme* and replace it with *community* each time it occurs.

5. Apply the Foundry theme to the document.

6. Key the table and adjust column widths to remove extra space. Format the table as follows:

   a. Apply Medium Grid 3 – Accent 2 to the table. Bold the headings in cells B2–D2.

   b. Change the height of row 1 to 0.4". Change the main heading to uppercase, 16-point font, and center it vertically and horizontally in the row.

   c. Change the height of rows 2–5 to 0.3". Center the copy vertically in the cells.

   d. Center the table horizontally on the page.

7. Insert a clip art photograph using *pond* as a keyword.

   a. Choose a clip that is taller than it is wide, and reduce the height to 3.3".

   b. Apply Tight text wrapping and the Center Shadow Rectangle picture style. Position the clip to the right of the first two paragraphs of the report, under the title.

   c. Compress the picture.

8. Below the last paragraph of the report, insert a Vertical Block List SmartArt diagram. Key the following information in the shapes:

Westlake	**Accessible**
	Relatively flat and wooded
	Pond
Woodcreek	**Accessible**
	Attractive creek
Southside	**Not as accessible**
	Difficult terrain

9. Reduce the height of the diagram to 2.8" so it fits on page 2 of the report.

10. Check and close. (*55-d3*)

3d Rhythm Builder

Think and key phrases. Do not key the vertical rules separating the phrases.

phrases (think and key phrases)

19 and and land land el el elf elf self self ail nail

20 as as ask ask ad ad lad lad id id lid lid kid kids

21 if if|is is|jak jak|all all|did did|nan nan|elf elf

22 as a lad| ask dad| fed a jak| as all ask| sales fad

23 sell a lead|seal a deal|feel a leaf|if a jade sale

24 is a|is as if|a disk|aid all kids|did ski|is a silk

3e Textbook Keying

Key each line once; DS between 2-line groups.

★ TECHNIQUE TIP

Tap keys quickly.
Tap the Space Bar with down-and-in motion.
Tap Enter with a quick flick of the little finger.

reach review

25 ea sea lea seas deal leaf leak lead leas flea keas

26 as ask lass ease as asks ask ask sass as alas seas

DS

27 sa sad sane sake sail sale sans safe sad said sand

28 le sled lead flee fled ale flea lei dale kale leaf

DS

29 jn jn nj nj in fan fin an; din ink sin and inn an;

30 de den end fen an an and and ken knee nee dean dee

3f Timed Writing

1. Key lines 35–38 for 1'. If you finish before time is up, repeat the lines.
2. Practice the remaining lines in the game.
3. End your lesson.
4. Clean up your work area.

d/e 31 den end fen ken dean dens ales fend fens keen knee

32 a deed; a desk; a jade; an eel; a jade eel; a dean

n/a 33 an an in in and and en end end sane sane sand sand

34 a land; a dean; a fan; a fin; a sane end; end land

e/n 35 el eel eld elf sell self el dell fell elk els jell

36 in fin inn inks dine sink fine fins kind line lain

all reaches 37 an and fan dean elan flan land lane lean sand sane

38 sell a lead; sell a jade; seal a deal; feel a leaf

© CENGAGE LEARNING

Check your document against the illustrations below.

**Expansion of
Leppard Outpatient
Center**

Student Name
2/18/2010

LEPPARD OUTPATIENT CENTER

Today, doctors perform a significant segment of all health-care procedures on an outpatient basis. The outpatient volume at Leppard increased 62 percent over the past five years.[1] The Strategic Planning Committee reviewed the Metro Analysis Feasibility Study[2] and determined that the expansion of Leppard Outpatient Center could be justified. The Strategic Planning Committee then directed the Outpatient Expansion Task Force to prepare a general business plan for the expansion of the Leppard Outpatient Center.

Development of the Business Plan

This study focused on identifying the specific facilities needed, preparing the cost justification, and obtaining the Certification of Need from the Department of Health. Data were collected from Leppard Center records, Department of Health records, interviews with administrators of area hospitals, questionnaires sent to doctors and other local health-care providers, and industry literature.

Leppard Medical Center is more than double the size of its closest competitor in bed capacity, hospital utilization, Medicare utilization, and revenue generated. Also, Leppard was compared to Babcock Hospital, Juk Medical Center, and InstaCare. InstaCare has only a ten-bed capacity and was dropped from the analysis because it has no impact on Leppard Medical Center.

Bed Capacity and Utilization

Table 1 presents all data required for the Certification of Need.

Table 1. Bed Capacity and Utilization

Capacity	Juk	Babcock	Leppard
Number of beds	165	184	385
Hospital utilization average daily census	136	94	326
Medicare utilization average daily census	60	53	104
Full-time equivalent	615	364	1,682

[1] Isabella Miguel, *Hospital Growth Analysis* (Atlanta, 2010), p. 6.

[2] Andrew Glenn, *Metro Analysis Feasibility Study—Leppard Outpatient Center* (Atlanta, 2010), p. 8.

Cover page and Page 1

Leppard clearly is the primary provider of medical care in the regional area served. Leppard also provides a large number of specialized units, including Psychiatric Service Unit, Pediatric Unit, Level III Neonatal Intensive Care Unit, Level II Emergency Service Unit, and floors dedicated to various specialties.

Revenue Generated

Last year, Leppard had $6,842,000 excess of revenue over expenses. In comparison, Juk had $2,359,000 excess of revenue over expenses, and Babcock had $1,748,000 excess of revenue over expenses.[3]

Outpatient Expansion Proposed

The proposed facilities have received tentative approval. The top priorities are to provide 30 additional outpatient surgery beds and a cancer clinic with a full range of outpatient diagnostic and treatment services, including surgery, radiation oncology, and chemotherapy. Specific units given tentative approval included a G. I. lab, an endoscopy lab, a plastic surgery unit, a burn unit, six therapy rooms, and a large reception room.

Financial Evaluation

The project was evaluated from both a cost perspective and a revenue generation perspective. A projected annual budget was prepared for three years. (See Appendix A.)

Projected Costs

The proposed cost of the 26,000-square-foot expansion project is $2,165,960. This cost equates to $83.31 per square foot. The bed capacity increases by 48 with a resulting cost of $45,124 per bed.

Projected Revenue

The revenue projections were based on a 75 percent occupancy rate the first year, netting a gain of $52,847. The occupancy rate the second year is projected at 85 percent, netting a gain of $78,542. The occupancy rate for the third year is projected to be 95 percent, netting a gain of $143,985.

Time Frame

The projected time frame is based on having the Certification of Need and all other approvals within three months. The estimated time is ten months for construction of facilities, two

[3] Mark Gibson, "Outpatient Costs in the Southeast," *Health Care News*, January 2010, p. 36.

months for furnishing laboratories, and one month for testing laboratory equipment. This time frame also assumes that federal funds are not involved in the project.

Results of Analysis

The outpatient expansion is justified both on a needs basis and on a cost basis. The project is projected to have a positive cash flow in the first year. The current facilities cannot accommodate the growing demand for outpatient medical service. Other hospitals in the area cannot meet the needs of the region.

Action Recommended

The Leppard Outpatient Center is critically needed and will enhance the current services offered to patients in the region. The project should be implemented as soon as the necessary approvals are obtained.

Pages 2–3

Lesson 4 | *Left Shift, H, T, Period*

WARMUP

Lessons/4a Warmup

Key each line twice. Keep eyes on copy.

home row	1	al as ads lad dad fad jak fall lass asks fads all;
e/i/n	2	ed ik jn in knee end nine line sine lien dies leis
all reaches	3	see a ski; add ink; fed a jak; is an inn; as a lad
easy	4	an dial id is an la lake did el ale fake is land a

New Keys

4b Left **Shift** and **h**

Key each line once.

Follow the "Standard Procedures for Learning New Keyreaches" on p. 4 for all remaining reaches.

left shift Reach *down* with *left fourth* (little) finger; shift, tap, release.

© CENGAGE LEARNING

h Reach to *left* with *right first* finger.

© CENGAGE LEARNING

left shift

5 J Ja Ja Jan Jan Jane Jana Ken Kass Lee Len Nan Ned

6 and Ken and Lena and Jake and Lida and Nan and Ida

7 Inn is; Jill Ina is; Nels is; Jen is; Ken Lin is a

h

8 h hj hj he he she she hen aha ash had has hid shed

9 h hj ha hie his half hand hike dash head sash shad

10 aha hi hash heal hill hind lash hash hake dish ash

all reaches learned

11 Nels Kane and Jake Jenn; she asked Hi and Ina Linn

12 Lend Lana and Jed a dish; I fed Lane and Jess Kane

13 I see Jake Kish and Lash Hess; Isla and Helen hike

4c   Textbook Keying

Key the drill once: Strive for good control.

14 he she held a lead; she sells jade; she has a sale

15 Ha Ja Ka La Ha Hal Ja Jake Ka Kahn La Ladd Ha Hall

16 Hal leads; Jeff led all fall; Hal has a safe lead

17 Hal Hall heads all sales; Jake Hess asks less fee;

5. Format the caption of Table 1 using Heading 2 style and center it. Add space before the paragraph that follows the table.

6. Use the Light List – Accent 1 table style. Center column headings.

7. Insert a column to the left of *Babcock*; key the column head **Juk**, and insert the following data in the column, from top to bottom:

   165

   136

   60

   615

8. Adjust column widths so all information is on one line. Remove any extra space in the columns and center the table horizontally.

9. Replace each of the citations (for example: Miguel, 2010, 6) in the report with the following footnotes. Insert a blank line between footnotes 1 and 2.

Isabella Miguel, *Hospital Growth Analysis* (Atlanta, 2010), p. 6.

Andrew Glenn, *Metro Analysis Feasibility Study—Leppard Outpatient Center* (Atlanta, 2010), p. 8.

Mark Gibson, "Outpatient Costs in the Southeast," *Health Care News*, January 2010, p. 36.

10. Insert the Sideline cover page. Key the title **Expansion of Leppard Outpatient Center**, and replace the author name near the bottom of the page with your name. Insert the current date in the date field, and delete the other fields you do not need.

11. Insert a Continuous section break at the top of the first page of the report.

12. Position the insertion point in the header of Section 2. Deselect Different First Page if it is selected. Break the links between the headers for both sections. Go to the footer of Section 2. Break the link between the footers for both sections.

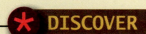
13. Go to the header of Section 2 and number the pages of the report at the top right using the Accent Bar 2 page number style. Change the page number format to begin with page 1. Click Different First Page to suppress the page numbers on the first page of the report.

14. Use Spelling & Grammar to check the document; proofread using Full Screen Reading view.

15. Click Next to continue. (*55-d2*)

4d **t** and **.** (period)
Key each line once.

t Reach *up* with *left first* finger.

. (period) Reach *down* with *right third* finger.

Period: Space once after a period that follows an initial or an abbreviation. To increase readability, space twice after a period that ends a sentence.

t

18 t tf tf aft aft left fit fat fete tiff tie the tin

19 tf at at aft lit hit tide tilt tint sits skit this

20 hat kit let lit ate sit flat tilt thin tale tan at

. (period)

21 .l .l l.l fl. fl. L. L. Neal and J. N. List hiked.

22 Hand J. H. Kass a fan. Jess did. I need an idea.

23 Jane said she has a tan dish; Jae and Lee need it.

all reaches learned

24 I did tell J. K. that Lt. Li had left. He is ill.

25 tie tan kit sit fit hit hat; the jet left at nine.

26 I see Lila and Ilene at tea. Jan Kane ate at ten.

Skill Building

4e Reinforcement
Key with control; concentrate as you practice the new reaches.

reach review
27 tf .l hj ft ki de jh tf ik ed hj de ft ki l. tf ik

28 elf eel left is sis fit till dens ink has delt ink

h/e
29 he he heed heed she she shelf shelf shed shed she

30 he has; he had; he led; he sleds; she fell; he is

i/t
31 it is if id did lit tide tide tile tile list list

32 it is; he hit it; he is ill; she is still; she is

shift
33 Hal and Nel; Jade dishes; Kale has half; Jed hides

34 Hi Ken; Helen and Jen hike; Jan has a jade; Ken is

enter
35 Nan had a sale.

36 He did see Hal.

37 Lee has a desk.

38 Ina hid a dish.

★ **TECHNIQUE TIP**

Tap Enter without pausing or looking up from the copy.

The Foundation owns both out-of-state and in-state property. However, the bulk of the property is located within South Carolina. Properties are acquired either by gift or purchase.

Insert side heading:
Out-of-State Property →

Virtually all of the out-of-state property is acquired by gift. Occasionally, a parcel of undeveloped or developed land will be offered to the Foundation at a bargain price. The Foundation then sells the property as soon as it is feasible to do so and retains the profit. The total value of the out-of-state property is $2,145,000.

Insert side heading:
South Carolina Property →

Some of the in-state property is purchased by the Foundation for future use. Other property is donated to the Foundation. Donated property may be retained for future use or sold. In-state property is divided into three regions—Coastal, Midlands, and Other. The following table shows the distribution of the property by region:

Bold

Bold and Center
headings →

Property Location and Value		
South Carolina Regions	Value of Property in Region	Percentage of Total Property
Coastal Region	$18,325,000	53%
Midlands Region	12,650,000	36%
Other Regions—In-State	3,840,000	11%

Right align   *Center align*

The total value of the in-state property is $34,815,000. More than half of the property is located in the Coastal region. The next largest concentration is in the Midlands region. The property values are based on the appraisal price at the time of the acquisition. Most real estate professionals estimate that the current value is more than double the value shown in the table.

55-d2

Report with Table

leppard

1. In the open document, format the report as a leftbound report.

2. Position the headings on the first and last pages at 2" from the top of the page and apply Title style to both headings.

3. Use Heading 1 format for all side headings. Capitalize main words in all side headings.

4. Insert the table shown below under the table caption on the first page.

Capacity	Babcock	Leppard
Number of beds	184	385
Hospital utilization average daily census	94	326
Medicare utilization average daily census	53	104
Full-time equivalent	364	1,682

Lesson 5 | R, Right Shift, C, O

Key each line twice.

home keys	1	a; ad add al all lad fad jak ask lass fall jak lad
t/h/i/n	2	the hit tin nit then this kith dint tine hint thin
left shift/.	3	I need ink. Li has an idea. Hit it. I see Kate.
all reaches	4	Jeff ate at ten; he left a salad dish in the sink.

New Keys

5b r and Right Shift
Key each line once.

r Reach *up* with *left first* finger.

right shift Reach *down* with *right fourth* finger; shift, tap, release.

r

5 r rf rf riff riff fir fir rid ire jar air sir lair
6 rf rid ark ran rat are hare art rant tire dirt jar
7 rare dirk ajar lark rain kirk share hart rail tart

right shift

8 D D Dan Dan Dale Ti Sal Ted Ann Ed Alf Ada Sid Fan
9 and Sid and Dina and Allen and Eli and Dean and Ed
10 Ed Dana; Dee Falk; Tina Finn; Sal Alan; Anna Deeds

all reaches learned

11 Jane and Ann hiked in the sand; Asa set the tents.
12 a rake; a jar; a tree; a red fire; a fare; a rain;
13 Fred Derr and Rai Tira dined at the Tree Art Fair.

5c Textbook Keying
Key each line once; DS between 2-line groups.

14 ir ir ire fir first air fair fire tire rid sir
15 fir jar tar fir flit rill till list stir dirt fire
DS

16 Feral is ill. Dan reads. Dee and Ed Finn see Dere.
17 All is still as Sarah and I fish here in the rain.
DS

18 I still see a red ash tree that fell in the field.
19 Lana said she did sail her skiff in the dark lake.

Lesson 55 | Review Reports

WARMUP

Lessons/55a Warmup

A ALL LETTERS

Skill Building

55b Timed Writing
Key two 3' timed writings.
Strive for control.

	gwam	3'	5'

Voting is a very important part of being a good citizen. **4 | 2**
However, many young people who are eligible to vote choose not **8 | 5**
to do so. When asked to explain or justify their decision, many **12 | 7**
simply shrug their shoulders and reply that they have no particular **16 | 10**
reason for not voting. The explanation others frequently give is **21 | 13**
that they just did not get around to going to the voting polls. **25 | 15**

A good question to consider concerns ways that we can motivate **29 | 18**
young people to be good citizens and to go to the polls and to vote. **34 | 21**
Some people approach this topic by trying to determine how satisfied **39 | 23**
people are who do not vote with the performance of their elected **43 | 26**
officials. Unfortunately, those who choose not to vote are just as **48 | 29**
satisfied with their elected officials as are those who voted. **52 | 31**

One interesting phenomenon concerning voting relates to the **56 | 34**
job market. When the job market is strong, fewer young people vote **61 | 36**
than when the job market is very bad. They also tend to be less **65 | 39**
satisfied with their elected officials. Self-interest seems to **69 | 41**
be a powerful motivator. Unfortunately, those who do not choose **74 | 44**
to vote miss the point that it is in their best interest to be a **78 | 47**
good citizen. **79 | 47**

| 3' | 1 | 2 | 3 | 4 |
| 5' | 1 | 2 | 3 | |

Applications

55-d1

Report with Table

References/Document Formats/Report

1. Key the report on the next page.
2. Key the main heading **Foundation Property** at 2" and apply Title style.
3. Apply Heading 1 style to the side headings.
4. Edit and format the table:
   a. Make the edits shown in the table.
   b. Apply 14-point font to the main heading in the table. Change the height of row 1 to 0.35". Center the heading vertically and horizontally.
   c. Add a row at the bottom of the table. Key in the three columns:
      Total | $34,815,000 | 100%
   d. Adjust column widths to remove extra space and center the table horizontally.
5. Proofread and check; click Next to continue. *(55-d1)*

5d c and o
Key each line once.

c Reach *down* with *left second* finger.

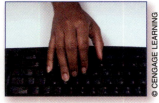

o Reach *up* with *right third* finger.

c

20 c c cd cd cad cad can can tic ice sac cake cat sic
21 clad chic cite cheek clef sick lick kick dice rice
22 call acid hack jack lack lick cask crack clan cane

o

23 o ol ol old old of off odd ode or ore oar soar one
24 ol sol sold told dole do doe lo doll sol solo odor
25 onto door toil lotto soak fort hods foal roan load

all reaches learned

26 Carlo Rand can call Rocco; Cole can call Doc Cost.
27 Trina can ask Dina if Nick Corl has left; Joe did.
28 Case sent Carole a nice skirt; it fits Lorna Rich.

Skill Building

5e Keyboard Reinforcement
Key each line once; key at a steady pace. Strive for control.

TECHNIQUE TIP

Reach up without moving hands away from your body. Use quick keystrokes.

o/r
29 or or for for nor nor ore ore oar oar roe roe sore
30 a rose|her or|he or|he rode|or for|a door|her doll

i/t
31 is is tis tis it it fit fit tie tie this this lits
32 it is|it is|it is this|it is this|it sits|tie fits

e/n
33 en en end end ne ne need need ken ken kneel kneels
34 lend the|lend the|at the end|at the end|need their

c/o
35 ch ch check check ck ck hack lack jack co co cones
36 the cot|the cot|a dock|a dock|a jack|a jack|a cone

all reaches
37 Jack and Rona did frost nine of the cakes at last.
38 Jo can ice her drink if Tess can find her a flask.
39 Ask Jean to call Fisk at noon; he needs her notes.

1. Key the letter shown below in modified block style and mixed punctuation to:
   Ms. Anne R. Marshall | **3088 Myrtle Street** | **Evansville, IN 47710-3060**
2. Supply all necessary letter parts. The letter is from **Lynn P. Timmons**.
3. Find all occurrences of *quotation* and replace with *proposal*.
4. Check and close. (*54-d4*)

Thank you for ~~letting~~ *giving* us *the opportunity to* analyze the three proposals ~~you wanted us to~~ *submitted in response* ~~review~~ *to your Request for Quotation* and to give you our recommendations. Two of the three proposals were written by consultants who are experienced *and* who have ~~reasonably~~ good reputations *in the specific area of work to be performed*.

The Bradford quotation misses the target. Even though it ~~matched your~~ ~~RFP and~~ focuse*s* on productivity and cost reduction *as specified in your Request for Quotation*, the approach is a standard industrial engineering approach with emphasis on efficiency. This type of approach *is more effective for factory and clerical work than it is for work done* ~~does not work well for your type of employees.~~ *by professionals.*

The Eastman quotation uses an approach that is better suited to your employees and should ~~accomplish what you expect it to.~~ *meet your expectations.* However, we have concerns about the price quoted. The ~~1st~~ *first* phase of the program costs $20,000 and the ~~2nd~~ *second* phase cost depends on the results of the ~~1st~~ *first* phase. The ~~1st~~ *first* phase is too high, and you need more specifics on the ~~2nd~~ *second* phase costs.

The McAlexander quotation was submitted by a group that specializes in employee benefits. We *would prefer to recommend a group with more* ~~question their~~ expertise in productivity and cost reduction.

We recommend that you negotiate the price on the Eastman quotation *and will be happy to assist you with that process*.

Lesson 6 | W, Comma, B, P

Key each line twice; avoid pauses.

home row 1 ask a lad; a fall fad; had a salad; ask a sad jak;

o/t 2 to do it; to toil; as a tot; do a lot; he told her

c/r 3 cots are; has rocks; roll cot; is rich; has an arc

all reaches 4 Holt can see Dane at ten; Jill sees Frank at nine.

New Keys

6b w and , (comma)
Key each line once.

Comma: Space once after a comma.

w Reach *up* with *left third* finger.

, (comma) Reach *down* with *right second* finger.

w

5 w ws ws was was wan wit low win jaw wilt wink wolf

6 sw sw ws ow ow now now row row own own wow wow owe

7 to sew; to own; was rich; was in; is how; will now

, (comma)

8 k, k, k, irk, ilk, ask, oak, ark, lark, jak, rock,

9 skis, a dock, a fork, a lock, a fee, a tie, a fan,

10 Jo, Ed, Ted, and Dan saw Nan in a car lift; a kit

all reaches learned

11 Win, Lew, Drew, and Walt will walk to West Willow.

12 Ask Ho, Al, and Jared to read the code; it is new.

13 The window, we think, was closed; we felt no wind.

6c Textbook Keying
Key each line once.

14 walk wide sown wild town went jowl wait white down

15 a dock, a kit, a wick, a lock, a row, a cow, a fee

16 Joe lost to Ron; Fiji lost to Cara; Don lost to Al

17 Kane will win; Nan will win; Rio will win; Di wins

18 Walter is in Reno; Tia is in Tahoe; then to Hawaii

Block Letter

*References/Document
Formats/Block Letter*

1. Prepare a letter using block letter style and open punctuation to:

   Mr. Kazuki Wang | **2170 Bryant Street** | **San Francisco, CA 94110-2128**

2. Date the letter **October 11, 201-,** use an appropriate salutation and complimentary close, and use your name as the signature.

3. Search for *section* each time it appears and replace it with *phase*.

4. Use the Thesaurus to find a synonym for *prolific*. Select the first option.

5. Proofread and check; click Next to continue. (*54-d3*)

Our team completed its preliminary review of your proposal today. Overall, we are very pleased with the approach you have taken.

Please plan to provide the following information at our October 18 meeting:

1. Please provide a more detailed pricing plan. We would like to have each section of the project priced separately specifying hourly rate and expenses rather than the one total sum quoted.

2. How many hours do you estimate will be necessary to complete each section of the project? When would your firm be able to begin the project?

We look forward to a very prolific meeting on October 18.

QUICK ✔

Check your documents against the illustrations below.

TO: Planning Commission

FROM: Community Park Site Committee

DATE: Current date

SUBJECT: Community Park Site Assessment

The Community Park Site Committee has completed its assessment of the potential sites for the new park. Our report is attached.

The Committee unanimously recommends that the Westlake site be used for the new park. The Woodcreek site was considered acceptable, but it is not as desirable as the Westlake site. The Southside site was the least desirable of the three sites.

Please contact us if you have any questions.

xx

Attachment: Community Park Site Assessment Report

c   Mayor Charles Morgan

October 11, 201-

Mr. Kazuki Wang
2170 Bryant Street
San Francisco, CA 94110-2128

Dear Mr. Wang

Our team completed its preliminary review of your proposal today. Overall, we are very pleased with the approach you have taken.

Please plan to provide the following information at our October 18 meeting:

1. Please provide a more detailed pricing plan. We would like to have each phase of the project priced separately specifying hourly rate and expenses rather than the one total sum quoted.
2. How many hours do you estimate will be necessary to complete each phase of the project? When would your firm be able to begin the project?

We look forward to a very productive meeting on October 18.

Sincerely

Student's Name

54-d2

54-d3

6d b and p
Key each line once.

b Reach *down* with *left first* finger.

p Reach *up* with *right fourth* (little) finger.

b

19 bf bf bf biff fib fib bib bib boa boa fib fibs rob
20 bf bf bf ban ban bon bon bow bow be be rib rib sob
21 a dob, a cob, a crib, a lab, a slab, a bid, a bath

p

22 p; p; pa pa; pal pal pan pan pad par pen pep paper
23 pa pa; lap lap; nap nap; hep ape spa asp leap clap
24 a park, a pan, a pal, a pad, apt to pop, a pair of

all reaches learned

25 Barb and Bob wrapped a pepper in paper and ribbon.
26 Rip, Joann, and Dick were all closer to the flash.
27 Bo will be pleased to see Japan; he works in Oslo.

Skill Building

6e Keyboard Reinforcement
Key each line once; key at a steady pace.

reach review

28 ki kid did aid lie hj has has had sw saw wits will
29 de dell led sled jn an en end ant hand k, end, kin

s/w

30 ws ws lows now we shown win cow wow wire jowl when
31 Wes saw an owl in the willow tree in the old lane.

b/p

32 bf bf fib rob bid ;p p; pal pen pot nap hop cap bp
33 Rob has both pans in a bin at the back of the pen.

6f Speed Builder
Key each line twice. Work for fluency.

34 to do|can do|to bow|ask her|to nap|to work|is born
35 for this|if she|is now|did all|to see|or not|or if

all reaches

36 Dick owns a dock at this lake; he paid Ken for it.
37 Jane also kept a pair of owls, a hen, and a snake.

38 Blair soaks a bit of the corn, as he did in Japan.
39 I blend the cocoa in the bowl when I work for Leo.

Document Review

LEARNING OUTCOMES

- Review and edit memos and letters.
- Review, edit, and format reports with tables and graphics.
- Build keying and editing skills.

Lesson 54 *Review Memos and Letters*
Lesson 55 *Review Reports*

Lesson 54 | *Review Memos and Letters*

WARMUP

KEYBOARDING PRO DELUXE 2 | *Lessons/54a Warmup*

Applications

54-d1

Memo

 edit memo

1. Revise the open document to make it a memo to **Richard M. Taylor** from **Dianne C. Gibson**.
   a. Use **November 1, 201-** as the date.
   b. The subject of the memo is **Trail Design Meeting**.
   c. Send a copy of the memo to **Bruce R. Diamond, NatureLink, Inc.**
2. Proofread and check; click Next to continue. (*54-d1*)

54-d2

Memo

KEYBOARDING PRO DELUXE 2

References/Document Formats/Memo

1. Key the memo shown below; supply all necessary parts.
2. Check your memo against the Quick Check on the next page.
3. Proofread and check; click Next to continue. (*54-d2*)

Planning Commission | Community Park Site Committee | Current date | Community Park Site Assessment | Attachment: Community Park Site Assessment Report | Copy to Mayor Charles Morgan

The Community Park Site Committee has completed its assessment of the potential sites for the new park. Our report is attached.

The Committee unanimously recommends that the Westlake site be used for the new park. The Woodcreek site was considered acceptable, but it is not as desirable as the Westlake site. The Southside site was the least desirable of the three sites.

Please contact us if you have any questions.

Lesson 7 | Review

Key each line twice; begin new lines promptly.

all	1	We often can take the older jet to Paris and back.
home	2	a; sl dk fj a;sl dkfj ad as all ask fads adds asks
1st row	3	Ann Bascan and Cabal Naban nabbed a cab in Canada.
3rd row	4	Rip went to a water show with either Pippa or Pia.

Skill Building

7b Textbook Keying
Key each line once; DS between 3-line groups.

5	ws ws was was wan wan wit wit pew paw nap pop bawl
6	bf bf fb fb fob fob rib rib be be job job bat back
7	p; p; asp asp pan pan ap ap ca cap pa nap pop prow

DS

8	Barb and Bret took an old black robe and the boot.
9	Walt saw a wisp of white water renew ripe peppers.
10	Pat picked a black pepper for the picnic at Parks.

7c Textbook Keying
Key each line once; DS between 3-line groups.

words	11	a an pan so sot la lap ah own do doe el elf to tot
phrases	12	if it|to do|it is|do so|for the|he works|if he bid
sentences	13	Jess ate all of the peas in the salad in the bowl.

DS

words	14	bow bowl pin pint for fork forks hen hens jak jaks
phrases	15	is for|did it|is the|we did a|and so|to see|or not
sentences	16	I hid the ace in a jar as a joke; I do not see it.

DS

words	17	chap chaps flak flake flakes prow prowl work works
phrases	18	as for the|as for the|and to the|to see it|and did
sentences	19	As far as I know, he did not read all of the book.

 TECHNIQUE TIP

words: key as a single unit rather than letter by letter;
phrases: say and key fluently;
sentences: work for fluency.

Memo with Picture and Shapes

rct inn

patio plan

1. In the open document, key the memo from the information below.

Management Team | Sherry Frazier | Current date | Patio Plans

The picture shown below illustrates the patio style that we plan to use for our new patio. Our fountain lends to this type of design.

We can choose other options for laying the blocks if we wish to do so. One example would be a diamond pattern rather than the square pattern. Other samples will be presented at our next meeting.

2. After the first paragraph, tap ENTER eight times before keying the second paragraph. Then tap ENTER seven times and key the reference initials.

3. In the space below the first paragraph, insert the *patio plan* picture. Crop the left side of the picture to the rounded edge of the patio; crop the top of the picture to the top of the brick column. Size the picture 2.5" high and compress it. Center the picture horizontally.

4. Insert four Diamond shapes below the second paragraph; size them 1" by 1" and apply Colored Outline – Green, Accent 4 Shape Style.

5. Position the second Diamond shape directly below the first with the points touching; position the third Diamond shape to the right of the first shape with the points touching; position the fourth Diamond shape directly below the third shape with the points touching. Group the shapes and center horizontally. See the Quick Check below.

6. Preview, print, and check. (*53-d2*)

7. Check test and close.

TIP

Insert the first Diamond shape and format it; then press CTRL and drag to copy the shape. You can also use Copy and Paste.

QUICK ✔

Check your documents against the ones shown below.

53-d1

53-d2

BOOKMARK

www.collegekeyboarding.com
Module 7 Practice Quiz

7d Technique Practice

Key each set of lines once.

▼ Space once after a period following an abbreviation.

spacing: space *immediately* after each word

20 ad la as in if it lo no of oh he or so ok pi be we
21 an ace ads ale aha a fit oil a jak nor a bit a pew
22 ice ades born is fake to jail than it and the cows

spacing/shifting

▼ ▼

23 Ask Jed. Dr. Han left at ten; Dr. Crowe, at nine.
24 I asked Jin if she had ice in a bowl; it can help.
25 Freda, not Jack, went to Spain. Joan likes Spain.

7e Timed Writing

1. Take two 1' writings. If you finish before time is up, begin again. Do not tap ENTER at the ends of the lines.

2. End the lesson. Go to the Word Processor and complete 7f.

Goal: 12 *gwam*.

gwam

It is hard to fake a confident spirit. We will do 10
better work if we approach and finish a job and 20
know that we will do the best work we can and then 30
not fret. 32

| 1 | 2 | 3 | 4 | 5 | 6 | 7 | 8 | 9 | 10 |

7f Using the Word Processor Timer

Exercises to be keyed in the Word Processor are identified with the Word Processor icon. Key the timing in 7e. Follow the instructions in the textbook and key from the textbook.

STANDARD PLAN for Using the Word Processor Timer

You can check your speed in the Word Processor using the Timer.

1. In the Word Processor, click the Timer button on the status bar.

2. The Timer begins once you start to key and stops automatically.

3. To save the timing, click the File menu and Save as. Use your initals (*xx*), the exercise number, and number of the timing as the filename. Example: *xx-7f-t1* (your initials, exercise 7f, timing1).

4. Click the Timer button again to start a new timing.

5. Each new timing must be saved with its own name.

7g Word Processor

1. In the Word Processor, key each line once for fluency. Do not save your work.

2. Set the Timer in the Word Processor for 30". Take two 30" writings on each line. Do not save the timings.

Goal: to reach the end of the line before time is up.

gwam

26 Dan took her to the show. 12
27 Jan lent the bowl to the pros. 14
28 Hold the wrists low for this drill. 16
29 Jessie fit the black panel to the shelf. 18
30 Jake held a bit of cocoa and an apricot for Diane. 20
31 Dick and I fish for cod on the docks at Fish Lake. 20
32 Kent still held the dish and the cork in his hand. 20

| 1 | 2 | 3 | 4 | 5 | 6 | 7 | 8 | 9 | 10 |

Newsletter

 central portfolio

✱ DISCOVER

Insert/Text/Object

1. Position insertion point where you wish to insert the diagram.
2. Select Text from File.

★ TIP

Use Show/Hide. When you insert the diagram, only one paragraph marker (¶) should appear below the Continuous section break. Delete any other paragraph markers that display. You may have to move the diagram over until the columns are balanced again and then position it at the center.

1. Prepare the newsletter using the information that follows:
   a. Set custom margins at 0.75" for all margins; tap ENTER three times, enter a Continuous section break, and key the text. Apply Heading 2 style to all headings.
   b. Format the text using two equal-width columns. Balance the columns.
   c. Use Fill – Red, Accent 2, Matte Bevel WordArt to create the banner heading, **Central Foundation Update**; position in Top Center with Square Text Wrapping and size the WordArt 0.8" high.
   ✱d. Insert the *Word* data file *central portfolio* below the columns and center the diagram. Make sure that the columns remain balanced and the newsletter fits on one page. See the Quick Check on the next page.
2. Proofread; check Spelling and Grammar; correct all errors. (*53-d1*).
3. Continue to the next document.

Central Foundation Update

Central University Foundation committees met this past week, and this newsletter is designed to update all Board Members of the actions taken by the Investment Committee. At its last meeting, the Foundation Board charged the Investment Committee to work with its consultants to diversify the Foundation's investment portfolio and present the proposed portfolio structure to the full Board for its approval at its next meeting.

Asset Allocation

The Investment Committee agreed on an aggressive asset allocation of 75% equity and 25% fixed income securities. The Foundation endows its assets in perpetuity and spends only 5% of the income earned on these assets each year. Therefore, the extremely long time horizon of the investment portfolio justifies the aggressive investment in equities.

Asset Classes

The Committee considered eight classes of assets: large cap core, large cap value, large cap growth, small cap value, small cap growth, international equities, fixed income, and alternative assets. The Committee included all classes of assets except alternative investments in its recommendation. Alternative investments are so named because these assets have not traditionally been included in the portfolios of foundations. Alternative investments include assets such as hedge funds, venture capital funds, real estate funds, and direct investment in startup ventures. The Committee recommends that investments in alternative investments be deferred for at least a year.

Asset Weightings

Obviously, some of the equity classes deserve higher weightings than other classes. Small cap stocks and international stocks play a less predominant role in traditional foundation portfolios than large cap stocks. The portfolio structure diagram shown below contains the Investment Committee's recommendations for the various asset classes. Weighting is dependent on the economy.

Lesson 8 | G, Question Mark, X, U

WARMUP

Lessons/8a Warmup

Key each line twice. Keep eyes on copy.

all 1 Dick will see Job at nine if Rach sees Pat at one.

w/b 2 As the wind blew, Bob Webber saw the window break.

p/, 3 Pat, Pippa, or Cap has prepared the proper papers.

all 4 Bo, Jose, and Will fed Lin; Jack had not paid her.

New Keys

8b g and ?

Key each line once; repeat.

Question mark: The question mark is usually followed by two spaces.

g Reach to *right* with *left first* finger.

? Left SHIFT; reach *down* with *right fourth* finger.

g

5 g g gf gaff gag grog fog frog drag cog dig fig gig

6 gf go gall flag gels slag gala gale glad glee gals

7 golf flog gorge glen high logs gore ogle page grow

?

8 ? ?; ?; ? ? Who? When? Where? Who is? Who was?

9 Who is here? Was it he? Was it she? Did she go?

10 Did Geena? Did he? What is that? Was Jose here?

all reaches learned

11 Has Ginger lost her job? Was her April bill here?

12 Phil did not want the boats to get here this soon.

13 Loris Shin has been ill; Frank, a doctor, saw her.

8c Textbook Keying

Key each line once; DS between groups.

reach review

14 ws ws hj hj tf tf ol ol rf rf ed ed cd cd bf bf p;

15 wed bid has old hold rid heed heed car bed pot pot

g

16 gf gf gin gin rig ring go gone no nog sign got dog

17 to go|to go|go on|go in|go in|to go in|in the sign

One space after question mark.

? 18 ?; ?;? who? when? where? how? what? who? It is I?

19 Is she? Is he? Did I lose Jo? Is Gal all right?

TECHNIQUE TIP

Concentrate on correct reaches.

Lesson 53 | Assessment

Skill Building

53b   Timed Writing
Key two 3' timed writings.

	gwam	1'	3'
Most people today realize that they cannot count on their		12	4	79

Most people today realize that they cannot count on their employer or on the government to provide for their retirement. They must plan for their own future. Young people who are healthy and are not concerned about retirement often do not consider the value of benefits when they compare job offers they have. They tend to focus more on the salary they will earn.

Most companies provide some type of health benefits. The portion that the employee has to pay tends to vary widely, however. Therefore, it is wise to analyze the quality, the type of coverage provided, and the cost of the benefits to the employee. A lower salary with benefits paid by the company may produce more net income than a higher salary with high benefit costs to the employee.

To recruit bright, young people who are likely to change jobs many times, companies set up portable savings plans that defer taxes on income. The company matches a certain percentage of the savings to provide incentives for the employee to contribute to the plan. Usually the plan vests in less than five years, and employees can take the entire amount with them when they leave.

gwam	1'	3'
12	4	79
25	8	84
39	13	89
52	17	93
66	22	97
73	24	100
13	29	104
27	33	109
42	38	114
56	43	119
69	47	123
77	50	126
12	54	130
26	59	134
40	63	139
54	68	144
69	73	149
76	76	151

```
1' |  1  |  2  |  3  |  4  |  5  |  6  |  7  |  8  |  9  |  10  |  11  |  12  |  13  |
3' |        1        |        2        |        3        |        4        |
```

Applications

53c

Assessment

 Continue

 Check

When you complete a document, proofread it, check the spelling, and preview for placement. When you are completely satisfied, click the Continue button to move to the next document. Click the Check button when you are ready to error-check the test. Review and/or print the document analysis results.

8d x and u

Key each line once; repeat.

x Reach *down* with *left third* finger.

u Reach *up* with *right first* finger.

x

20 x x xs xs ox ox lox sox fox box ex hex lax hex fax
21 sx six sax sox ax fix cox wax hex box pox sex text
22 flax next flex axel pixel exit oxen taxi axis next

u

23 u uj uj jug jut just dust dud due sue use due duel
24 uj us cud but bun out sun nut gun hut hue put fuel
25 dual laud dusk suds fuss full tuna tutus duds full

all reaches learned

26 Paige Power liked the book; Josh can read it next.
27 Next we picked a bag for Jan; then she, Jan, left.
28 Is her June account due? Has Lou ruined her unit?

Skill Building

8e Reinforcement

Key each line once; work for control.

29 nut cue hut sun rug us six cut dug axe rag fox run
30 out of the sun|cut the action|a fox den|fun at six
31 That car is not junk; it can run in the next race.

32 etc. tax nick cure lack flex walls uncle clad hurt
33 lack the cash|not just luck|next in line|just once
34 June Dunn can send that next tax case to Rex Knox.

Use wordwrap ↓

8f Timed Writing

Take two 1' timings. If time permits, continue to paragraph 2. **Use wordwrap.**

★ TECHNIQUE TIP

Wordwrap: Text within a paragraph moves automatically to the next line. Tap ENTER only to begin a new paragraph.

```
            •           4          •           8          •
How a finished job will look often depends on how
       12          •          16          •          20
we feel about our work as we do it.  Attitude has
          •          24          •          28          •
a definite effect on the end result of work we do.
```
Tap ENTER once
```
            •           4          •           8          •
When we are eager to begin a job, we relax and do
       12          •          16          •          20
better work than if we start the job with an idea
          •          24          •          28          •
that there is just nothing we can do to escape it.
```

for the lot immediately adjacent to the arena. If you would like more information about the Cornerstone Club and how you can become a charter member, call the Cougars Club office during regular business hours.

What View Would You Like?

Most of us would like to sit in our seats and try them out before we select them rather than look at a diagram of the seating in the new arena. Former Cougar players make it easy for you to select the perfect angle to watch the ball go in the basket. Mark McKay and Jeff Dunlap, using their patented Real View visualization software, make it possible for you to experience the exact view you will have from the seats you select. In fact, they encourage you to try several different views. Most of the early testers of the new seat selection software reported that they came in with their minds completely made up about the best seats in the house. However, after experiencing several different views with the Real View software, they changed their original seat location request.

QUICK ✔

Check your document against the one shown below.

ARENA UPDATE

Get Your Shovels Ready!

The architects have put the final touches on the arena plans, and the groundbreaking has been scheduled for March 18. Put the date on your calendar and plan to be a part of this exciting time. The Groundbreaking Ceremony will begin at 5:00 at the new arena site. After the ceremony, you will join the architects in the practice facility for refreshments and an exciting visual presentation of the new arena. The party ends when we all join the Western Cougars as they take on the Central Lions for the final conference game.

Cornerstone Club Named

Robbie Holiday of the Cougars Club submitted the winning name for the new premium seating and club area of the new arena. Thanks to all of you who

submitted suggestions for naming the new club. For his suggestion, which was selected from over 300 names submitted, Robbie has won season tickets for next year and the opportunity to make his seat selection first. The Cornerstone Club name was selected because members of our premium club play a crucial role in making our new arena a reality. Without the financial support of this group, we could not lay the first cornerstone of the arena.

Cornerstone Club members have first priority in selecting their seats for both basketball and hockey in a specially designated section of the new arena. This section provides outstanding seats for both basketball games and hockey matches. Club members also have access to the Cornerstone Club before the game, during halftime, and after the game. They also receive a parking pass for the lot immediately adjacent to the arena. If you would like more information about the Cornerstone Club and how you can become a charter member, call the Cougars Club office during regular business hours.

What View Would You Like?

Most of us would like to sit in our seats and try them out before we select them rather than look at a diagram of the seating in the new arena. Former Cougar players make it easy for you to select the perfect angle to watch the ball go in the basket. Mark McKay and

Jeff Dunlap, using their patented Real View visualization software, make it possible for you to experience the exact view you will have from the seats you select. In fact, they encourage you to try several different views. Most of the early testers of the new seat selection software reported that they came in with their minds completely made up about the best seats in the house. However, after experiencing several different views with the Real View software, they changed their original seat location request.

Lesson 9 | *Q, M, V, Apostrophe*

Key each line twice.

all letters	1	Lex gripes about cold weather; Fred is not joking.
space bar	2	Is it Di, Jo, or Al? Ask Lt. Coe, Bill; he knows.
easy	3	I did rush a bushel of cut corn to the sick ducks.
easy	4	He is to go to the Tudor Isle of England on a bus.

New Keys

9b q and m
Key each line once; repeat.

q Reach *up* with *left fourth* finger.

m Reach *down* with *right first* finger.

q

5 q qa qa quad quad quaff quant queen quo quit quick
6 qa qu qa quo quit quod quid quip quads quote quiet
7 quite quilts quart quill quakes quail quack quaint

m

8 m mj mj jam man malt mar max maw me mew men hem me
9 m mj ma am make male mane melt meat mist amen lame
10 malt meld hemp mimic tomb foam rams mama mire mind

all reaches learned

11 Quin had some quiet qualms about taming a macaque.
12 Jake Coxe had questions about a new floor program.
13 Max was quick to join the big reception for Lidia.

9c Textbook Keying
Key each line once for control.
DS between 2-line groups.

m/x 14 me men ma am jam am lax, mix jam; the hem, six men
15 Emma Max expressed an aim to make a mammoth model.
DS

q/u 16 qa qu aqua aqua quit quit quip quite pro quo squad
17 Did Quin make a quick request to take the Qu exam?
DS

g/n 18 fg gn gun gun dig dig nag snag snag sign grab grab
19 Georgia hung a sign in front of the union for Gib.

Applications

52-d1

Newsletter

1. Apply the Grid theme and Narrow margins.

2. Tap ENTER four times and key the newsletter as it is shown. Do not format as you key.

3. Select the text and format it into two equal-width columns. Note that a Continuous section break is positioned above the columns.

4. Apply a Tan, Accent 1, Darker 50%, 1½-point double-line page border.

5. Insert Gradient Fill – Brown, Accent 4, Reflection WordArt, and key the title **Arena Update**. Apply Square text wrapping and position the WordArt between the top border and the Continuous section break. Size the WordArt 1" high and 4" wide. Center the WordArt horizontally.

6. Click in the first heading and apply Heading 1 style. Click Remove Space Before Paragraph and then Add Space After Paragraph. Repeat these steps for the second and third headings.

7. Insert the clip art indicated below; use Square text wrapping and position each clip as shown on the next page.

   a. Use keyword *shovel* for the first clip; size the clip 1.5" high.

   b. Use keywords *building blocks* for the second clip; size the clip 2.3" high.

   c. Use keywords *stadium seats* for the third clip; size the clip 2.5" high.

8. Check and close. (*52-d1*)

Arena Update

Get Your Shovels Ready!

The architects have put the final touches on the arena plans, and the groundbreaking has been scheduled for March 18. Put the date on your calendar and plan to be a part of this exciting time. The Groundbreaking Ceremony will begin at 5:00 at the new arena site. After the ceremony, you will join the architects in the practice facility for refreshments and an exciting visual presentation of the new arena. The party ends when we all join the Western Cougars as they take on the Central Lions for the final conference game.

Cornerstone Club Named

Robbie Holiday of the Cougars Club submitted the winning name for the new premium seating and club area of the new arena. Thanks to all of you who submitted suggestions for naming the new club. For his suggestion, which was selected from over 300 names submitted, Robbie has won season tickets for next year and the opportunity to make his seat selection first. The Cornerstone Club name was selected because members of our premium club play a crucial role in making our new arena a reality. Without the financial support of this group, we could not lay the first cornerstone of the arena.

Cornerstone Club members have first priority in selecting their seats for both basketball and hockey in a specially designated section of the new arena. This section provides outstanding seats for both basketball games and hockey matches. Club members also have access to the Cornerstone Club before the game, during halftime, and after the game. They also receive a parking pass

9d v and ' (apostrophe)

Key each line once; repeat.

Apostrophe: The apostrophe shows (1) omission (as Rob't for Robert or it's for it is) or (2) possession when used with nouns (as Joe's hat).

v Reach *down* with *left first* finger.

' Reach to the *right* with the *right fourth* finger.

v

20 v vf vf vie vie via via vim vat vow vile vale vote
21 vf vf ave vet ova eve vie dive five live have lave
22 cove dove over aver vivas hive volt five java jive

' (apostrophe)

23 '; '; it's it's Rod's; it's Bo's hat; we'll do it.
24 We don't know if it's Lee's pen or Norma's pencil.
25 It's ten o'clock; I won't tell him that he's late.

all reaches learned

26 It's Viv's turn to drive Iva's van to Ava's house.
27 Qua, not Vi, took the jet; so did Cal. Didn't he?
28 Wasn't Fae Baxter a judge at the post garden show?

Skill Building

9e Reinforcement

Key each line once.

TECHNIQUE TIP

Keep your hands still as you reach to the third or bottom rows.

v/?
29 Viola said she has moved six times in five months.
30 Does Dave live on Vine Street? Must he leave now?

q/?
31 Did Viv vote? Can Paque move it? Could Val dive?
32 Didn't Raquel quit Carl Quent after their quarrel?

direct reach
33 Fred told Brice that the junior class must depart.
34 June and Hunt decided to go to that great musical.

double letter
35 Harriette will cook dinner for the swimming teams.
36 Bill's committee meets in an accounting classroom.

9f Timed Writing

Key the paragraph once for control. Key it again a little faster. **Use wordwrap.**

Use wordwrap ↓

```
          .         4         .         8         .
We must be able to express our thoughts with ease
     12        .         16        .         20
if we desire to find success in the business world.
     .         24        .         28
It is there that sound ideas earn cash.
```

CAPITALIZATION

52c1

KEYBOARDING PRO DELUXE 2

References/Communication Skills/Capitalization

1. Review the capitalization rules and examples in *Keyboarding Pro DELUXE 2*.
2. Key the sentences, correcting all capitalization errors. Use the Numbering command to number the sentences.
3. Proofread and check; click Next to continue. *(52c1)*

1. according to one study, the largest ethnic minority group online is hispanics.
2. the american author mark twain said, "always do right; this will gratify some people and astonish the rest."
3. the grand canyon was formed by the colorado river cutting into the high-plateau region of northwestern arizona.
4. the president of russia is elected by popular vote.
5. the hubble space telescope is a cooperative project of the european space agency and the national aeronautics and space administration.
6. the train left north station at 6:45 this morning.
7. the trademark cyberprivacy prevention act would make it illegal for individuals to purchase domains solely for resale and profit.
8. consumers spent $7 billion online between november 1 and december 31, 201-, compared to $3.1 billion for the same period in 2010.
9. new students should attend an orientation session on wednesday, august 15, at 8 a.m. in room 252 of the perry building.
10. the summer book list includes *where the red fern grows* and *the mystery of the missing baseball.*

52c2

1. Key the sentences, correcting all capitalization errors. Use the Numbering command to number the sentences.
2. Proofread and check; click Next to continue. *(52c2)*

1. buckminster fuller has been called a renaissance man and has been compared to ben franklin.
2. the first paperback books, introduced in 1935, included works by agatha christie and ernest hemingway.
3. the great scientist albert einstein said, "anyone who has never made a mistake has never tried anything new."
4. margaret thatcher was the first woman to be elected prime minister of great britain.
5. the marketing department closes its search for new employees on friday, march 15.
6. aunt jane and my mother are flying to paris for thanksgiving.
7. several sites to see in washington, d.c. include the smithsonian institute, the jefferson memorial, and the washington monument.
8. the movie, *the pelican brief*, was set in a large city in the south.
9. the attorney quoted from section 2 of the code.
10. the twin cities futbol club and the north dallas baseball association are combining efforts to raise money for the american red cross.

Lesson 10 | Z, Y, Quotation Mark, Tab

Key each line twice.

all letters	1	Quill owed those back taxes after moving to Japan.
spacing	2	Didn't Vi, Sue, and Paul go? Someone did; I know.
q/v/m	3	Marv was quite quick to remove that mauve lacquer.
easy	4	Lana is a neighbor; she owns a lake and an island.

New Keys

10b z and y
Key each line once; repeat.

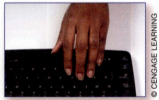

z Reach *down* with *left fourth* finger.

z

5 za za zap zap zing zig zag zoo zed zip zap zig zed
6 doze zeal zero haze jazz zone zinc zing size ozone
7 ooze maze doze zoom zarf zebus daze gaze faze adze

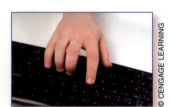

y Reach *up* with *right first* finger.

y

8 y yj yj jay jay hay hay lay nay say days eyes ayes
9 yj ye yet yen yes cry dry you rye sty your fry wry
10 ye yen bye yea coy yew dye yaw lye yap yak yon any

all reaches learned

11 Did you say Liz saw any yaks or zebus at your zoo?
12 Relax; Jake wouldn't acquire any favorable rights.
13 Has Mazie departed? Tex, Lu, and I will go alone.

14 Cecilia brings my jumbo umbrella to every concert.

10c Textbook Keying
Key each line once. DS between groups.

direct reach
15 John and Kim recently brought us an old art piece.
16 I built a gray brick border around my herb garden.

DS

17 sa ui hj gf mn vc ew uy re io as lk rt jk df op yu

adjacent reach
18 In Ms. Lopez' opinion, the opera was really great.
19 Polly and I were joining Walker at the open house.

WRAP TEXT AROUND GRAPHICS

When graphic elements are used in documents formatted in columns, the text usually wraps around the graphic. A graphic can be positioned in one column or may overlap multiple columns. You can position the graphic with the mouse or Position command.

To wrap text around graphics and position graphics:

Picture Tools Format/Arrange/Wrap Text or Position

1. Select the graphic, choose Wrap Text, and select the desired wrapping style.
2. Use the mouse to drag the graphic to the position in a column. -or-
   Click Position and select the desired position.

You can also add lines between columns to separate the text in the columns.

To add a line between columns:

Page Layout/Page Setup/Columns

1. Display the options and choose More Columns to display the Columns dialog box.
2. Click Line between. To remove the line, remove the check from the box.

DRILL 2 — LINE BETWEEN COLUMNS

1. Open *52-drill1*; search for clip art using the keywords *business men computers*; select a clip like the one shown below.

2. Apply Position in Middle Left with Square Text Wrapping; then drag the clip to the horizontal center of the column.

3. Size the picture to 1.6" high and 2.4" wide; add a line between the columns.

4. Proofread and check; click Next to continue. (*52-drill2*)

DRILL 3 — GRAPHICS

1. Open *52-drill2* and remove the line between columns.

2. Position the graphic in Middle Center with Square Text Wrapping.

3. Use Rotate to flip the clip horizontally.

4. Preview, check, and close. (*52-drill3*)

QUICK ✓

Check your documents against those shown below.

52-drill2

52-drill3

10d " (quotation mark) and TAB

Key each line once; repeat.

TAB Reach *up* with *left fourth* finger.

" Shift; then reach to the *right* with the *right fourth* finger.

" (quotation mark)

20 "; "; " " "lingo" "bugs" "tennies"   I like "malts."
21 "I am not," she said, "going."   I just said, "Oh?"

tab key

22   The tab key is used for indenting paragraphs and aligning columns.
23   Tabs that are set by the software are called default tabs, which are usually a half inch.

Skill Building

10e Textbook Keying

Key lines 24–30 once. Tap TAB to indent each paragraph. Use wordwrap, tapping ENTER only at the end of each paragraph.

24   The expression "I give you my word," or put another
25 way, "Take my word for it," is just a way I can say, "I
26 prize my name; it clearly stands in back of my words."
27 I offer "honor" as collateral.
tab 28   Tap the tab key and begin the line without a pause to maintain fluency.
29   She said that this is the lot to be sent; I agreed with her.
30   Tap Tab before starting to key a timed writing so that the first line is indented.

10f Timed Writing

Take two 1' timings beginning with paragraph 1. If you finish before time is up, continue with paragraph 2. **Use wordwrap.**

Goal: 15 gwam

TECHNIQUE TIP

Wordwrap: Text within a paragraph moves automatically to the next line. Tap ENTER only to begin a new paragraph.

wordwrap ↓

gwam 1'

Tab → All of us work for progress, but it is not   8
always easy to analyze "progress." We work hard   18
for it; but, in spite of some really good efforts,   28
we may fail to receive just exactly the response we   39
want.   40
Tab → When this happens, as it does to all of us,   9
it is time to cease whatever we are doing, have   18
a quiet talk with ourselves, and face up to the   28
questions about our limited progress. How can we   38
do better?   40

| 1 | 2 | 3 | 4 | 5 | 6 | 7 | 8 | 9 | 10 |

Lesson 52 | *Documents with Columns*

New Commands
- Equal-Width Columns
- Balance Columns
- Revise Column Structure
- Format Banner
- Wrap Text Around Graphics

New Commands

52b

KEYBOARDING PRO DELUXE 2

*References/Word 2010
Commands/Lesson 52*

COLUMNS OF EQUAL WIDTH

Columns

Text may be formatted in multiple columns on a page to make it easier to read. The text flows down one column and then to the top of the next column. Often the heading on documents with columns spans multiple columns. The heading is called a banner or masthead. Programs, newsletters, flyers, and brochures are typically formatted in columns. Columns may be of equal width or of varying widths. In this lesson, you will work with equal-width columns. Columns may be formatted before or after keying text. Generally, it is easier to format text in columns after it has been keyed. Columns are often balanced or forced to end at approximately the same point on the page.

To format equal-width columns:

Page Layout/Page Setup/Columns

1. Select the text you want to format in columns; click Columns, and select the desired number of columns.

2. To balance columns on a page, click at the end of the columns and insert a Continuous section break.

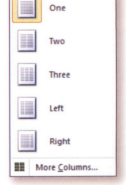
One
Two
Three
Left
Right
More Columns...

DRILL 1 COLUMNS

productivity

1. In the open document, select the title and apply Gradient Fill – Orange, Accent 6, Inner Shadow Text Effect from the Font group on the Home tab.

2. Select the text, click Columns, and select Three.

3. Preview the document and then revise the column structure; select the text again and click Two columns.

Page Layout/Page Setup/Breaks

4. Add a Continuous section break at the end of the columns to balance them.

5. Proofread and check; click Next to continue. (*52-drill1*)

Lesson 11 | Review

Key line twice (slowly, then faster).

alphabet 1 Zeb had Jewel quickly give him five or six points.

" (quote) 2 Can you spell "chaos," "bias," "bye," and "their"?

y 3 Ty Clay may envy you for any zany plays you write.

easy 4 Did he bid on the bicycle, or did he bid on a map?

| 1 | 2 | 3 | 4 | 5 | 6 | 7 | 8 | 9 | 10 |

Skill Building

11b Keyboard Reinforcement

Key each line once; repeat the drill to increase fluency.

TECHNIQUE TIP

Work for smoothness, not speed.

5 za za zap az az maze zoo zip razz zed zax zoa zone

6 Liz Zahl saw Zoe feed the zebra in an Arizona zoo.

7 yj yj jy jy joy lay yaw say yes any yet my try you

8 Why do you say that today, Thursday, is my payday?

9 xs xs sax ox box fix hex ax lax fox taxi lox sixes

10 Roxy, you may ask Jay to fix any tax sets for you.

11 qa qa aqua quail quit quake quid equal quiet quart

12 Did Enrique quietly but quickly quell the quarrel?

13 fv fv five lives vow ova van eve avid vex vim void

14 Has Vivi, Vada, or Eva visited Vista Valley Farms?

11c Speed Builders

Key each balanced-hand line twice, as quickly as you can.

15 is to for do an may work so it but an with them am

16 am yam map aid zig yams ivy via vie quay cob amend

17 to do is for an may work so it but am an with them

18 for it|for it|to the|to the|do they|do they|do it

19 Pamela may go to the farm with Jan and a neighbor.

20 Rod and Ty may go by the lake if they go downtown.

| 1 | 2 | 3 | 4 | 5 | 6 | 7 | 8 | 9 | 10 |

51-d1

Announcement with WordArt and Drop Cap

1. Apply custom margins of 0.75" top, bottom, and sides; apply landscape orientation.

2. Tap ENTER 11 times and key the announcement text using 26-point font; justify text, and apply a drop cap to the first letter. Select the drop cap and apply Dark Blue, Text 2 font color.

3. Select the clip art shown in the left margin. Crop the black border from all sides; then resize the clip art to 2" high. Position in Top Center with Square Text Wrapping.

4. Use Fill – White, Outline – Accent 1 WordArt for the title; apply Red from Standard Colors Text Fill, and 1½ point weight Text Outline; then click Transform Text Effects and apply Triangle Up. Size the WordArt 1.25" high and 9" wide and center it.

5. Apply a Dark Blue, Text 2, double-line, 1½-point page border.

6. Proofread and check; click Next to continue. (*51-d1*)

Fourth of July Celebration

Pack your lawn chairs or blankets and bring the entire family to join your friends and neighbors for the annual Fourth of July celebration at City Park. Music and festivities begin at 7:30 and end with a spectacular fireworks display at 10:30.

Fourth of July Celebration

Pack your lawn chairs or blankets and bring the entire family to join your friends and neighbors for the annual Fourth of July celebration at City Park. Music and festivities begin at 7:30 and end with a spectacular fireworks display at 10:30.

51-d2

Character Spacing, Symbols, and Special Characters

1. Tap ENTER three times and key the text shown below, inserting the symbols or special characters shown.

2. Apply 16-point, bold font to the title and use character spacing to expand it by 2 points.

3. Apply 16-point, bold, Red text to the Wingdings 2 and Wingdings symbols in the first sentence and the special character in the second sentence. Space twice before and after each symbol or special character.

4. Select all of the text and add a 3-D paragraph border; use Red Standard Color and a 3-point thick-and-thin line. Then add Red, Accent 2, Lighter 80% shading to the text.

5. Check and close. (*51-d2*).

Symbols and Special Characters

My instructor put the symbols ✗ and ☹ on my paper.

Then she wrote, "What does this special character © mean when it is placed on the title of an article?"

11d Textbook Keying

Key each line once. Tap ENTER at the end of each line. DS between the groups of lines.

enter: key smoothly without looking at fingers

21 Make the return snappily

22 and with assurance; keep

23 your eyes on your source

24 data; maintain a smooth,

25 constant pace as you key.

DS

space bar: use down-and-in motion

26 us me it of he an by do go to us if or so am ah el

27 Have you a pen? If so, print "Free to any guest."

DS

caps lock: press to toggle it on or off

28 Use ALL CAPS for items such as TO, FROM, or SUBJECT.

29 Did Kristin mean Kansas City, MISSOURI, or KANSAS?

© CENGAGE LEARNING

11e Timed Writing

1. Take two 2' timings on all paragraphs. If you finish before time is up, start over with paragraph 1. Use wordwrap. Key fluently but with control. **Use wordwrap.**

   Goal: 16 *gwam*

2. End the lesson but do not exit the software.

To determine gross-words-a-minute (*gwam*) rate for 2':

Follow these steps if you are *not* using *Keyboarding Pro*.

1. Note the figure at the end of the last line completed.

2. For a partial line, note the figure on the scale direcly below the point at which you stopped keying.

3. Add these two figures to determine the total gross words a minute (*gwam*) you keyed.

gwam 2'

Have we thought of communication as a kind   4 | 31

of war that we wage through each day?   8 | 35

When we think of it that way, good language   12 | 39

would seem to become our major line of attack.   17 | 44

Words become muscle; in a normal exchange or in   22 | 49

a quarrel, we do well to realize the power of words. 27 | 54

11f Enrichment

1. Click the Skill Building tab from the main menu and choose Technique Builder; select Drill 1a.

2. Key Drill 1a from page 31. Key each line once striving for good accuracy.

3. The results will be listed on the Skill Building Report.

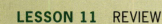

SYMBOLS AND SPECIAL CHARACTERS

Symbols and special characters that are not on your keyboard can be inserted using the Symbol command. Different types of symbols can be inserted depending on the font selected. Some symbols are scientific or mathematical and are generally located on the Symbols font. Other symbols are decorative and are generally located on the Wingdings fonts.

To insert symbols:
Insert/Symbols/Symbol

1. Click in the document where the symbol is to be inserted.

2. Follow the path to display the gallery of symbols. The Gallery generally contains the symbols that have been recently used on that computer. If the symbol you want to insert is not among the options, click More Symbols to display the Symbol dialog box.

3. Make sure the Symbols tab is selected, and then check the Font box for the appropriate font. If Symbol (or the font you want to use) is not displayed, click the drop-list arrow and scroll to the desired font and select it.

4. Scroll down to locate the desired symbol and select it.

5. Click Insert and Close.

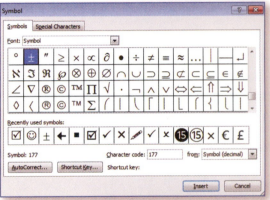

Special characters not located on the keyboard are located on the Special Characters tab. Examples of some of the special characters include Em Dash, Nonbreaking Hyphen, Registered, Trademark, and Paragraph.

To insert special characters:
Insert/Symbols/Symbol/More Symbols

1. Position the insertion point where you want to insert the special character.

2. Click the Special Characters tab in the Symbol dialog box.

3. Select the special character desired; click Insert and Close.

DRILL 6   SYMBOLS AND SPECIAL CHARACTERS

1. Apply Verdana 16-point font.

2. Insert the following symbols; tap ENTER after each symbol.

   a. Plus or minus symbol (±) from the Symbol font

   b. Smiley face (☺) from the Wingdings font

   c. Check box (☑) from the Wingdings 2 font

3. Key text when indicated and insert the following special characters; tap ENTER after each character.

   a. Key: **Farbe Microfiber**™ (Trademark)

   b. Section (§)

   c. Paragraph (¶)

4. Proofread and check; click Next to continue. (*51-drill6*)

Lesson 12 | Review

Key each line twice (slowly, then faster).

alphabet	1	Jack won five quiz games; Brad will play him next.
q	2	Quin Racq quickly and quietly quelled the quarrel.
z	3	Zaret zipped along sizzling, zigzag Arizona roads.
easy	4	Did he hang the sign by the big bush at the lake?

| 1 | 2 | 3 | 4 | 5 | 6 | 7 | 8 | 9 | 10 |

Skill Building

12b New Key Review

Key each line once; DS between groups. Work for smoothness, not speed.

b/f	5	bf bf fab fab ball bib rf rf rib rib fibs bums bee
	6	Did Buffy remember that he is a brass band member?
z/y	7	za za zag zig zip yj yj jay eye day lazy hazy zest
	8	Liz amazed us with the zesty pizza on a lazy trip.
q/u	9	qa qa quo qt. quit quay quad quarm que uj jug quay
	10	Where is Quito? Qatar? Boqueirao? Quebec? Quilmes?
v/m	11	vf vf valve five value mj mj ham mad mull mass vim
	12	Vito, enter the words vim, vivace, and avar; save.
all	13	I faced defeat; only reserves saved my best crews.
	14	In my opinion, I need to rest in my reserved seat.
all	15	Holly created a red poppy and deserves art awards.
	16	My pump averages a faster rate; we get better oil.

12c Textbook Keying

Key each line once; DS between groups. Work for smooth, unhurried keying.

★ **TECHNIQUE TIP**

Keep fingers curved and body aligned properly.

de/ed	17	ed fed led deed dell dead deal sled desk need seed
	18	Dell dealt with the deed before the dire deadline.
ol/lo	19	old tolls doll solo look sole lost love cold stole
	20	Old Ole looked for the long lost olive oil lotion.
op/po	21	pop top post rope pout port stop opal opera report
	22	Stop to read the top opera opinion report to Opal.
we/ew	23	we few wet were went wears weather skews stew blew
	24	Working women wear sweaters when weather dictates.

To apply a paragraph border and shading:

Page Layout/Page Background/Page Borders

1. Click in the paragraph or select the text to be formatted with a border.

2. On the Borders tab, select the style, color, and setting. Apply to paragraph or text.

3. On the Shading tab, select the desired color in the Fill box and apply to paragraph or text.

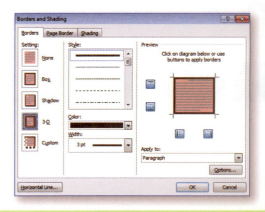

DRILL 4   PARAGRAPH BORDERS

1. Key the paragraph shown on the right.

2. Apply a thin-and-thick box border, with Red color from the Standard Colors and 3-point line width.

3. Apply Dark Blue, Text 2, Lighter 60% shading to the paragraph.

4. Proofread and check; click Next to continue. (51-drill4)

This paragraph is formatted with a 3-point red, thin-and-thick box border, and Dark Blue, Text 2, Lighter 60% shading.

CHARACTER SPACING

Character spacing is used to expand or condense text. It is useful in spreading out a heading or compacting text when space is limited.

To apply character spacing:

Home/Font/Font Dialog Box Launcher

1. Select the text and click the Advanced tab on the Font dialog box.

2. Click Spacing; select Expanded or Condensed and use the spin arrows to specify the points.

★ TIP

Note that text effects can be applied to text and to WordArt. In Drill 5, the effect is applied to text and should be selected from the Font group.

DRILL 5   CHARACTER SPACING

1. Key the text shown at the right; apply Cambria 16-point font. Center and tap ENTER twice after each line.

2. Expand the first line by 2 points and the second line by 1 point; condense the third line by 1 point.

3. Apply Gradient Fill – Purple, Accent 4, Reflection Text Effect to the second line.

4. Proofread and check; click Next to continue. (51-drill5)

Expanding Character Spacing with Heading Font

Expanding Character Spacing with Text Effects

Condensing Character Spacing with Heading Font

12d Textbook Keying

Key each line once; DS between 3-line groups. Concentrate and key with control.

25 a for we you is that be this will be a to and well
26 as our with I or a to by your form which all would
27 new year no order they so new but now year who may

DS

28 This is Lyn's only date to visit their great city.
29 I can send it to your office at any time you wish.
30 She kept the fox, owls, and fowl down by the lake.

DS

31 Harriette will cook dinner for the swimming teams.
32 Annette will call at noon to give us her comments.
33 Johnny was good at running and passing a football.

| 1 | 2 | 3 | 4 | 5 | 6 | 7 | 8 | 9 | 10 |

12e Timed Writing

Key a 2' timing on both paragraphs. If you finish before time is up, start again with paragraph 1. Key fluently but not rushed. Repeat the timing again for 2'. **Use wordwrap.**

Goal: 16 gwam

Copy Difficulty

What factors determine whether copy is difficult or easy? Research shows that difficulty is influenced by syllables per word, characters per word, and percent of familiar words. Carefully controlling these three factors ensures that speed and accuracy scores are reliable— that is, increased scores reflect increased skill.

In Level 1, all timings are easy. Note "E" inside the triangle at left of the timing. Easy timings contain an average of 1.2 syllables per word, 5.1 characters per word, and 90 percent familiar words. Easy copy is suitable for the beginner who is mastering the keyboard.

E ALL LETTERS

gwam 2'

	gwam	2'
There should be no questions, no doubt, about	5	35
the value of being able to key; it's just a matter	10	40
of common sense that today a pencil is much too slow.	15	45
Let me explain. Work is done on a keyboard	19	49
three to six times faster than other writing and	24	54
with a product that is a prize to read. Don't you	29	59
agree?	30	60

2' | 1 | 2 | 3 | 4 | 5 |

PAGE BORDERS

Page Borders

In Module 5, you applied borders and shading to tables. In this module, you will apply borders to pages and borders and shading to paragraphs. Page borders can be formatted using a variety of line styles, weights, and colors.

To apply a page border:

Page Layout/Page Background/Page Borders

1. Click Page Borders to display the Borders and Shading dialog box.
2. Make sure the Page Border tab is active.
3. Choose the desired setting, line style, color, and width.
4. In the Apply to box ❶, choose the desired option.

⭐ **TIP**

Note that the line color displayed is determined by the theme colors.

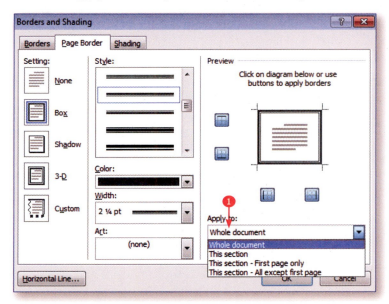

DRILL 3   PAGE BORDERS

1. Open *50-d2* and apply a Box page border.
2. Choose a thick-and-thin line style, 2¼ pt width shown in the illustration above.
3. Choose Gray, 80%, Text 2 color.
4. Apply to Whole document.
5. Proofread and check; click Next to continue. (*51-drill3*)

KEYBOARDING PRO DELUXE 2

References/Word 2010 Commands/Lesson 51

PARAGRAPH BORDERS AND SHADING

Borders and shading may be applied to paragraphs or to selected text as shown in the illustration below.

> This paragraph illustrates a 3-D border with a 3-point, Red, Text 2, Darker 50% line. The shading for the paragraph is Red, Text 2, Lighter 60%. The document theme is Clarity.

Lesson 13 | Review

Key each line twice (slowly, then faster).

alphabet	1	Bev quickly hid two Japanese frogs in Mitzi's box.
shift	2	Jay Nadler, a Rotary Club member, wrote Mr. Coles.
, (comma)	3	Jay, Ed, and I paid for plates, knives, and forks.
easy	4	Did the amendment name a city auditor to the firm?

| 1 | 2 | 3 | 4 | 5 | 6 | 7 | 8 | 9 | 10 |

Skill Building

13b Textbook Keying

Key each line once; DS between groups of lines. Key the text as suggested:

Lines 5–7: Key the words as a single unit.

Lines 8–10: Key the words letter by letter.

Lines 11–13: Vary your keying as your fingers find the right rhythm.

word-level response: key short, familiar words as units

5 is to for do an may work so it but an with them am
6 Did they mend the torn right half of their ensign?
7 Hand me the ivory tusk on the mantle by the bugle.

letter-level response: key more difficult words letter by letter

8 only state jolly zest oil verve join rate mop card
9 After defeat, look up; gaze in joy at a few stars.
10 We gazed at a plump beaver as it waded in my pool.

combination response: use variable speed; your fingers will let you feel the difference

11 it up so at for you may was but him work were they
12 It is up to you to get the best rate; do it right.
13 Sami greeted reporters as stars got ready at home.

| 1 | 2 | 3 | 4 | 5 | 6 | 7 | 8 | 9 | 10 |

13c Keyboard Reinforcement

Key each line once; fingers well curved, wrists low.

p	14	Pat appears happy to pay for any supper I prepare.
x	15	Knox can relax; Alex gets a box of flax next week.
v	16	Vi, Ava, and Viv move ivy vines, leaves, or stems.
'	17	It's a question of whether they can't or won't go.
?	18	Did Jan go? Did she see Ray? Who paid? Did she?
.	19	Ms. E. K. Nu and Lt. B. A. Walz had the a.m. duty.
"	20	"Who are you?" he asked. "I am," I said, "Marie."
;	21	Find a car; try it; like it; work a price; buy it.

WordArt can be formatted by using the tools on the Drawing Tools Format tab.

- *Styles*—can be changed to any style in the gallery.
- *Text Fill*—used to add color or change the color of the interior of the letters.
- *Text Outline*—used to change the color, style, or weight of the lines of the exterior border of the letters.
- *Text Effects*—add depth or emphasis to text, such as Shadow, Glow, Bevel, 3-D Rotation, or Transform.

To apply WordArt formats:

Drawing Tools Format/WordArt Styles/Text Fill, Text Outline, Text Effects, or WordArt Styles

1. To change to a new WordArt style, preview and click the desired style.
2. To change Text Fill, Text Outline, or Text Effects, select the text, click the appropriate drop-list arrow, and select the desired color, line, or effect.

DRILL 1   WORDART

1. Select the Fill – White, Warm Matte Bevel WordArt style; select the text; and key **Happy Birthday to You!**

2. Position at Top Center with Square Text Wrapping. Select the text and apply Red, Accent 2, Darker 50% Text Outline. Then apply Red, Accent 2, Lighter 60% Text Fill.

3. Click the Text Effects drop-list arrow to display the Text Effect options and select Transform; then click Triangle Up to apply it.

4. Proofread and check; click Next to continue. (*51-drill1*)

DROP CAP

A drop cap is a large capital letter at the beginning of a text block that is used to draw the reader's attention. The dropped cap usually extends down three or four lines. The text of the paragraph can wrap around the dropped cap or extend to the right of it. Use the Drop Cap Options to change the font style or number of lines to drop.

To create a dropped cap:

Insert/Text/Drop Cap

1. Click in the paragraph that you want to begin with a drop cap.
2. Click Drop Cap and select Dropped or In margin.

DRILL 2   DROP CAP

 portfolio structure

1. In the open file, select the first letter of the first paragraph, and apply an In margin cap.

2. Repeat step 1 for the first letter of the second paragraph.

3. Select the first letter of each paragraph and change the In margin cap to a Dropped cap.

4. Proofread and check; click Next to continue. (*51-drill2*)

13d Textbook Keying

Troublesome Pairs: Key each line once; DS between groups.

t 22 at fat hat sat to tip the that they fast last slat
r 23 or red try ran run air era fair rid ride trip trap
t/r 24 A trainer sprained an arm trying to tame the bear.

DS

m 25 am me my mine jam man more most dome month minimum
n 26 no an now nine once net knee name ninth know never
m/n 27 Many men and women are important company managers.

DS

o 28 on or to not now one oil toil over only solo today
i 29 it is in tie did fix his sit like with insist will
o/i 30 Joni will consider obtaining options to buy coins.

DS

a 31 at an as art has and any case data haze tart smart
s 32 us as so say sat slap lass class just sassy simple
a/s 33 Disaster was averted as the steamer sailed to sea.

DS

e 34 we he ear the key her hear chef desire where there
i 35 it is in tie did fix his sit like with insist will
e/i 36 An expression of gratitude for service is desired.

E   ALL LETTERS

13e Timed Writing

Key a 2' writing on both paragraphs. If you finish before time is up, start again with paragraph 1. Key fluently but not rushed. Repeat the timing again for 2'. **Use wordwrap.**

Goal: 16 gwam

gwam 2'

          •   4   •   8
    The questions of time use are vital ones; we   5
    •   12   •   16
miss so much just because we don't plan.   9
          •   4   •   8
    When we organize our days, we save time for   13
    •   12   •   16
those extra premium things we long to do.   17

2' | | 1 | 2 | 3 | 4 | 5 |

Lesson 51 | *Format Text Graphically*

New Commands
- Insert WordArt
- Create Drop Cap
- Borders and Shading
- Character Spacing
- Symbols and Special Characters

Skill Building

51b Textbook Keying

1. Key each line once, concentrating on using good keying techniques. Tap ENTER twice after each 2-line group.
2. Repeat the drill if time permits.

1st finger
1 Freddie just gave a friend that nice ring for her fifth birthday.
2 Ginger and Gretchen recently found three cute bunnies in my yard.

2nd finger
3 Quinn will fix an old radio so Paul can play popular jazz loudly.
4 Alexa was at the zoo with six polo players who quit playing polo.

double letters
5 Jarrett cheerfully killed millions of bugs near the pool at noon.
6 All planning committees have four dinner meetings with key staff.

New Commands

51c

WORDART

WordArt consists of decorative text that can be added to documents. WordArt is often used in announcements, flyers, casual letterhead, and newsletters to make the documents more interesting. A variety of styles and visual effects can be added to WordArt.

To insert WordArt:

Insert/Text/WordArt

1. Follow the path to display the WordArt gallery.
2. Preview and select the desired option.
3. Select the text in the text box that displays and replace it with your text.
4. Size and position the WordArt as desired.

Skill Builder 1

From the Skill Building tab, select Technique Builder and then the drill. Key each line once at a comfortable rate. Tap ENTER at the end of each line. Single-space the drill. Concentrate and key accurately. Repeat if desired.

DRILL 1

Goal: reinforce key locations

Key each line once at a comfortable, constant rate.

© CENGAGE LEARNING

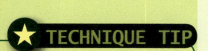

★ TECHNIQUE TIP

Keep
- your eyes on source copy
- your fingers curved, upright
- your wrists low but not touching
- your elbows hanging loosely
- your feet flat on the floor

Drill 1a

A We saw that Alan had an alabaster vase in Alabama.
B My rubber boat bobbed about in the bubbling brook.
C Ceci gave cups of cold cocoa to Rebecca and Rocco.
D Don's dad added a second deck to his old building.
E Even as Ellen edited her document, she ate dinner.
F Our firm in Buffalo has a staff of forty or fifty.
G Ginger is giving Greg the eggs she got from Helga.
H Hugh has eighty high, harsh lights he might flash.

Drill 1b

I Irik's lack of initiative is irritating his coach.
J Judge J. J. Jore rejected Jeane and Jack's jargon.
K As a lark, Kirk kicked back a rock at Kim's kayak.
L Lucille is silly; she still likes lemon lollipops.
M Milt Mumm hammered a homer in the Miami home game.
N Ken Linn has gone hunting; Stan can begin canning.
O Jon Soto rode off to Otsego in an old Morgan auto.
P Philip helped pay the prize as my puppy hopped up.
Q Quiet Raquel quit quoting at an exquisite marquee.

Drill 1c

R As Mrs. Kerr's motor roared, her red horse reared.
S Sissie lives in Mississippi; Lissa lives in Tulsa.
T Nat told Betty not to tattle on her little sister.
U Ula has a unique but prudish idea on unused units.
V Eva visited every vivid event for twelve evenings.
W We watched as wayworn wasps swarmed by the willow.
X Tex Cox waxed the next box for Xenia and Rex Knox.
Y Ty says you may stay with Fay for only sixty days.
Z Hazel is puzzled about the azure haze; Zack dozes.

Document with Graphics

 training notes

1. In the open document, apply Black Tie document theme.

2. Position the title on the first line so that the document will fit on one page. Apply Title style to the title and Subtitle style to the subtitle.

3. After the first paragraph, insert six blank paragraphs and center the graphics described in the next step vertically.

4. Insert Rounded Rectangle and Oval shapes as shown in the Quick Check below. Apply Shape Style Light 1 Outline, Colored Fill – Black, Dark 1 to both shapes. Size the shapes 9" high by 1.7" wide. Insert the text as shown; increase font size to 16 point and apply bold.

5. Insert Arrow shapes as shown below and apply Intense Line – Dark 1 Shape Style to both arrows. Size .7" wide.

6. Search Clip Art using the keywords *global communication* and insert a clip similar to the one shown below. Size it 1.5" high and apply Square text wrapping.

7. After the last paragraph, insert the Alternating Flow SmartArt from the Process category and size it 6.5" wide. Apply Light 1 Outline, Colored Fill – Black, Dark 1 Shape Style to the three main shapes. Size the shapes for bulleted text to about 2" wide. Apply Black Shape Outline to the under and over arrows in the SmartArt. Then key the text provided in the data file in the shapes.

8. Use the Quick Check below to compare your document.

9. Preview, check, and close. *(50-d2)*

QUICK ✔

Check your document against the illustration below.

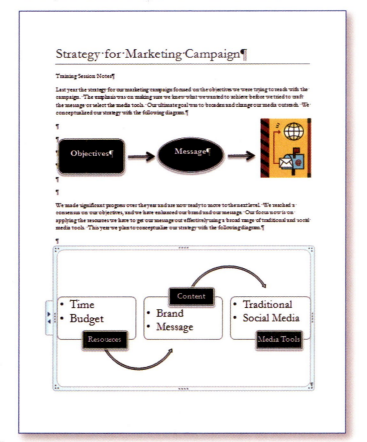

DRILL 2

Goal: strengthen up and down reaches

Keep hands and wrists quiet; fingers well curved in home position; stretch fingers up from home or pull them palmward as needed.

home position

1 Hall left for Dallas; he is glad Jake fed his dog.
2 Ada had a glass flask; Jake had a sad jello salad.
3 Lana Hask had a sale; Gala shall add half a glass.

down reaches

4 Did my banker, Mr. Mavann, analyze my tax account?
5 Do they, Mr. Zack, expect a number of brave women?
6 Zach, check the menu; next, beckon the lazy valet.

up reaches

7 Prue truly lost the quote we wrote for our report.
8 Teresa quietly put her whole heart into her words.
9 There were two hilarious jokes in your quiet talk.

DRILL 3

Goal: strengthen individual finger reaches

1st finger

1 Bob Mugho hunted for five minutes for your number.
2 Juan hit the bright green turf with his five iron.
3 The frigates and gunboats fought mightily in Java.

2nd finger

4 Dick said the ice on the creek had surely cracked.
5 Even as we picnicked, I decided we needed to diet.
6 Kim, not Mickey, had rice with chicken for dinner.

3rd/4th finger

7 Pam saw Roz wax an aqua auto as Lex sipped a cola.
8 Wally will quickly spell Zeus, Apollo, and Xerxes.
9 Who saw Polly? Zoe Pax saw her; she is quiet now.

DRILL 4

Goal: strengthen special reaches

Emphasize smooth stroking. Avoid pauses, but do not reach for speed.

adjacent reaches

1 Falk knew well that her opinions of art were good.
2 Theresa answered her question; order was restored.
3 We join there and walk north to the western point.

direct reaches

4 Barb Nunn must hunt for my checks; she is in debt.
5 In June and December, Irvin hunts in Bryce Canyon.
6 We decided to carve a number of funny human faces.

double letters

7 Anne stopped off at school to see Bill Wiggs cook.
8 Edd has planned a small cookout for all the troop.
9 Keep adding to my assets all fees that will apply.

| 1 | 2 | 3 | 4 | 5 | 6 | 7 | 8 | 9 | 10 |

DRILL 3   SMARTART

 Insert/Illustrations/SmartArt

1. Apply the Hardcover theme.

2. Insert the Converging Radial SmartArt layout.

3. Click in the shape at the right side and then click Add Shape three times to add three more shapes.

4. Click the Text Pane and key the text shown at the right.

5. Proofread and check; click Next to continue. *(50-drill3)*

Effective Decision Making

    Identify Decision to Be Made

    Determine Options

    Analyze Options

    Select Best Option

    Implement Option

    Evaluate Decision Made

Applications

50-d1

Document with Graphics

 farbe memo
credenza

1. In the open document, note that Farbe uses the Black Tie document theme.

2. Key the memo shown below, inserting the Name and Title Organization Chart where noted.

3. Click in the top shape and add another Assistant shape. Use the Text Pane to key the names in the organization chart. Click in the Title boxes to key the titles. In the second Assistant shape, use **New** as the name.

4. Use In Line with Text wrapping and size the organization chart 3.8" high by 6.5" wide.

5. Tap ENTER after the reference initials and insert the *credenza* picture from the data files. Size it 5" high and position at Top Center with Square Text Wrapping. Compress the picture, accepting the defaults.

6. Proofread and check; click Next to continue. *(50-d1)*

Marketing Employees | Mark Redman | Current date | Feedback from Executive Management Retreat

The Executive Team approved the reorganization of the Marketing Department. The new organization chart is shown below. You will be pleased to note that our three area managers have been promoted to directors.

(Insert Name and Title Organization Chart here. Key the names and titles shown below in the chart.)

Mark Redman Vice President | Trista Blackmon Executive Assistant | New Executive Assistant | Andrea Kelly Director | Daniel Wexford Director | Jodye Bristow Director

The Communications, Advertising, and Public Relations Teams will report to Andrea, the Marketing and Strategic Planning Teams will report to Daniel, and the Inside Sales and the Field Sales Teams will report to Jodye. A new assistant will be hired to support the three directors.

The Executive Team also approved the purchase of credenzas that we requested for all of the Marketing Department offices. Of the three styles proposed, the team selected the style that is in Pat's office in the Finance Department. See the picture on the next page.

xx

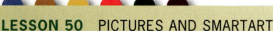

DRILL 5

Goal: improve troublesome pairs

Use a controlled rate without pauses.

1 ad add did does dish down body dear dread dabs bad

d/k 2 kid ok kiss tuck wick risk rocks kayaks corks buck

3 Dirk asked Dick to kid Drake about the baked duck.

4 deed deal den led heed made needs delay he she her

e/i 5 kit kiss kiln kiwi kick kilt kind six ribs kill it

6 Abie had neither ice cream nor fried rice in Erie.

7 fib fob fab rib beg bug rob bad bar bed born table

b/v 8 vat vet gave five ever envy never visit weave ever

9 Did Harv key jibe or jive, TV or TB, robe or rove?

10 aft after lift gift sit tot the them tax tutu tyro

t/r 11 for far ere era risk rich rock rosy work were roof

12 In Toronto, Ruth told the truth about her artwork.

13 jug just jury judge juice unit hunt bonus quiz bug

u/y 14 jay joy lay you your only envy quay oily whey body

15 Willy usually does not buy your Yukon art in July.

DRILL 6

Goal: fluency

1 Dian may make cocoa for the girls when they visit.

2 Focus the lens for the right angle; fix the prism.

3 She may suspend work when she signs the torn form.

4 Augment their auto fuel in the keg by the autobus.

5 As usual, their robot did half turns to the right.

6 Pamela laughs as she signals to the big hairy dog.

7 Pay Vivian to fix the island for the eighty ducks.

DRILL 7

Goal: eyes on the copy

Option: In the Word (WP) Processor, set the Timer for Variable and then either 20" or 30". Choose a *gwam* goal that is two to three words higher than your best rate. Try to reach your goal.

	words	30"	20"
1 Did she make this turkey dish? **ENTER**		12	18
2 Blake and Laurie may go to Dubuque.		14	21
3 Signal for the oak sleigh to turn right.		16	24
4 I blame Susie; did she quench the only flame?		18	27
5 She turns the panel dials to make this robot work.		20	30

SMARTART

 SmartArt consists of predesigned diagrams that help to simplify complex concepts. SmartArt layouts are grouped into nine categories: List, Process, Cycle, Hierarchy, Relationship, Matrix, Pyramid, Picture, and layouts from Office.com. You can elect to view all of the layouts or the layouts in one of the categories.

To insert and add text to SmartArt:

<mark>Insert/Illustrations/SmartArt</mark>

1. Position the insertion point where you want to add the graphic, and click SmartArt to open the Choose a SmartArt Graphic dialog box shown below. Categories of SmartArt are listed at the left, the layouts for each category display in the center, and the preview and description of the appropriate use appear in the right pane.

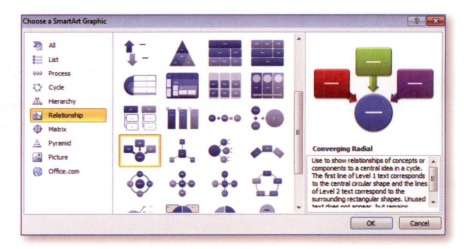

2. Click the SmartArt layout you wish to insert.

3. Click in each shape and key the desired text. -or-

   Key text in the Text Pane (shown at right) that displays along with the diagram.

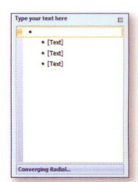

Each SmartArt diagram offers a few shapes by default. If you need more shapes than the diagram offers, you can add shapes to the diagram. If you are keying text in the Text Pane, tapping ENTER after your last entry adds a new shape. Or you can add a shape at a specific location in the diagram using the SmartArt Tools Design tab.

To add shapes to SmartArt:

<mark>SmartArt Tools Design/Create Graphic/Add Shape</mark>

1. Click in the shape before or after which you want to add another shape.

2. Follow the path to add a shape, or click the drop-list arrow and select an option from the Add Shape options.

3. Repeat the process until you have as many shapes as you need in the layout.

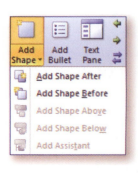

 TIP

If desired, apply a document theme so that the SmartArt layout will use the appropriate colors of the theme.

TIP

The options available on the Add Shape list depend on the type of diagram you are working with.

Any timed writing in the book can be completed using the Timed Writing feature.

TO USE THE TIMED WRITING FEATURE:

1. Select the Timed Writings tab from the Main screen.
2. Scroll to select the timed writing.
3. Select the source and the timing length. For example,
   - Select Paragraph 1 and 1'. Key paragraph 1; if you finish before time is up, repeat the same paragraph. Always use wordwrap when keying timed writings.
   - Select Paragraph 2 and 1'. Key paragraph 2; repeat the same paragraph if you finish before time is up.
   - Select the Entire Writing and 2'. Try to maintain your 1' rate. If you finish before time is up, start over, beginning with paragraph 1.
4. Timings save automatically.
5. The Timed Writing Report displays the results of the last 40 timed writings and the best 3 timings at each speed.

wordwrap ↓

E ALL LETTERS

Goal: build staying power
1. Key each paragraph as a 1' timing. **Use wordwrap.**
2. Key a 2' timing on both paragraphs. **Use wordwrap.**

Writing 1: **18 gwam**

	gwam 2'
Why spend weeks with some problem when just a few quiet	6
minutes can help us to resolve it.	9
If we don't take time to think through a problem, it will	15
swiftly begin to expand in size.	18

Writing 2: **20 gwam**

We push very hard in our quest for growth, and we all	5
think that only excellent growth will pay off.	10
Believe it or not, one can actually work much too hard,	16
be much too zealous, and just miss the mark.	20

Writing 3: **22 gwam**

A business friend once explained to me why he was often	6
quite eager to be given some new project to work with.	11
My friend said that each new project means he has to	16
organize and use the best of his knowledge and his skill.	22

Writing 4: **24 gwam**

Don't let new words get away from you. Learn how to spell	6
and pronounce new words and when and how finally to use them.	12
A new word is a friend, but frequently more. New words	18
must be used lavishly to extend the size of your own word power.	24

2' | 1 | 2 | 3 | 4 | 5 | 6 |

In previous drills, you have moved pictures with the mouse. You can also move pictures to specific places on the page by using the Position command options.

To position pictures on the page:

Picture Tools Format/Arrange/Position

1. Follow the path to display the options for positioning pictures on the page.

2. Preview and select the desired option.

Besides using the Rotate handle on a picture to rotate it, you can use the Rotate options on the Picture Tools Format tab. Pictures can be rotated to the left or right or can be flipped vertically or horizontally.

To rotate pictures:

Picture Tools Format/Arrange/Rotate

1. Follow the path to display the rotate options.

2. Preview and select the desired option.

3. To change the degrees of left or right rotation, click More Rotation Options.

DRILL 2 ARRANGE PICTURES rhino

1. Insert the *rhino* picture from your data files.

2. Size it 4" high.

3. Hover the mouse pointer over the various positions for a live preview and then position it in Middle Center with Square text wrapping.

4. Compress the picture, accepting the defaults.

5. Hover the mouse pointer over the rotate options for a live preview and then select Flip Horizontal.

6. Add a Bevel Rectangle picture style.

7. Preview the document.

8. Proofread and check; click Next to continue. (*50-drill2*)

Note: The dot above text represents two words.

Writing 5: 26 gwam

gwam 2'

We usually get best results when we know where we are 5

going. Just setting a few goals will help us quietly see what 12

we are doing. 13

Goals can help measure whether we are moving at a good 19

rate or dozing along. You can expect a goal to help you find 25

good results. 26

Writing 6: 28 gwam

To win whatever prizes we want from life, we must plan to 6

move carefully from this goal to the next to get the maximum 12

result from our work. 14

If we really want to become skilled in keying, we must 19

come to see that this desire will require of us just a little 26

patience and hard work. 28

Writing 7: 30 gwam

Am I an individual person? I'm sure I am; still, in a 5

much, much bigger sense, other people have a major voice in 12

thoughts I think and actions I take. 15

Although we are each a unique person, we all work and 21

play in organized groups of people who do not expect us to 26

dismiss their rules of law and order. 30

2' | 1 | 2 | 3 | 4 | 5 | 6 |

To crop pictures:

Picture Tools Format/Size/Crop

1. To crop one side of a picture, click Crop and drag the cropping handle on the side inward.

2. To crop the same amount on two sides, press CTRL while you drag the handle. The cropping line will illustrate what is being cut off.

3. To finish, click off the picture.

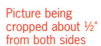

Picture being cropped about ½" from both sides

Picture being cropped about ¾" from the bottom

To compress pictures:

Picture Tools Format/Adjust/Compress Pictures

1. Select the picture and click Compress Pictures.

2. You can change the defaults, but it usually is not necessary to do so. Click OK to compress the picture and reduce file size.

Note that if you have cropped the picture, compressing it will remove the cropped areas. Until you compress, you can use the Crop tool to restore parts of the picture that were originally cropped.

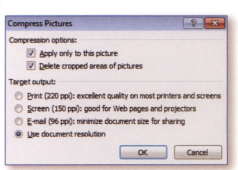

DRILL 1　　　　**PICTURES**　　　　hippo with baby

1. Insert the *hippo with baby* picture from your data files.

2. Crop the picture about 0.5" from both sides and 0.75" from the bottom.

3. Size the picture about 3" high; use Square text wrapping, and move it to the top center of the page.

Picture Tools Format/Picture Styles/Picture Styles

4. Apply the first picture style, Simple Frame, White.

5. Compress the picture, accepting the defaults.

6. Proofread and check; click Next to continue. (*50-drill1*)

Figure and Symbol Keys

Lessons 14–18   *Figure Keys*
Lessons 19–24   *Symbol Keys*
Lessons 25   *Assessment*

LEARNING OUTCOMES

- Key the numeric keys by touch.
- Use symbol keys correctly.
- Build keying speed and accuracy.
- Apply correct number expression.
- Apply proofreaders' marks.

Lesson 14 | *1 and 8*

WARMUP

KEYBOARDING PRO DELUXE 2 ▶ *Lessons/14a Warmup*

Key each line twice.

Line 2: Space once after a series of brief questions within a sentence.

alphabet	1	Jessie Quick believed the campaign frenzy would be exciting.
space bar	2	Was it Mary? Helen? Pam? It was a woman; I saw one of them.
3rd row	3	We were quietly prepped to write two letters to Portia York.
easy	4	Kale's neighbor works with a tutor when they visit downtown.

| 1 | 2 | 3 | 4 | 5 | 6 | 7 | 8 | 9 | 10 | 11 | 12 |

Skill Building

14b Textbook Keying

The words at the right are from the 100 most used words.

Key each line once; work for fluency.

Top 100 High-Frequency Words

5 a an it been copy for his this more no office please service

6 our service than the they up was work all any many thank had

7 business from I know made more not me new of some to program

8 such these two with your about and have like department year

9 by at on but do had in letter most now one please you should

10 their order like also appreciate that there gentlemen letter

11 be can each had information letter may make now only so that

12 them time use which am other been send to enclosed have will

Lesson 50 | Pictures and SmartArt

New Commands

- Insert Pictures
- Size Pictures
- Adjust Pictures
- Arrange Pictures
- Create SmartArt
- Modify SmartArt
- Format SmartArt

WARMUP

Lessons/50a Warmup

Skill Building

50b   Textbook Keying

1. Key each line once, concentrating on using good keying techniques. Tap ENTER twice after each 2-line group.
2. Repeat the drill if time permits.

1st row
1 Max, Zam, and a local man saw an amazing cave on a long bus ride.
2 Janna came back home six times to visit the bat caves at the zoo.

3rd row
3 We wrote Terry to try to get a quote; Perry tried to get a quote.
4 Perry peeped at Terry's quote; were you there with Perry or Pete?

home row
5 Kala was glad Alyssa sold a glass flask at a gala sale in Dallas.
6 Jack Hall's dad was in Dallas at a glass sale; a sad lad saw him.

one hand
7 Jimmy saw him carve a great pumpkin; John deserved better awards.
8 Nikki saved a million as a minimum reserve on debt; Jimmy agreed.

balanced hand
9 Jamale Rodney, a neighbor, and Sydney may go to the lake by auto.
10 Bud got the tub of big worms to go to the dock to fish with them.

New Commands

50c

KEYBOARDING PRO DELUXE 2

References/Word 2010 Commands/Lesson 50

PICTURES

Pictures are photographs or other images created in software other than *Word*. The format and design tools for pictures are very similar to those you have used in the previous lesson. The same principle applies: To format the picture, click in it and apply the appropriate design or format from the tools that display. Pictures frequently need to be cropped to remove unwanted portions and to be compressed to reduce the file size. As with all graphics, pictures can be sized and moved. Picture styles can be applied, and a number of adjustments can be made.

To insert and format pictures:

Insert/Illustrations/Picture

1. **Click at the position you wish to insert a picture, and then click Picture to browse your files and select the picture to be inserted.**
2. **Click the picture and use the tools on the Picture Tools Format tab to apply a picture style, arrange the picture, or size it.**

New Keys

14c [1] and [8]

Key each line once.

Note: The digit "1" and the letter "l" have separate values on a computer keyboard. Do not interchange these characters.

1 Reach *up* with *left fourth* finger.

8 Reach *up* with *right second* finger.

Abbreviations: Do not space after a period within an abbreviation, as in Ph.D., U.S., C.O.D., a.m.

1

13 1 1a a1 1 1; 1 and a 1; 1 add 1; 1 aunt; 1 ace; 1 arm; 1 aye

14 1 and 11 and 111; 11 eggs; 11 vats; Set 11A; May 11; Item 11

15 The 11 aces of the 111th Corps each rated a salute at 1 p.m.

8

16 8 8k k8 8 8; 8 kits; ask 8; 8 kites; kick 8; 8 keys; spark 8

17 OK 88; 8 bags; 8 or 88; the 88th; 88 kegs; ask 88; order 888

18 Eight of the 88 cars score 8 or better on our Form 8 rating.

all figures learned

19 She did live at 818 Park, not 181 Park; or was it 181 Clark?

20 Put 1 with 8 to form 18; put 8 with 1 to form 81. Use 1881.

21 On May 1 at 8 a.m., 18 men and 18 women left Gate 8 for Rio.

Skill Building

14d Reinforcement

Key each line. Key with accuracy.

figures

22 Our 188 trucks moved 1881 tons on August 18 and December 18.

23 Send Mary 181 No. 188 panes for her home at 8118 Oak Street.

24 The 188 men in 8 boats left Docks 1 and 18 at 1 p.m., May 1.

25 pop was lap pass slaw wool solo swap Apollo wasp load plaque

26 Was Polly acquainted with the skillful jazz player in Texas?

27 The computer is a useful tool; it helps you to perform well.

14e Speed Builder

Key these lines in the game.

28 Did their form entitle them to the land?

29 Did the men in the field signal for us to go?

30 I may pay for the antique bowls when I go to town.

31 The auditor did the work right, so he risks no penalty.

32 The man by the big bush did signal us to turn down the lane.

| 1 | 2 | 3 | 4 | 5 | 6 | 7 | 8 | 9 | 10 | 11 | 12 |

Check your documents against the illustrations below.

49-d1

49-d2

49-d2

Document with Graphics

 rct inn

1. In the open document, key the memo shown below.

2. Use *plaque* as the keyword to search and insert a clip of a plaque similar to the one shown above before the last paragraph of the memo. Size it 2.5" high; apply Square text wrapping.

3. Draw a Bevel shape and size it 1.5" high by 3" wide. Key **Jane P. Smith** in the shape; increase the font size to 24 point. Click below the plaque and key the last paragraph.

4. Compare your document to the Quick Check above.

5. Preview, proofread, print, check, and close. (*49-d2*)

Mason M. White | Maria C. Tighe | Current date | Employee of the Month Plaque

Effective next month, we plan to name an RCT Inn Employee of the Month. The plaque will be placed behind the registration desk for the entire month. Then it will be given to the employee.

Please have a plaque designed and get quotes for the cost. We plan to use the plaque for a number of years. Therefore, please request that the quote be based on a three-year supply. A sample design shown below on the left illustrates the style we would like. Our name, logo, and Employee of the Month need to be incorporated in the design of the plaque. Then the name of the employee would be engraved and attached to the plaque as shown below on the right side.

(Tap ENTER 10 times to leave space for illustrations)

Please bring a sketch of the plaque to our meeting next week for the management team to review.

xx

Lesson 15 | 5 and 0

Key each line twice.

For a series of capital letters, tap CAPS LOCK with the left little finger. Tap again to release.

alphabet	1 John Quigley packed the zinnias in twelve large, firm boxes.
1/8	2 Idle Motor 18 at 8 mph and Motor 81 at 8 mph; avoid Motor 1.
caps	3 Lily read BLITHE SPIRIT by Noel Coward. I read VANITY FAIR.
lock	4 Did they fix the problem of the torn panel and worn element?

| 1 | 2 | 3 | 4 | 5 | 6 | 7 | 8 | 9 | 10 | 11 | 12 |

15b Technique Reinforcement

Reach up or down without moving your hands. Key each line once; repeat drill.

adjacent reaches

5 as oil red ask wet opt mop try tree open shred operas treaty

6 were pore dirt stew ruin faster onion alumni dreary mnemonic

7 The opened red hydrants were powerful, fast, and very dirty.

outside reaches

8 pop zap cap zag wasp equip lazy zippers queue opinion quartz

9 zest waste paper exist parquet azalea acquaint apollo apathy

10 The lazy wasp passed the potted azalea on the parquet floor.

New Keys

15c 5 and 0

Key each line once.

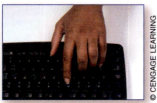

5 Reach *up* with *left first* finger.

0 Reach *up* with *right fourth* finger.

5

11 5 5f f5 5 5; 5 fans; 5 feet; 5 figs; 5 fobs; 5 furs; 5 flaws

12 5 o'clock; 5 a.m.; 5 p.m.; is 55 or less; buy 55; 5 and 5 is

13 Call Line 555 if 5 fans or 5 bins arrive at Pier 5 by 5 p.m.

0

14 0 0; ;0 0 0; skip 0; plan 0; left 0; is below 0; I scored 0;

15 0 degrees; key 0 and 0; write 00 here; the total is 0 or 00;

16 She laughed at their 0 to 0 score; but ours was 0 to 0 also.

all figures learned

17 I keyed 550 pages for Invoice 05, or 50 more than we needed.

18 Pages 15 and 18 of the program listed 150, not 180, members.

19 On May 10, Rick drove 500 miles to New Mexico in car No. 08.

49-d1

Document with Graphics

1. Tap ENTER three times to position the title at 2".
2. Key the report shown below and then apply the formats listed after the report.

Trend Analysis Report

Market Trends

The population in the metropolitan area is growing both in the college's service area and in the demographic segments that represent the greatest market enrollment.

The metropolitan area continues to add employment opportunities at a growth rate of 22 percent, but the area economy suffers from some of the same insecurities about the future as do other areas.

Information technology is creating more customer potential and new demands for the delivery of coursework as well as generating new opportunities for competitors to enter this educational market.

The pace of change is forcing people at all levels of the economy to learn new skills at the same time they are being asked to work harder—and sometimes hold more than one job.

The new school improvement plan has not taken shape as quickly as anticipated, but a move toward mastering skills and testing for proficiencies—not rote knowledge—is gaining momentum.

3. Apply the Essential theme to the document.
4. Apply Title style to the title and Subtitle style to the subtitle.
5. Use a checkbox symbol (☑) from the Wingdings font and apply bullets to the five paragraphs.
6. Tap ENTER 11 times following the last paragraph and key: **Understanding our community to prepare for our future!** Apply 18-point Brush Script MT font and center the paragraph.
7. Search for a clip using the keyword *Trends*. Select and insert the clip that shows a computer keyboard with a key named *Trends*.
8. Apply Square text wrapping and size the clip 2.5" high; position it below the bulleted text about 1.5" from the left edge of the paper.
9. Insert a Cloud Callout shape and size it 2" high; position it below the bulleted text about 1.5" from the right edge of the paper. Use the adjustment handle to connect the cloud to the *Trends* key in the clip art.
10. Add text to the callout: **Market Trends Affecting Academia**
11. Use the Quick Check on the next page to compare your document.
12. Proofread and check; click Next to continue. (*49-d1*)

Skill Building

15d Textbook Keying
Key each line once; DS between 3-line groups.

improve figures

20 Read pages 5 and 8; duplicate page 18; omit pages 50 and 51.

21 We have Model 80 with 10 meters or Model 180 with 15 meters.

22 After May 18, French 050 meets in room 15 at 10 a.m. daily.

improve long reaches

23 Barb Abver saw a vibrant version of her brave venture on TV.

24 Call a woman or a man who will manage Minerva Manor in Nome.

25 We were quick to squirt a quantity of water at Quin and West.

E | ALL LETTERS

15e Timed Writing
Take a 2' writing on both paragraphs. End the lesson; go to the Word Processor to complete 15e. **Use wordwrap.**

	gwam 2'	3'
I thought about Harry and how he had worked for me for	6	4
10 years; how daily at 8 he parked his worn car in the lot;	12	8
then, he left at 5. Every day was almost identical for him.	18	12
In a quiet way, he did his job well, asking for little	23	15
attention. So I never recognized his thirst for travel. I	29	19
didn't expect to find all of those maps near his workplace.	35	23

2' | 1 | 2 | 3 | 4 | 5 | 6 |
3' | 1 | 2 | 3 | 4 |

15f Tab Review

1. Read the instructions to clear and set tabs.

2. Go to the Word Processor. Set a left tab at 4".

3. Practice the lines; tap TAB without watching your keyboard.

STANDARD PLAN for Setting and Clearing Tabs in the Word Processor

Preset or default tabs are displayed on the Ruler. If necessary, display the Ruler in the Word Processor. (Choose Horizontal Ruler on the View menu.) Sometimes you will want to remove or clear existing tabs before setting new ones.

To clear and set tabs:

1. On the menu bar, click Format, and then Clear All Tabs.

2. To set tabs: From the Format menu, select Set Tab. Select the type of tab you want to set (left, center, decimal, or right); enter the position and click OK.

Option: Click the left or right mouse button directly on the Ruler to set either a left or right tab.

Set tab 4"

►Tab	Keyboarding
has become ►Tab	the primary
means of ►Tab	written communication
in business and ►Tab	in our personal lives.
Keyboarding is ►Tab	used by persons
in every profession ►Tab	and most job levels.

To size a clip:

Picture Tools Format/Size/Height or Width

- Click the clip in the document and use the Height or Width arrows in the Size group to adjust the clip to the desired size. -or-
- Click the clip and position the pointer over the handles and drag to increase or decrease the size as you did with shapes.

DRILL 2   CLIP ART

1. Key your name, right-align it, tap ENTER twice, and change to left-alignment.

2. Click Clip Art to display the task pane and search for a laptop computer clip.

3. Select a clip and click it to insert it in the document.

4. Apply Square text wrapping to the clip.

5. Size it to 4" by 4".

6. Drag the clip to the approximate horizontal center of the page.

7. Proofread and check; click Next to continue. (49-drill2)

JGI/JAMIE GRILL/BLEND IMAGES/JUPITER IMAGES

! WORKPLACE SUCCESS

Positive Attitude

What makes a successful employee? Many employers respond to that question with a list of characteristics that are often referred to as "soft skills." Having the skills and knowledge necessary to do your job is always expected, and most employers can determine if a potential employee has the necessary technical skills before hiring that person. Trying to determine whether a potential employee has the necessary soft skills is much more difficult.

Most employers list a positive attitude as one of the top five characteristics that they seek in a potential employee. They believe that a positive attitude enhances performance. Although people with positive attitudes tend to smile more and be more optimistic, the primary reason employers seek people with a positive attitude is that they tend to be problem solvers. They look at problems as challenges that also come with opportunities and try to find ways to solve them.

Self-confidence is also linked to a positive attitude. If you think you can do something, you are quite likely to do it. If you do not think you can do something and have doubts about your ability, you are not likely to do things you are capable of doing very well. Workers with a poor self-image are more likely to look for faults than strengths.

Another very important reason for developing a positive attitude is that other employees prefer to work with individuals who have a positive attitude. Most companies require employees to work on teams; thus, having a positive attitude enhances teamwork and contributes to the success of the team.

Lesson 16 | 2 and 7

Key each line twice.

alphabet	1	Perry might know I feel jinxed because I have missed a quiz.
figures	2	Channels 5 and 8, on from 10 to 11, said Luisa's IQ was 150.
caps lock	3	Ella Hill will see Chekhov's THE CHERRY ORCHARD on Czech TV.
easy	4	The big dog by the bush kept the ducks and hen in the field.

| 1 | 2 | 3 | 4 | 5 | 6 | 7 | 8 | 9 | 10 | 11 | 12 |

New Keys

16b 2 and 7
Key each line once.

2 Reach *up* with *left third* finger.

7 Reach *up* with *right first* finger.

2

5 2 2s s2 2 2; has 2 sons; is 2 sizes; was 2 sites; has 2 skis
6 add 2 and 2; 2 sets of 2; catch 22; as 2 of the 22; 222 Main
7 Exactly at 2 on April 22, the 22nd Company left from Pier 2.

7

8 7 7j j7 7 7; 7 jets; 7 jeans; 7 jays; 7 jobs; 7 jars; 7 jaws
9 ask for 7; buy 7; 77 years; June 7; take any 7; deny 77 boys
10 From May 7 on, all 77 men will live at 777 East 77th Street.

all figures learned

11 I read 2 of the 72 books, Ellis read 7, and Han read all 72.
12 Tract 27 cites the date as 1850; Tract 170 says it was 1852.
13 You can take Flight 850 on January 12; I'll take Flight 705.

16c Number Reinforcement
Key each line. Concentrate as you reach to the top row.

8/1	14	line 8; Book 1; No. 88; Seat 11; June 18; Cart 81; date 1881
2/7	15	take 2; July 7; buy 22; sell 77; mark 27; adds 72; Memo 2772
5/0	16	feed 5; bats 0; age 50; Ext. 55; File 50; 55 bags; band 5005
all	17	I work 18 visual signs with 20 turns of the 57 lenses to 70.
all	18	Did 17 boys fix the gears for 50 bicycles in 28 racks or 10?

CLIP ART

Clip
Art

Clip art is a media file that may be an illustration, photograph, video, or audio file. A large collection of clips is provided with *Office* software, and additional clips are available online. Clip art can be located by using keywords that describe the type of clip you are trying to find.

To add a clip to a document:

Insert/Illustrations/Clip Art

1. Click Clip Art to display the Clip Art task pane. Key a word or phrase in the Search for box to locate the desired type of clip art. Accept the defaults and click Go.

2. Scroll to locate the desired clip and click it to insert it in the document.

Note: If you do not find an appropriate clip, position the pointer over one or more clips, click the drop-list arrow ❶ at the right of it, and then click Preview/Properties ❷. Note that other keywords are suggested that may help you locate a clip that meets your needs.

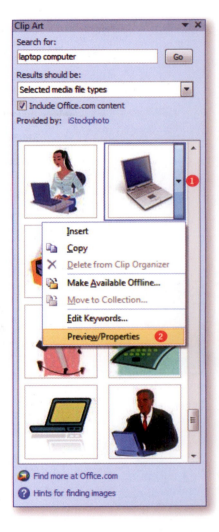

A new clip is inserted in a blank paragraph, like text. To move it easily, you must change the text wrapping option.

To change text wrapping and move a clip:

Picture Tools Format/Arrange/Wrap Text

1. Click the clip in the document, and then click Wrap Text and select a style such as Square.

2. Drag the clip to the desired position.

TIP

Check Include Office.com content in the Clip Art task pane to obtain clips from the Microsoft online gallery. If you do not locate the clip illustrated, substitute a similar one. Use other keywords if necessary to locate an appropriate clip.

Skill Building

16d Textbook Keying

Key each line once to review reaches; fingers curved and relaxed; wrists low. DS between groups.

3rd/4th
19 pop was lap pass slaw wool solo swap apollo wasp load plaque
20 Al's quote was, "I was dazzled by the jazz, pizza, and pool."

1st/2nd
21 bad fun nut kick dried night brick civic thick hutch believe
22 Kim may visit her friends in Germany if I give her a ticket.

3rd/1st
23 cry tube wine quit very curb exit crime ebony mention excite
24 To be invited, petition the six executive committee members.

16e Textbook Keying

Key each line once; DS between 3-line groups. Do not pause at the end of lines.

TECHNIQUE TIP

Think and key the words and phrases as units rather than letter by letter.

words: *think, say,* and *key* words

25 is do am lay cut pen dub may fob ale rap cot hay pay hem box
26 box wit man sir fish also hair giant rigor civic virus ivory
27 laugh sight flame audit formal social turkey bicycle problem

phrases: *think, say,* and *key* phrases

28 is it│is it│if it is│if it is│or by│or by│or me│or me│for us
29 and all│for pay│pay dues and│the pen│the pen box│the pen box
30 such forms│held both│work form│then wish│sign name│with them

easy sentences

31 The man is to do the work right; he then pays the neighbors.
32 Sign the forms to pay the eight men for the turkey and hams.
33 The antique ivory bicycle is a social problem for the chair.

│ 1 │ 2 │ 3 │ 4 │ 5 │ 6 │ 7 │ 8 │ 9 │ 10 │ 11 │ 12 │

16f Timed Writing

Take a 2' timing on both paragraphs. Repeat the timing. **Use wordwrap.**

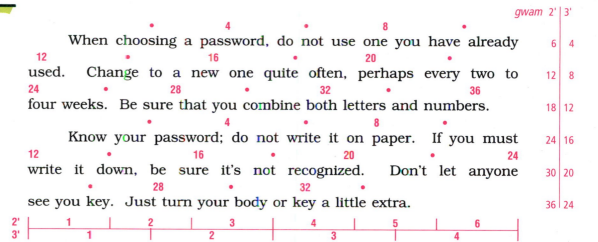

	gwam 2'	3'
When choosing a password, do not use one you have already	6	4
used. Change to a new one quite often, perhaps every two to	12	8
four weeks. Be sure that you combine both letters and numbers.	18	12
Know your password; do not write it on paper. If you must	24	16
write it down, be sure it's not recognized. Don't let anyone	30	20
see you key. Just turn your body or key a little extra.	36	24

2' 1   2   3   4   5   6
3' 1   2   3   4

Drawing tools can be used to apply a Shape Style; to change the shape fill, outline, or effects; to size the shape to specific dimensions; to position it; and to group multiple shapes. Position the mouse over each of the commands on the Drawing Tools Format tab to preview the description and other information about the commands. On the commands with drop-list arrows, click the arrow to view the gallery of options available. Some of the commands are shown below.

More button

To format a shape using the Drawing Tools commands:

Drawing Tools Format/Shape Styles/Shape Fill, Shape Outline, Shape Effects, Shape Styles

1. Select the shape and then click the Shape Styles More button to display the Shape Styles gallery.

2. Click the desired style to apply it. -or-

3. Click the drop-list arrow on Shape Fill, Shape Outline, or Shape Effects and choose a fill color, outline color and weight, or a shape effect.

Grouping shapes enables you to move all of the shapes in the group as one object. Groups can be ungrouped to make changes in an individual shape. Then they can be regrouped.

To group shapes:

Drawing Tools Format/Arrange/Group

1. Press and hold the SHIFT key as you click each object that is to be a part of the group.

2. Click Group and then select Group.

3. To make changes to a shape in the group, click Group and then Ungroup.

4. After the changes have been made, select the shapes and group them.

DRILL 1 — SHAPES

1. Key your name and right-align it. Tap ENTER and return to left-align.

2. From the gallery of shapes, insert a Diamond, a Striped Right Arrow, a Rounded Rectangle, a Striped Right Arrow, and an Oval. Use the mouse to size the shapes about 1" high and the arrows 0.25" high.

3. Apply the Light 1 Outline, Colored Fill – Olive Green, Accent 3 Shape Style to the shapes that are not arrows.

4. Add the text **Plan**, **Execute**, and **Evaluate** as shown below; apply bold to the text.

5. Apply Shape Fill – Olive Green, Accent 3, Lighter 80% and Shape Outline – Olive Green, Accent 3, Darker 50% to both arrows.

6. Group the shapes, and then move the group down so the top of the group is at about 2" on the Vertical Ruler.

7. Proofread and check; click Next to continue. (49-drill1)

Lesson 17 | *4 and 9*

WARMUP

Warmup 17a

Key each line twice.

alphabet	1	Bob realized very quickly that jumping was excellent for us.
figures	2	Has each of the 18 clerks now corrected Item 501 on page 27?
shift keys	3	L. K. Coe, M.D., hopes Dr. Lopez can leave for Maine in May.
easy	4	The men paid their own firms for the eight big enamel signs.

New Keys

17b   **4** and **9**
Key each line once.

4 Reach *up* with *left first* finger.

9 Reach *up* with *right third* finger.

4

5 4 4f f4 4 4 4; if 4 furs; off 4 floors; gaff 4 fish; 4 flags

6 44th floor; half of 44; 4 walked 44 flights; 4 girls; 4 boys

7 I order exactly 44 bagels, 4 cakes, and 4 pies before 4 a.m.

9

8 9 9l l9 9 9 9; fill 9 lugs; call 9 lads; Bill 9 lost; dial 9

9 also 9 oaks; roll 9 loaves; 9.9 degrees; sell 9 oaks; Hall 9

10 Just 9 couples, 9 men and 9 women, left at 9 on our Tour 99.

all figures learned

11 Memo 94 says 9 pads, 4 pens, and 4 ribbons were sent July 9.

12 Study Item 17 and Item 28 on page 40 and Item 59 on page 49.

13 Within 17 months he drove 85 miles, walked 29, and flew 490.

Skill Building

17c   **Textbook Keying**
Key each line once.

14 My staff of *18* worked *11* hours a day from May *27* to June *12*.

15 There were *5* items tested by Inspector *7* at *4* p.m. on May *8*.

16 Please send her File *10* today at *8*; her access number is *97*.

17 Car *47* had its trial run. The qualifying speed was *198* mph.

18 The estimated score? *485*. Actual? *190*. Difference? *295*.

SHAPES

Individual shapes can be added to a document, or a number of shapes can be combined to create a more complex drawing. Review the illustration at the right to view the different groups of preformatted shapes that are built into the software. Note that once you have used a shape, it is added to the group of Recently Used Shapes. It is also retained in the group in which it is normally located. You can add text to most shapes by clicking in the shape and keying the text.

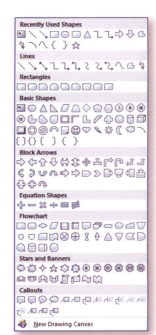

To add a shape to a document:
Insert/Illustrations/Shapes

1. Click Shapes to display the gallery of Shapes available.
2. Click the shape desired; then click in the document where you want to position the shape and drag diagonally to draw the shape the desired size.
3. To add text to the shape, click on it and key the text.

TIP

To create a perfect circle or square (or to constrain the dimensions of other shapes), press and hold SHIFT while you drag.

FORMAT SHAPES

The size and layout of a shape can be changed with the mouse. The appearance of shapes can be changed by using a variety of drawing tools.

To change shape size or location with the mouse:
Select the shape to display the sizing handles located in the corners and center of the borders.

- To increase or decrease the shape size, hold the insertion point over a sizing handle; when the pointer turns to a double-headed arrow, drag to the size desired.
- To move a shape, hold the insertion point over one of the borders; when the pointer turns to a four-headed arrow, drag to the position desired.
- To rotate the shape, turn the rotation handle to the desired position.
- To adjust the image's appearance, drag the adjustment handle.

TIP

Dragging the sizing handles at the corners will retain the proportion of the shape; dragging the sizing handles at the center will distort the proportion of the shape.

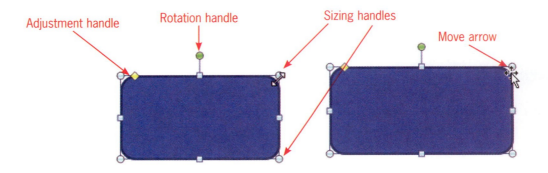

17d Technique Reinforcement

Key smoothly; tap the keys at a brisk, steady pace.

first finger

19 buy them gray vent guy brunt buy brunch much give huge vying
20 Hagen, after her July triumph at tennis, may try volleyball.
21 Verna urges us to buy yet another of her beautiful rag rugs.

second finger

22 keen idea; kick it back; ice breaker; decide the issue; cite
23 Did Dick ask Cecelia, his sister, if she decided to like me?
24 Suddenly, Micki's bike skidded on the Cedar Street ice rink.

third/fourth finger

25 low slow lax solo wax zip zap quips quiz zipper prior icicle
26 Paula has always allowed us to relax at La Paz and at Quito.
27 Please ask Zale to explain who explores most aquatic slopes.

E **ALL LETTERS**

17e Timed Writing

Take a 2' timing on both paragraphs. Repeat the timing. **Use wordwrap.**

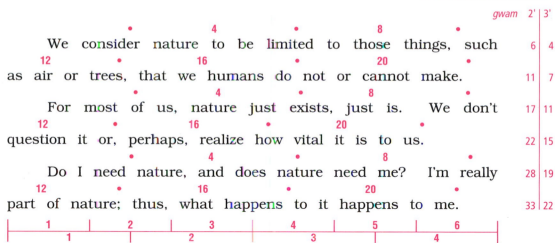

	gwam	2'	3'
We consider nature to be limited to those things, such		6	4
as air or trees, that we humans do not or cannot make.		11	7
For most of us, nature just exists, just is. We don't		17	11
question it or, perhaps, realize how vital it is to us.		22	15
Do I need nature, and does nature need me? I'm really		28	19
part of nature; thus, what happens to it happens to me.		33	22

2' | 1 | 2 | 3 | 4 | 5 | 6 |
3' | 1 | 2 | 3 | 4 |

17f Enrichment

★ TECHNIQUE TIP

Keep hands quiet and fingers well curved over the keys. Do not allow your fingers to bounce.

1. Click the Skill Building tab from the main menu and choose Technique Builder; select Drill 2.
2. Key Drill 2 from page 32. Key each line once striving for good accuracy.
3. The results will be listed on the Skill Building Report.

49c Timed Writing

1. Key a 1' writing on each paragraph; work to increase speed. Use wordwrap.
2. Key a 3' timing on all paragraphs.

	gwam	1'	3'

Homeownership is the dream of most Americans. Yet only about   12 4 79
two-thirds of all people are able to achieve that dream. Many young   26 9 84
people who are single do not think of buying a home; they live in rental   40 13 89
units. The reasons for their choice vary widely. Many recognize that   54 18 93
owning a home comes with major responsibilities. Others just have   67 22 98
never thought about the idea.   73 25 100

Why do families tend to focus more on owning their homes than   12 29 104
single people? Most seem to think that owning a home requires a   25 33 108
commitment to stay in the same location for a long period of time.   39 37 113
Single people are often not ready to make that commitment. They want   52 42 117
to be free to move on when opportunity knocks. Another reason is that   66 47 122
apartments provide more social outlets for singles.   77 50 126

A home can be a very good financial investment. Typically, a   12 54 130
down payment is required when you buy a home. Significant tax   25 58 134
benefits accrue from owning a home. The mortgage payment consists   38 63 138
of both the interest on the loan and principal repayment. The interest   52 68 143
is tax deductible. The down payment and the portion of the payment   65 72 147
that goes to the principal are the owner's equity.   76 75 151

```
1' |  1  |  2  |  3  |  4  |  5  |  6  |  7  |  8  |  9  | 10  | 11  | 12  | 13  |
3' |        1        |        2        |        3        |        4        |
```

New Commands

49d

KEYBOARDING PRO DELUXE 2

References/Word 2010
Commands/Lesson 49

LEARNING ABOUT GRAPHICS

Many different types of graphics can be used to enhance documents. Typically, graphics are used in documents such as announcements, invitations, flyers, brochures, reports, and newsletters. However, they can be used in virtually any type of document to enhance the document and to clarify or simplify concepts. For example, a picture may convey a concept that would take many words to describe adequately. It is important to use graphics strategically and not to overuse them. The overuse of graphics can be distracting to the reader.

In this lesson, you will insert and format shapes and clip art. Shapes are actually drawing tools. They can be combined to create complex drawings. *Office 2010*'s clip art files include illustrations (created by hand or computer software), photographs, and audio and video clips.

Lesson 18 | *3 and 6*

WARMUP

Warmup 18a

Key each line twice.

alphabet 1 Jim Kable won a second prize for his very quixotic drawings.

figures 2 If 57 of the 105 boys go on July 29, 48 of them will remain.

easy 3 With the usual bid, I paid for a quantity of big world maps.

| 1 | 2 | 3 | 4 | 5 | 6 | 7 | 8 | 9 | 10 | 11 | 12 |

New Keys

18b 3 and 6

Key each line once.

3 Reach *up* with *left second* finger.

6 Reach *up* with *right first* finger.

Note: Ergonomic keyboard users will use *left first* finger to key 6.

3

4 3 3d d3 3 3; had 3 days; did 3 dives; led 3 dogs; add 3 dips

5 we 3 ride 3 cars; take 33 dials; read 3 copies; save 33 days

6 On July 3, 33 lights lit 33 stands holding 33 prize winners.

6

7 6 6j 6j 6 6; 6 jays; 6 jams; 6 jigs; 6 jibs; 6 jots; 6 jokes

8 only 6 high; on 66 units; reach 66 numbers; 6 yams or 6 jams

9 On May 6, Car 66 delivered 66 tons of No. 6 shale to Pier 6.

all figures learned

10 At 6 p.m., Channel 3 reported the August 6 score was 6 to 3.

11 Jean, do Items 28 and 6; Mika, 59 and 10; Kyle, 3, 4, and 7.

12 Cars 56 and 34 used Aisle 9; Cars 2 and 87 can use Aisle 10.

Skill Building

18c Keyboard Reinforcement

Key each line once.

⭐ **TECHNIQUE TIP**

Make long reaches without returning to home row between reaches.

long reaches

13 ce cede cedar wreck nu nu nut punt nuisance my my amy mystic

14 ny ny any many company mu mu mull lumber mulch br br furbish

15 Cecil received a large brown umbrella from Bunny and Hunter.

number review

16 set 0; push 4; Car 00; score 44; jot 04; age 40; Billet 4004

17 April 5; lock 5; set 66; fill 55; hit 65; pick 56; adds 5665

18 Her grades are 93, 87, and 100; his included 82, 96, and 54.

Graphics

LEARNING OUTCOMES

- Learn to create and format graphics.
- Enhance documents with graphics.
- Create documents with columns and graphics.
- Build keyboarding skills.

Lesson 49 | *Basic Graphics*

New Commands

- Insert Shapes
- Format Shapes
- Insert Clip Art
- Format Clip Art

KEYBOARDING PRO DELUXE 2

WARMUP

Lessons/49a Warmup

Skill Building

49b Textbook Keying

1. Key each line, concentrating on using good keying techniques. Tap ENTER after each 3-line group.
2. Repeat the drill if time permits.

adjacent keys

1 were pool fast join tree guy trait cruise walk fare port trio buy

2 mere try career trade polka excite joint report revere riot quiet

3 Polly and Guy were trying to prepare a joint report very quickly.

long, direct reaches

4 braced munch decide jumped many brave curve numb young hunt brunt

5 jungle nut glum bun precede muck break junk must plum nerve bunch

6 Cecilia munched on junk food while she hunted for her cat, Brent.

| 1 | 2 | 3 | 4 | 5 | 6 | 7 | 8 | 9 | 10 | 11 | 12 | 13 |

18d Textbook Keying

Key each line once; DS between 2-line groups.

word response: *think* and *key* words

19 he el id is go us it an me of he of to if ah or bye do so am

20 Did she enamel emblems on a big panel for the downtown sign?

stroke response: *think* and *key* each stroke

21 kin are hip read lymph was pop saw ink art oil gas up as mop

22 Barbara started the union wage earners tax in Texas in July.

combination response: vary speed but maintain rhythm

23 upon than eve lion when burley with they only them loin were

24 It was the opinion of my neighbor that we may work as usual.

E   ALL LETTERS

18e Timed Writing

1. Key two 3' writings.
   Use wordwrap.

2. End the lesson but do not exit the software.

Goals: 1', 17–23 *gwam*
       2', 15–21 *gwam*
       3', 14–20 *gwam*

gwam 2' | 3'

	4	8		
I am something quite precious. Though millions of people			6	4
12	16	20		
in other countries might not have me, you likely do. I have			12	8
24	28	32	36	
a lot of power. For it is I who names a new president every			18	12
	40	44	48	
four years. It is I who decides if a tax shall be levied.			24	16
	52	56	60	
I even decide questions of war or peace. I was acquired at			30	20
	64	68	72	
a great cost; however, I am free to all citizens. And yet,			36	24
	76	80	84	
sadly, I am often ignored; or, still worse, I am just taken			42	28
	88	92	96	
for granted. I can be lost, and in certain circumstances I			48	32
	100	104	108	
can even be taken away. What, you may ask, am I? I am your			54	36
	112	116		
right to vote. Don't take me lightly.			58	39

2' | 1 | 2 | 3 | 4 | 5 | 6 |
3' | 1 | 2 | 3 | 4 |

Communication

18f Composition

1. Go to the Word Processor.

2. Introduce yourself to your instructor by composing two paragraphs, each containing about three sentences. Use proper grammatical structure. Do not worry about keying errors at this time.

3. Save the document as *xx-profile*. (Remember to replace *xx* with your initials.) It is not necessary to print the document. You will open and print it in a later lesson.

graphics, sound and video clips, and/or photographs copied from a Web page.

- Duplicating and distributing copies of music downloaded from the Web.

Know the Copyright Laws

To avoid copyright infringement, the designer must be knowledgeable about copyright law. Two important laws include The Copyright Law of 1976 and the Digital Millennium Copyright Act of 1998, which was enacted to update the copyright law for the digital age.

> **The Copyright Law of 1976:** Original works are protected by copyright at the moment they are first originated—printed, drawn, captured, or saved to a digital storage area. The copyright protection is automatic when the original work is first established in the real medium of expression.[1]

With an understanding of the copyright laws, users/designers now realize that materials placed on a website may be copyrighted and are not available for downloading or copying and pasting into other documents. Sound advice is always to seek permission from the original copyright owner before using the material. Purchasing royalty-free content is another excellent way to avoid any question of copyright infringement.

Protocol for Copyright Decisions

Employment at Okhuysen Design Company requires your full understanding of the challenges designers face related to copyright infringement and knowledge of all copyright laws. Should you have questions about an action in which you are unclear, practice the following protocol:

1. Refer to the copyright section of our company handbook (www.okhuysen.com/copyright).

2. Contact Carole Okhuysen for company approval.

Best of luck as you join our group of outstanding designers.

Footnote

[1]For full discussion, see *ODC Employee Handbook,* Section 12, page 59.

48-d2

Edit Report

BOOKMARK

www.collegekeyboarding.com
Module 6 Practice Quiz

1. Open *48-d1* and format as an unbound report.
2. Find all occurrences of the word *challenges* and replace the second occurrence with the word **opportunities**.
3. Delete the footnote.
4. Check the test and close. (*48-d2*)

Lesson 19 | $ and - (hyphen), Number Expression

WARMUP

Warmup 19a

Key each line twice.

alphabet	1	Why did the judge quiz poor Victor about his blank tax form?
figures	2	J. Boyd, Ph.D., changed Items 10, 57, 36, and 48 on page 92.
3rd row	3	To try the tea, we hope to tour the port prior to the party.
easy	4	Did he signal the authentic robot to do a turn to the right?

| 1 | 2 | 3 | 4 | 5 | 6 | 7 | 8 | 9 | 10 | 11 | 12 |

New Keys

19b $ and -

Key each line once; DS between 2-line groups.

- = hyphen
-- = dash
Do not space before or after a hyphen or a dash.

$ Shift; then reach *up* with *left first* finger.

- (hyphen) Reach *up* with *right fourth* finger.

$

5 $ $f f$ $ $; if $4; half $4; off $4; of $4; $4 fur; $4 flats

6 for $8; cost $9; log $3; grab $10; give Rolf $2; give Viv $4

7 Since she paid $45 for the item priced at $54, she saved $9.

- (hyphen)

8 - -; ;- - - -; up-to-date; co-op; father-in-law; four-square

9 pop-up foul; big-time job; snap-on bit; one- or two-hour ski

10 You need 6 signatures--half of the members--on the petition.

all symbols learned

11 I paid $10 for the low-cost disk; high-priced ones cost $40.

12 Le-An spent $20 for travel, $95 for books, and $38 for food.

13 Mr. Loft-Smit sold his boat for $467; he bought it for $176.

Skill Building

19c Keyboard Reinforcement

Key each line once; repeat the drill.

e/d	14	Edie discreetly decided to deduct expenses in making a deal.
w/e	15	Working women wear warm wool sweaters when weather dictates.
r/e	16	We heard very rude remarks regarding her recent termination.
s/d	17	Daily sudden mishaps destroyed several dozens of sand dunes.
v/b	18	Beverley voted by giving a bold beverage to every brave boy.

48-d1

Leftbound Report

★ TIP

Remember to proofread and preview each document for placement before you move to the next one.

1. Key the leftbound report shown below. Apply the Equity document theme.
2. Indent the long quotation appropriately. Remove the hyperlink to the website.
3. Create a cover page using the Pinstripes cover page style. Key the following:

   Document Title: Key main heading.

   Document subtitle: **Orientation Session for New Employees**

   Date: Select the current date.

   Company Name: **Okhuysen Design Company**

   Author Name: **Carole Okhuysen, President**
4. Insert a Continuous section break at the top of the first page of the report.
5. Position the insertion point in the header of Section 2. Deselect Different First Page if it is selected. Break the links between the headers for both sections. Go to the footer of Section 2. Break the link between the footers for both sections.
6. Go to the header of Section 2 and number the pages of the report at the top right using the Plain Number 3 page number style. Change the page number format to begin with page 1. Click Different First Page to suppress the page numbers on the first page of the report.
7. Continue to the next document. (48-d1)

Copyright Directives

Welcome to Okhuysen Design Company and to our fine group of design specialists. Orientation to a design company requires a review of copyright law and directives related to copyright issues you will encounter. Please read carefully the information provided in this report.

Understand Technology Infringements

As technology advances more rapidly than ever before, designers are faced with new challenges related to copyright compliance. History shows us that copyright infringements occur at the introduction of each new invention or emerging technology. Examples include the phonograph and tape recorder and mimeograph and copy machines. Today, the ease of copying Web materials and distributing electronic files provides even greater challenges.

Authors who publish content on the Web, photographers who post their pictures on Web pages, and recording artists whose music is downloaded from the Web are only a few examples of copyright challenges resulting from this technology and the ease in which it can be done. Compounding the issue is that many designers may not be aware they are violating copyright law. The following list shows actions taken daily that are considered copyright infringements:

- Copying content from a Web page and pasting it into documents.
- Distributing handouts that contain cartoon characters or other graphics copied from a Web page.
- Presenting originally designed electronic presentations that contain

(continued)

19d Textbook Keying

Key each line once, working for fluid, consistent stroking.

★ TECHNIQUE TIP

- Key the easy words as "words" rather than stroke by stroke.
- Key each phrase (marked by a vertical line) without pauses between words.

easy words

19 am it go bus dye jam irk six sod tic yam ugh spa vow aid dug

20 he or by air big elf dog end fit and lay sue toe wit own got

21 six foe pen firm also body auto form down city kept make fog

easy phrases

22 it is | if the | and also to me | the end | to us | if it | it is | to the

23 if it is | to the end | do you wish | to go to | for the end | to make

24 lay down | he or she | make me | by air | end of | by me | kept it | of me

easy sentences

25 Did the chap work to mend the torn right half of the ensign?

26 Blame me for their penchant for the antique chair and panel.

27 She bid by proxy for eighty bushels of a corn and rye blend.

Communication

19e Textbook Keying

1. Study the rules and examples at the right.
2. Key the sample sentences 28–33.
3. Change figures to words as needed in sentences 34–36.

NUMBER EXPRESSION: SPELL OUT NUMBERS

1. **First word in a sentence.** Key numbers ten and lower as words unless they are part of a series of related numbers, any of which are over ten.

   Three of the four members were present.

   She wrote 12 stories and 2 plays in five years.

2. The **smaller of two adjacent numbers** as words.

   SolVir shipped six 24-ton engines.

3. **Isolated fractions and approximate numbers.** Key as words **large round numbers that can be expressed as one or two words**. Hyphenate fractions expressed as words.

   She completed one-fourth of the experiments.

   Val sent out three hundred invitations.

4. **Preceding "o'clock."**

   John's due at four o'clock. Pick him up at 4:15 p.m.

28 **Six** or **seven** older players were cut from the **37**-member team.

29 I have **2** of **14** coins I need to start my set.   Kristen has **9**.

30 Of **nine 24**-ton engines ordered, we shipped **six** last Tuesday.

31 Shelly has read just **one-half** of about **forty-five** documents.

32 The **six** boys sent well over **two hundred** printed invitations.

33 **One** or **two** of us will be on duty from **two** until **six** o'clock.

34 The meeting begins promptly at 9.   We plan 4 sessions.

35 The three-person crew cleaned 6 stands, 12 tables, and 13 desks.

36 The 3rd meeting is at 3 o'clock on Friday, February 2.

Lesson 48 | Assessment

Skill Building

gwam 3' | 5'

48b Timed Writing
Take two 5' timed writings.

Whether any company can succeed depends on how well it fits   4 | 2
into the economic system. Success rests on certain key factors   8 | 5
that are put in line by a management team that has set goals for   13 | 8
the company and has enough good judgment to recognize how best to   17 | 10
reach these goals. Because of competition, only the best-organized   21 | 13
companies get to the top.   23 | 14

A commercial enterprise is formed for a specific purpose: 27 | 16
that purpose is usually to equip others, or consumers, with   31 | 19
whatever they cannot equip themselves. Unless there is only one   36 | 21
provider, a consumer will search for a company that returns the   40 | 24
most value in terms of price; and a relationship with such a   43 | 27
company, once set up, can endure for many years.   47 | 28

Thus our system assures that the businesses that manage to   51 | 31
survive are those that have been able to combine successfully an   56 | 33
excellent product with a low price and the best service—all in a   60 | 36
place that is convenient for the buyers. With no intrusion from   64 | 39
outside forces, the buyer and the seller benefit both themselves   69 | 41
and each other.   70 | 42

3' | 1   2   3   4
5' | 1   2   3

Applications

48c

Assessment

 Continue

 Check

When you complete a document, proofread it, check the spelling, and preview for placement. When you are completely satisfied, click the Continue button to move to the next document. Click the Check button when you are ready to error-check the test. Review and/or print the document analysis results.

Lesson 20 | # and /

WARMUP

Warmup 20a

Key each line twice (slowly, then faster).

alphabet	1 Freda Jencks will have money to buy six quite large topazes.
symbols	2 I bought 10 ribbons and 45 disks from Cable-Han Co. for $78.
home row	3 Dallas sold jade flasks; Sal has a glass flask full of salt.
easy	4 He may cycle down to the field by the giant oak and cut hay.

New Keys

20b # and /

Key each line once.

= number sign, pounds
/ = diagonal, slash

Shift; then reach *up* with *left second* finger.

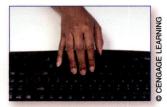

/ Reach *down* with *right fourth* finger.

#

5 # #e e# # # #; had #3 dial; did #3 drop; set #3 down; Bid #3

6 leave #82; sold #20; Lyric #16; bale #34; load #53; Optic #7

7 Notice #333 says to load Car #33 with 33# of #3 grade shale.

/

8 / /; ;/ / / /; 1/2; 1/3; Mr./Mrs.; 1/4/12; 22 11/12; and/or;

9 to/from; /s/ William Smit; 2/10, n/30; his/her towels; 6 1/2

10 The numerals 1 5/8, 3 1/4, and 60 7/9 are "mixed fractions."

all symbols learned

11 Invoice #737 cites 15 2/3# of rye was shipped C.O.D. 4/6/11.

12 B-O-A Company's Check #50/5 for $87 paid for 15# of #3 wire.

13 Our Co-op List #20 states $40 for 16 1/2 crates of tomatoes.

Skill Building

20c Keyboard Reinforcement

Key each line once; work for fluency.

Option: In the Word Processor, key 30" writings on both lines of a pair. Work to avoid pauses.

		gwam 30"
14	She did the key work at the height of the problem.	20
15	Form #726 is the title to the island; she owns it.	20
16	The rock is a form of fuel; he did enrich it with coal.	22
17	The corn-and-turkey dish is a blend of turkey and corn.	22
18	It is right to work to end the social problems of the world.	24
19	If I sign it on 3/19, the form can aid us to pay the 40 men.	24

47-d1

continued

○　Prepare online materials that more clearly explain the areas of the dress code that appeared in the study as violations.

In summary, the current dress code is fulfilling the company philosophy to provide a comfortable work environment and to project a positive corporate image. Professional development is recommended in selected areas.

Footnote text:

[1]Policy #105-12 Dress Code, Adopted October 15, 2000, Revised January 1, 2010.

[2]Study of five hundred companies revealed that 80% of the companies reported a 60% level of compliance by employees to established company dress policies.

47-d2

Edit report

1. Reformat *47-d1* as an unbound report.
2. Change the bulleted list to a numbered list.
3. Delete the second footnote. Scroll down to the bottom of page 2 and verify that the footnote is deleted.
4. Proofread and check; click Next to continue. (*47-d2*)

47-d3

Document with Endnotes

 checklist

1. In the open document, insert the following explanatory endnotes to this administration checklist. Be sure to add a blank line between endnotes.

   a. 18 computers[1]

   [1] All computers are installed with the *Windows* 7 operating system and *Office 2010*.

   b. Door prize—Joey's Steak House Gift Certificate[2]

   [2] Instructors must pick up the gift certificate from Mary Katherine Morgan, Office 208.

2. Check and close. (*47-d3*)

Communication

20d Textbook Keying: Number Usage Review

Key each line once. Decide whether the circled numbers should be keyed as figures or as words and make needed changes. Check your finished work with 19e, page 47.

20 Six or ⑦ older players were cut from the �37-member team.

21 I have ② of 14 coins I need to start my set. Kristen has ⑨.

22 Of ⑨ 24-ton engines ordered, we shipped ⑥ last Tuesday.

23 Shelly has read just ① half of about ㊺ documents.

24 The ⑥ boys sent well over ⑳⓪⓪ printed invitations.

25 ① or ② of us will be on duty from ② until ⑥ o'clock.

Skill Building

20e Timed Writing

1. Take a 3' writing on both paragraphs. If you finish the timing before time is up, repeat the timing. **Use wordwrap.**

2. End the lesson but do not exit the software.

E ALL LETTERS

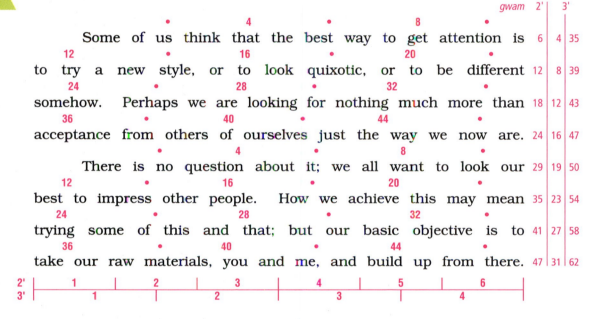

	gwam	2'	3'
Some of us think that the best way to get attention is		6	4	35
to try a new style, or to look quixotic, or to be different		12	8	39
somehow. Perhaps we are looking for nothing much more than		18	12	43
acceptance from others of ourselves just the way we now are.		24	16	47
There is no question about it; we all want to look our		29	19	50
best to impress other people. How we achieve this may mean		35	23	54
trying some of this and that; but our basic objective is to		41	27	58
take our raw materials, you and me, and build up from there.		47	31	62

20f Guided Writing

Go to the Word Processor, and follow the directions at the right to build your speed on each paragraph of the timing by four words.

Goal: 16 gwam

1/4'	1/2'	3/4'	gwam 1'
4	8	12	16
5	10	15	20
6	12	18	24
7	14	21	28
8	16	24	32
9	18	27	36
10	20	30	40

STANDARD PLAN   for Guided Writing Procedures

1. In the Word Processor, take a 1' writing on paragraph 1. Note your *gwam*.

2. Add four words to your 1' *gwam* to determine your goal rate.

3. Set the Timer for 1'. Set the Timer option to beep every 15".

4. From the table below, select from column 4 the speed nearest your goal rate. Note the ¼' point at the left of that speed. Place a light check mark within the paragraphs at the ¼' points.

5. Take two 1' guided writings on paragraphs 1 and 2. Do not save.

6. Turn the beeper off.

Preliminary Report of Dress Code Study

The Donovan National Bank Dress Code[1] outlines our company's philosophy to allow employees to work comfortably and to project a professional image to our publics within and outside the workplace. Although business casual is a term used by companies when describing business dress that is comfortable and professional, our employees still have difficulty in interpreting the dress code as intended by the current dress code policy. This report outlines the current findings of our employees' adherence to the dress code and recommendations for improvement.

Findings

According to company policy, a study of current practices related to the company dress code was authorized on February 15st, 2011. The study began on Monday, March 1st, and concluded on Friday, March 26st, which covered 4 full weeks. Observations were gathered from one hundred employees.

General findings showed that approximately 89% of all employees do follow the dress code as intended by the Executive Council. Males adhered to the policy 85% of the time while females adhered 75% of the time, indicating perhaps a need for more details in the female section of the dress code. Printed copies of the final report will be distributed on April 15th and findings presented at a meeting of the Executive Council.

Table one shows a cross tabulation of men and women who adhered to the policy and who did not follow the policy and their corresponding percentage of any instances of absenteeism and tardiness during that period.

Table 1
Comparison of Adherence of Dress Code Policy and Absenteeism and Tardiness

	Absenteeism		Tardiness	
	Male	Female	Male	Female
Adhered to policy	2%	2%	1%	0%
Did not adhere to policy	25%	30%	12%	10%

Merge cells *Merge cells* *Merge cells*

The findings clearly verify our review of the business literature that employees who dress more professionally are absent fewer days and are on time for work more often.

Recommendations

Although complete adherence to the dress code was not found, the findings of the study do show that the compliance to our policy (89%) is much better than companies included in the NABASW Study.[2] However, because the findings in our company show a correlation between absenteeism and tardiness, this subcommittee respectfully submits the following recommendations.

- Consider employing an image consultant to teach employees what is appropriate business casual and to plan the best business attire to project the image of our company.

(continued)

Lesson 21 | % and !

Key each line twice.

alphabet	1	Merry will have picked out a dozen quarts of jam for boxing.
fig/sym	2	Jane-Ann bought 16 7/8 yards of #240 cotton at $3.59 a yard.
1st row	3	Can't brave, zany Cave Club men/women next climb Mt. Zamban?
easy	4	Did she rush to cut six bushels of corn for the civic corps?

New Keys

21b % and !

Key each line once.

% = percent sign: Use % with business forms or where space is restricted; otherwise, use the word "percent." Space twice after the exclamation point!

% Shift; then reach *up* with *left first* finger.

© CENGAGE LEARNING

%

5	% %f f% % %; off 5%; if 5%; of 5% fund; half 5%; taxes of 5%
6	7% rent; 3% tariff; 9% F.O.B.; 15% greater; 28% base; up 46%
7	Give discounts of 5% on rods, 50% on lures, and 75% on line.

! reach *up* with the *left fourth* finger

8	! !a a! ! ! !; Eureka! Ha! No! Pull 10! Extra! America!
9	Listen to the call! Now! Ready! Get set! Go! Good show!
10	I want it now, not next week! I am sure to lose 50% or $19.

all symbols

11	The ad offers a 10% discount, but this notice says 15% less!
12	He got the job! With Clark's Supermarket! Please call Mom!
13	Bill #92-44 arrived very late from Zyclone; it was paid 7/4.

★ SPACING TIP

- Do not space between a figure and the % or $ signs.
- Do not space before or after the dash.

21c Keyboard Reinforcement

Key each line once; work for fluency.

all symbols

14	As of 6/28, Jeri owes $31 for dinner and $27 for cab fare.
15	Invoice #20--it was dated 3/4--billed $17 less 15% discount.
16	He deducted 2% instead of 6%, a clear saving of 6% vs. 7%.

combination response

17	Look at my dismal grade in English; but I guess I earned it.
18	Kris started to blend a cocoa beverage for a shaken cowhand.
19	Jan may make a big profit if she owns the title to the land.

47d

1. Complete the Number Expression pretest, rules, and posttest in *Keyboarding Pro DELUXE 2* before completing this exercise.

2. Key your name on the first line and right-align it.

3. Proofread each sentence on the right for errors in number expression. Then key each sentence, correcting error(s).

4. Proofread and check; click Next to continue. (*47d*)

NUMBER EXPRESSION

1. Address the letter to 1 Elm Street and postmark by April 15.

2. The retirement reception will be held on the 1st of May in Room Twelve at 5 o'clock.

3. Program participants included fifteen supervisors, five managers, and two vice presidents.

4. 12 boxes arrived damaged and about 2/3 of the contents were crushed.

5. The manager reported that 85% of the project was complete with 9 days remaining until the March 15th due date.

6. The presiding officer called the meeting to order at two p.m. and requested that the 2 50-page reports be distributed.

7. Nearly 10 million people visited the virtual museum this year.

8. Jim lives at nine 21st Street and works on 6th Avenue.

Applications

47-d1

Leftbound Report

1. Key the leftbound report on the next page. Correct the errors in number expression as you key. Choose the open circle bullet for the bulleted list.

2. Apply the Flow document theme and format the title and side headings.

3. Insert the two explanatory footnotes as marked in the report.

4. Insert the table shown below and apply the Medium Grid 3 – Accent 2. Merge the cells as shown. Insert a right tab at the approximate center of columns B–E to align the numbers in the approximate center of the column.

5. Insert an Austere cover page style. Key the following information:
   Date: Select the current year.

   Company: **Donovan National Bank**

   Author: **Tara Field, Human Resources Director**

   Document title: **Preliminary Report of Dress Code Study**

   Abstract: Copy the last paragraph of the report beginning with the word *the*.

6. Insert a Continuous section break at the top of the first page of the report.

7. Position the insertion point in the header of Section 2. Deselect Different First Page if it is selected. Break the links between the headers for both sections. Go to the footer of Section 2. Break the link between the footers for both sections.

8. Go to the header of Section 2 and number the pages of the report at the top right using the Rounded Rectangle 3 page number style. Change the page number format to begin with page 1. Click Different First Page to suppress the page numbers on the first page of the report.

9. Proofread and check; click Next to continue. (*47-d1*)

21d Textbook Keying

Key each line once; DS between groups; fingers curved, hands quiet. Repeat if time permits.

1st finger

20 by bar get fun van for inn art from gray hymn July true verb
21 brag human bring unfold hominy mighty report verify puny joy
22 You are brave to try bringing home the van in the bad storm.

2nd finger

23 ace ink did cad keyed deep seed kind Dick died kink like kid
24 cease decease decades kick secret check decide kidney evaded
25 Dedre likes the idea of ending dinner with cake for dessert.

3rd finger

26 oil sow six vex wax axe low old lox pool west loss wool slow
27 swallow swamp saw sew wood sax sexes loom stew excess school
28 Wes waxes floors and washes windows at low costs to schools.

4th finger

29 zap zip craze pop pup pan daze quote queen quiz pizza puzzle
30 zoo graze zipper panzer zebra quip partizan patronize appear
31 Czar Zane appears to be dazzled by the apple pizza and jazz.

E ALL LETTERS

21e Timed Writing

1. Key a 2' writing. Repeat.
2. End the lesson but do not exit the software.
3. Go to the Word Processor and complete 21f.

Goal: 16 gwam

	gwam	1'	2'
Teams are the basic unit of performance for a firm.	11	5	42
They are not the solution to all of the organizational needs.	23	12	48
They will not solve all of the problems, but it is known	35	17	54
that a team can perform at a higher rate than other groups.	47	23	60
It is one of the best ways to support the changes needed for	59	30	66
a firm. The team must have time in order to make	71	36	72
a quality working plan.	74	37	74

```
1' |   1   |   2   |   3   |   4   |   5   |   6   |   7   |   8   |   9   |  10   |  11   |  12   |
2' |       1       |       2       |       3       |       4       |       5       |       6       |
```

21f Speed Runs with Numbers

1. Set the Timer in the Word Processor for 1'.
2. Take two 1' writings; the last number you key when you stop is your approximate gwam. Do not save.

1 and 2 and 3 and 4 and 5 and 6 and 7 and 8 and 9 and 10 and 11 and 12 and 13 and 14 and 15 and 16 and 17 and 18 and 19 and 20 and 21 and 22 and 23 and 24 and 25 and 26 and 27 and

SHOW/HIDE WHITE SPACE

When in Print Layout View, the white space at the top and bottom of each page and the white space between pages can be hidden using the Show/Hide White Space feature. This saves screen space as you are viewing a document.

To hide white space, move the insertion point to the top or bottom of the page until the pointer becomes a double-pointed arrow and then double-click. To show the white space again, point to the top or bottom of the page until the double-pointed arrow appears and double-click.

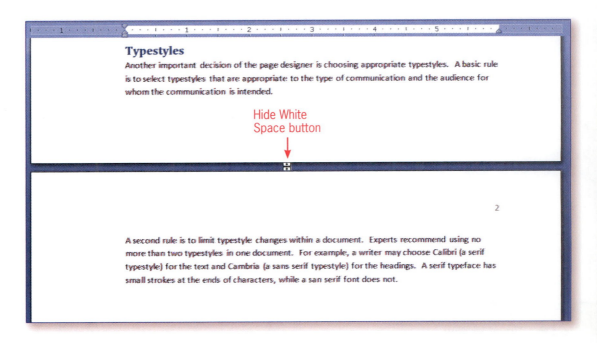

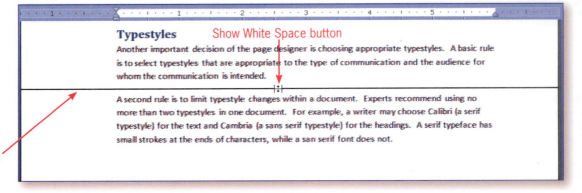

White space on pages 1 and 2 and blue space between pages are hidden.

DRILL 6	SHOW/HIDE WHITE SPACE

1. Open *47-drill5*, move the insertion point to the bottom of the first page, and hide the white space. The white space at the bottom of page 1 and the top of page 2 and the blue space are now hidden.

2. Move the insertion point to the same position and double-click to show the white space.

3. Proofread and check; click Next to continue. (*47-drill6*)

Lesson 22 | (and) and Backspace Key

Key each line twice.

alphabet	1	Avoid lazy punches; expert fighters jab with a quick motion.
fig/sym	2	Be-Low's Bill #483/7 was $96.90, not $102--they took 5% off.
caps lock	3	Report titles may be shown in ALL CAPS; as, BOLD WORD POWER.
easy	4	Do they blame me for their dismal social and civic problems?

| 1 | 2 | 3 | 4 | 5 | 6 | 7 | 8 | 9 | 10 | 11 | 12 |

New Keys

22b (and) (parentheses)
Key each line once.

( ) = parentheses
Parentheses indicate off-hand, aside, or explanatory messages.

(Shift; then reach *up* with the *right third* finger.

) Shift; then reach *up* with the *right fourth* finger.

5 ((l l((; (; Reach from l for the left parenthesis; as, ((.
6)); ;))); Reach from ; for the right parenthesis; as,)).

( )

7 Learn to use parentheses (plural) or parenthesis (singular).
8 The red (No. 34) and blue (No. 78) cars both won here (Rio).
9 We (Galen and I) dined (bagels) in our penthouse (the dorm).

all symbols learned

10 The jacket was $35 (thirty-five dollars)--the tie was extra.
11 Starting 10/29, you can sell Model #49 at a discount of 25%.
12 My size 8 1/2 shoe--a blue pump--was soiled (but not badly).

22c Textbook Keying
Key each line once, keeping eyes on copy.

13 Jana has one hard-to-get copy of her hot-off-the-press book.
14 An invoice said that "We give discounts of 10%, 5%, and 3%."
15 The company paid bill 8/07 on 5/2/11 and bill 4/9 on 3/6/11.
16 The catalog lists as out of stock Items #230, #710, and #13.
17 Elyn had $8; Sean, $9; and Cal, $7. The cash total was $24.

Insert/Header & Footer/Page Number/Format Page Numbers

7. Follow the path above and click the Start at up arrow until 1 displays ❺.

8. Check the numbers in Section 2. No number should appear on page 1, and remaining pages should be numbered at the top right.

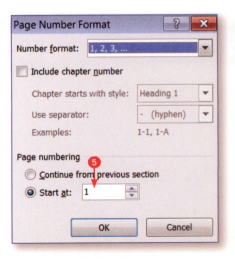

Troubleshooting Tips

Were your pages numbered correctly? If not, try these suggestions.
1. Remove all page numbers in header and footer.
2. Be sure the Different First Page command is not selected when you begin.
3. Check the Break the Link buttons in the header and footer to be sure the link is broken. Remember the Link to Previous button will display in gold until the link is successfully broken. The Same as Previous label will also display when there is a link between sections.

| DRILL 5 | NUMBER PAGES | report |

1. In the open document, position the insertion point at the beginning of page 2, which is page 1 of the report. *Hint:* Click Show/Hide and click on the first paragraph marker at 1".

2. Insert a Continuous section break.

3. Double-click in the header on page 1 of the report. Deselect Different First Page if it is selected.

4. Click Link to Previous to break the links between the headers in both sections. **Note:** This button should not display in gold if the link is correctly broken.

5. Click Go to Footer and click Link to Previous to break the links between the footers in both sections.

Insert/Header & Footer/Page Number

6. Click Page Number and Top of Page and select the Accent Bar 2 page number style.

7. Click Different First Page. You should now have a check mark in that option. This suppresses the page number on the first page of the report.

8. Click Page Number and Format Page Numbers. Change the page number format to begin with page 1.

9. Proofread and check; click Next to continue. (*47-drill5*)

22d Timed Writing

1. Take a 3' timing on both paragraphs.
2. End the lesson; then go to the Word Processor and complete 22e and 22f.

	1'	3'
Most people will agree that we owe it to our children — 10 | 4 | 28
to pass the planet on to them in better condition than we — 22 | 7 | 32
found it. We must take extra steps just to make the quality — 34 | 12 | 36
of living better. — 38 | 13 | 37

If we do not change our ways quickly and stop damaging — 11 | 16 | 41
our world, it will not be a good place to live. We can save — 12 | 21 | 45
the ozone and wildlife and stop polluting the air and water. — 35 | 25 | 49

Skill Building

22e BACKSPACE Key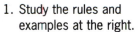

In the Word Processor, key the sentences using the BACKSPACE key to correct errors.

18 You should be interested in the special items on sale today.
19 If she is going with us, why don't we plan to leave now?
20 Do you desire to continue working on the memo in the future?
21 Did the firm or their neighbors own the autos with problems?
22 Juni, Vec, and Zeb had perfect grades on weekly query exams.
23 Jewel quickly explained to me the big fire hazards involved.

Communication

22f Word Processor

1. Study the rules and examples at the right.
2. In the Word Processor, key the information below at the left margin. Tap ENTER as shown.
Your name ENTER
Current date ENTER
Number Expression ENTER
3. Key the sample sentences 24–28. If you make an error, backspace to correct it.
4. Save the file as xx-22f.

NUMBER EXPRESSION: EXPRESS AS FIGURES

1. **Money amounts and percentages, even when appoximate.** Spell out cents and percent except in statistical copy.
   The 16 percent discount saved me $145; Bill, 95 cents.
2. **Round numbers expressed in millions or higher with their word modifier.**
   Ms. Ti contributed $3 million.
3. **House numbers** (except house number One) and street names over ten. If a street name is a number, separate it from the house number with a dash.
   1510 Easy Street   One West Ninth Avenue   1592--11th Street
4. **Date following a month.** A date preceding the month is expressed in figures followed by "rd" or "th."
   June 9, 2009   March 3   4th of July
5. **Numbers used with nouns.**
   Volume 1   Chapter 6

24 Ask **Group 2** to read **Chapter 7** of **Book 11** (**Shelf 19, Room 5**).
25 All **six** of us live at **One Bay Lane**, not at **142--59th Street**.
26 At **8 a.m.** the owners decided to close from **12 noon** to **1 p.m.**
27 Ms. Han leaves **June 3**; she returns the **14th or 15th of July**.
28 The **16 percent** discount saves **$115**. A stamp costs **44 cents**.

BREAK LINK BETWEEN SECTIONS AND INSERT PAGE NUMBERS

Numbering the pages of a report when the cover page is the first page requires a few extra steps but is well worth the effort to have the cover page and report in the same document.

To be successful on the first attempt every time, follow the directions below in the exact order. However, should the first attempt not work, follow the troubleshooting tips on the next page.

Step 1: To break the links in Section 2:

1. Move the insertion point to the top ½" of the page ❶ and double-click to position the insertion point in what is called the *header section*. Note the Header — Section 2 label displays at the left of the header and the Same as Previous label at the right.

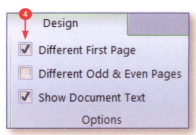

Header -Section 2-   Same as Previous

Header & Footer Tools Design/Navigation

2. Follow the path above and click the Link to Previous button ❷ to break the link for the header. Note the Go to Header button is dimmed, meaning the insertion point is in the header.

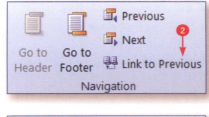

3. In the Navigation group, click Go to Footer to move to the footer of Section 2. Click the Link to Previous button ❸ to break the link for the footer.

   Note: The Link to Previous button will display in gold until the link is successfully broken.

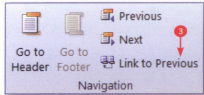

Step 2: To insert page numbers in Section 2:

4. Click Go to Header to return to the header section where the page number is to be inserted (Header & Footer Tools Design/Navigation/Go to Header).

5. In the Header & Footer group, click Page Number. Click Top Right and select a page number style that displays numbers at the top right.

6. From the Options group, click Different First Page ❹ to select the option to suppress page numbers on the first page.

Lesson 23 | & and : (colon), Proofreaders' Marks

WARMUP

Lessons/23a Warmup

Key each line twice.

alphabet	1	Roxy waved as she did quick flying jumps on the trapeze bar.
symbols	2	Ryan's--with an A-1 rating--sold Item #146 (for $10) on 2/7.
space bar	3	Mr. Fyn may go to Cape Cod on the bus, or he may go by auto.
easy	4	Susie is busy; may she halt the social work for the auditor?

| 1 | 2 | 3 | 4 | 5 | 6 | 7 | 8 | 9 | 10 | 11 | 12 |

New Keys

23b & and : (colon)

Key each line once.

& Shift; then reach *up* with *right first* finger.

: (colon) Left shift; then tap key with *right fourth* finger.

> **& = ampersand:** The ampersand is used only as part of company names.
> **Colon:** Space twice after a colon except when used within a number for time.

& (ampersand)

5 & &j j& & & &; J & J; Haraj & Jay; Moroj & Jax; Torj & Jones
6 Nehru & Unger; Mumm & Just; Mann & Hart; Arch & Jones; M & J
7 Rhye & Knox represent us; Steb & Doy, Firm A; R & J, Firm B.

: (colon)

8 : :; :: : : :; as: for example: notice: To: From: Date:
9 in stock: 8:30; 7:45; Age: Experience: Read: Send: See:
10 Space twice after a colon, thus: To: No.:   Time: Carload:

all symbols learned

11 Consider these companies: J & R, Brand & Kay, Uper & Davis.
12 Memo #88-89 reads as follows: "Deduct 15% of $300, or $45."
13 Bill 32(5)--it got here quite late--from M & N was paid 7/3.

23c Keyboard Reinforcement

Key each line twice; work for fluency.

double letters

14 Di Bennett was puzzled by drivers exceeding the speed limit.
15 Bill needs the office address; he will cut the grass at ten.
16 Todd saw the green car veer off the street near a tall tree.

figures and symbols

17 Invoice #84 for $672.90, plus $4.38 tax, was due on 5/19/11.
18 Do read Section 4, pages 60-74 and Section 9, pages 198-225.
19 Enter the following: (a) name, (b) address, and (c) tax ID.

To enter a section break:

Page Layout/Page Setup/Breaks

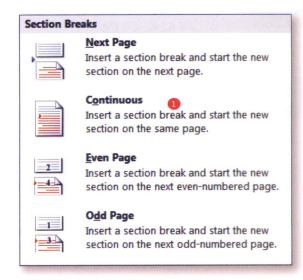

Section Breaks

Next Page
Insert a section break and start the new section on the next page.

Continuous ❶
Insert a section break and start the new section on the same page.

Even Page
Insert a section break and start the new section on the next even-numbered page.

Odd Page
Insert a section break and start the new section on the next odd-numbered page.

1. Follow the path to insert the section break.

2. From the Section Breaks category, click the desired section break ❶, and then click OK.

   Next Page: Begins a new page at the point the section break is entered.

   Continuous: Begins a new section on the same page.

   Even Page: Begins a new section on the next even-numbered page.

   Odd Page: Begins a new section on the next odd-numbered page.

In Draft View, section breaks appear as a dotted line with the type of break indicated. *Word* displays the current section number on the status bar.

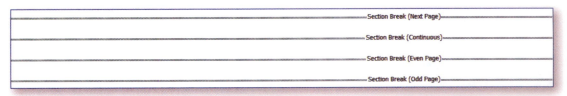

Section Break (Next Page)
Section Break (Continuous)
Section Break (Even Page)
Section Break (Odd Page)

Refer to the status bar to determine the section in which your insertion point is located. If you do not see the section number, place the insertion point on the status bar and right-click. Click Section.

Section: 1   Page: 1 of 5   At: 2"

To delete a section:

1. In Draft View, select the section break to be deleted.

2. Tap DELETE.

DRILL 4   **INSERT SECTION BREAK**   sections

1. In the open document, in Draft View, position the insertion point at the beginning of page 2, which is page 1 of the report. *Hint:* Click Show/Hide and click on the first paragraph marker at 1" (page 1 of the report).

2. Insert a Continuous section break.

3. Go to page 4 and position the insertion point at the 1" marker before Appendix A. Insert a Continuous section break.

4. Change to Print Layout View and check for Sections 1, 2, and 3.

5. In Draft View, delete the last section break for Section 3.

6. Proofread and check; click Next to continue. (*47-drill4*)

Skill Building

23d Textbook Keying
Key each line once; work for fluency.

20 Jane may work with an auditing firm if she is paid to do so.
21 Pam and eight girls may go to the lake to work with the dog.
22 Clancy and Claudia did all the work to fix the sign problem.
23 Did Lea visit the Orlando land of enchantment or a neighbor?
24 Ana and Blanche made a map for a neighbor to go to the city.
25 Sidney may go to the lake to fish with worms from the docks.
26 Did the firm or the neighbors own the auto with the problem?

| 1 | 2 | 3 | 4 | 5 | 6 | 7 | 8 | 9 | 10 | 11 | 12 |

E ALL LETTERS

23e Timed Writing
Take a 3' timing on both paragraphs. **Use wordwrap.** Repeat.

	gwam	1'	3'

Is how you judge my work important? It is, of course; — 11 | 4 | 26
I hope you recognize some basic merit in it. We all expect — 23 | 8 | 30
to get credit for good work that we conclude. — 32 | 11 | 33

I want approval for stands I take, things I write, and — 11 | 14 | 36
work I complete. My efforts, by my work, show a picture of — 23 | 18 | 41
me; thus, through my work, I am my own unique creation. — 34 | 22 | 44

| 1' | 1 | 2 | 3 | 4 | 5 | 6 | 7 | 8 | 9 | 10 | 11 | 12 |
| 3' | | 1 | | 2 | | 3 | | 4 | | | | |

Communication

23f Edit Text
1. Read the information about proofreaders' marks.
2. In the Word Processor, key your name, class, and **23f** at the left margin. Then key lines 27–32, making the revisions as you key. Use the BACKSPACE key to correct errors.
3. Save as *xx-23f* and print.

Proofreaders' marks are used to identify mistakes in typed or printed text. Learn to apply these commonly used standard proofreaders' marks.

Symbol	Meaning	Symbol	Meaning
——	Italic	◯ sp	Spell out
～～	Bold	¶	Paragraph
Cap or ≡	Capitalize	#	Add horizontal space
∧	Insert	/ or lc	Lowercase
℘	Delete	◡	Close up space
⊏	Move to left	～	Transpose
⊐	Move to right	stet	Leave as originally written

27 We miss 50% of in life's rewards by refusing to new try things.

28 do it now--today--then tomorrow's load will be 100%% lighter.

29 Satisfying work- whether it pays $40 or $400-is the pay off.

30 Avoid mistakes: confusing a #3 has cost thousands.

31 Pleased most with a first-rate job is the person who did it.

32 My wife and/or me mother will except the certificate for me.

SECTION BREAKS

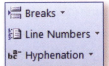

The title page of the report is considered as one of the preliminary pages of a report. Preliminary report pages may include the title page, letter of transmittal, and table of contents. These pages are numbered at the bottom center with lowercase Roman numerals. Often a page number is not printed at the bottom of the title page. Remember the pages in the body of a report are numbered in the upper right with Arabic numerals. Refer to the illustration below.

Problem: The preliminary and the report pages do not have the same page numbering format. Only one page numbering format is allowed per section.

Solution: Break the report into two sections.
Section 1—preliminary pages with lowercase Roman numerals at bottom
Section 2—report page with Arabic numerals at upper right

Section 1

Title Page

Letter of Transmittal

ii

Table of Contents

iii

Section 2
(Break link before changing page format)

Body of Report First Page

2

Body of Report Second Page

3

Body of Report Third Page

Important to Remember: Break the link or connection between the sections.

Mastering section breaks is very important as you advance to more complex documents. In this lesson, you will begin with a simple application of section breaks. You will insert a section break after the cover page and then number the pages of the report, beginning the report on page 1. In Book 2 you will add additional preliminary pages and number them as well as the report pages.

Lesson 24 | Other Symbols

Key each line twice.

alphabet 1 Pfc. Jim Kings covered each of the lazy boxers with a quilt.

figures 2 Do problems 6 to 29 on page 175 before class at 8:30, May 4.

" 3 They read the poems "September Rain" and "The Lower Branch."

easy 4 When did the busy girls fix the tight cowl of the ruby gown?

| 1 | 2 | 3 | 4 | 5 | 6 | 7 | 8 | 9 | 10 | 11 | 12 |

New Keys

24b   Textbook Keying

Key each pair of lines once; DS between 2-line groups.

Become familiar with these symbols:

@   at
<   less than
>   greater than
*   asterisk
+   plus sign (use a hyphen for minus and x for "times")
=   equals
[ ] left and right bracket

@   shift; reach *up* with *left third* finger to @

5 @ @s s@ @ @; 24 @ .15; 22 @ .35; sold 2 @ .87; were 12 @ .95

6 You may contact Luke @: LJP@rx.com or fax @ (602) 555-0101.

<   shift; reach *down* with *right second* finger to <
>   shift; reach *down* with *right third* finger to >

7 Can you prove "a > b"?   If 28 > 5, then 5a < x.   Is a < > b?

8 E-mail Al ajj@crewl.com and Matt mrw10@scxs.com by 9:30 p.m.

*   shift; reach *up* with *right second* finger to *

9 * *k k8* * *; aurelis*; May 7*; both sides*; 250 km.**; aka*

10 Note each *; one * refers to page 29; ** refers to page 307.

+   shift; reach *up* with *right fourth* finger to +

11 + ;+ +; + + +; 2 + 2; A+ or B+; 70+ F. degrees; +xy over +y;

12 The question was 8 + 7 + 51; it should have been 8 + 7 + 15.

=   reach *up* with *right fourth* finger to =

13 = =; = = =; = 4; If 14x = 28, x = 2; if 8x = 16, then x = 2.

14 Change this solution (where it says "= by") to = bx or = BX.

[ ]   reach *up* with *right fourth* finger to [and]

15 Mr. Wing was named.   [That's John J. Wing, ex-senator.   Ed.]

16 We [Joseph and I] will be in Suite #349; call us @ 555-0102.

ENDNOTES

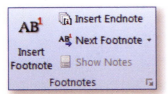

An endnote consists of two linked parts—the endnote reference in the text and the corresponding endnote with full information at the end of the last page of the report. *Word* automatically numbers endnotes with small Roman numerals (i, ii, iii), positions them at the end of the document, and applies 10-point style. You will be directed to change the number format to Arabic numerals (1, 2, 3) and to add one blank line between endnotes.

Word includes the endnote divider line to separate the report from the endnotes. Begin the reference page below the last endnote.

To insert and edit endnotes:

References/Footnotes/Insert Endnote

1. Switch to Print Layout View if you are working in a different view. Position the insertion point where the endnote reference is to be inserted.
2. Follow the path above and the reference number and the insertion point appear at the end of the last page of the document. Key the endnote.

To change the number format of the endnote:

References/Footnotes/Dialog Box Launcher

1. Follow the path above to display the Footnote and Endnote dialog box.
2. In the Number format box, click the down list arrow and select the Arabic numeral format (1, 2, 3).
3. Click Apply.

To edit an endnote, click in the endnote and revise. To delete an endnote, select the reference number in the text and tap DELETE. To move between endnotes, click the down list arrow next to the Next Footnote button. Select Next Endnote to move forward and Previous Endnote to move back.

To key the reference page, tap ENTER four times at the end of the last endnote. Key References as the title and apply Title style. Format the references using the hanging indent format.

TIP

The reason the reference page must start immediately below the endnotes and not on a new page is because a manual page break cannot be inserted after the endnotes. To key the reference page on a new page would necessitate it being keyed in a new file and inserting a page number that starts on the appropriate number—the number after the last page of the report.

DRILL 3   ENDNOTES endnotes

1. In the open document insert the three footnotes shown in Drill 2 as endnotes.
2. Change the number format to Arabic numerals (1, 2, 3).
3. Position the insertion point at the end of the last endnote. Tap ENTER four times to leave three blank lines. Turn on Show/Hide to see the paragraph markers.
4. Key **References** as the title; apply Title style.
5. Key the references in the hanging indent style.
6. Proofread and check; click Next to continue. (*47-drill3*)

Skill Building

24c Rhythm Builder

Key each line once.

double letters
17 feel pass mill good miss seem moons cliffs pools green spell
18 Assets are being offered in a stuffy room to two associates.

balanced hand
19 is if of to it go do to is do so if to to the it sign vie to
20 Pamela Fox may wish to go to town with Blanche if she works.

one hand
21 date face ere bat lip sew lion rear brag fact join eggs ever
22 get fewer on; after we look; as we agree; add debt; act fast

combination
23 was for | in the case of | they were | to down | mend it | but pony is
24 They were to be down in the fastest sleigh if you are right.

| 1 | 2 | 3 | 4 | 5 | 6 | 7 | 8 | 9 | 10 | 11 | 12 |

24d Timed Writing

Take a 3' timing on both paragraphs. **Use wordwrap.** Repeat.

	gwam	1'	3'

Why don't we like change very much? Do you think that — 11 | 4 | 26
just maybe we want to be lazy; to dodge new things; and, as — 23 | 8 | 30
much as possible, not to make hard decisions? — 32 | 11 | 33
We know change can and does extend new areas for us to — 11 | 14 | 36
enjoy, areas we might never have known existed; and to stay — 24 | 18 | 40
away from all change could curtail our quality of life. — 34 | 22 | 44

| 1' | 1 | 2 | 3 | 4 | 5 | 6 | 7 | 8 | 9 | 10 | 11 | 12 |
| 3' | | 1 | | 2 | | 3 | | 4 | | | |

24e Edited Copy

1. In the Word Processor, key your name, class, and date at the left margin, each on a separate line.
2. Key each line, making the corrections marked with proofreaders' marks.
3. Correct errors using the BACKSPACE key.
4. Save as xx-24e.

25 Ask Group 1 to read Chater 6 of Book 11 (Shelf 19, Room 5).

26 All 6 of us live at One Bay road, not at 126-56th Street. *six* *lc*

27 AT 9 a.m. the owners decided to close form 12 noon to 1 p.m.

28 Ms. Vik leaves June 9; she returns the 14 *th* or 15 *th* of July.

29 The 16 percent discount saves $115. A stamp costs 44 cents.

30 Elin gave $300,000,000; our gift was only 75 cents. *$3 million* *to charity*

Communication

24f Composition

1. In the Word Processor, open the file *xx-profile* that you created in Lesson 18.
2. Position the insertion point at the end of the last paragraph. TAP ENTER twice.
3. Key an additional paragraph that begins with the following sentence:
   Thank you for allowing me to introduce myself.
4. Finish the paragraph by adding two or more sentences that describe your progress and satisfaction with keyboarding.
5. Correct any mistakes you have made. Click Save to resave the document. Print.
6. Mark any mistakes you missed with proofreaders' marks. Revise the document, save, and reprint. Submit to your instructor.

DRILL 1 — FOOTNOTES

1. Key the paragraph in Drill 2. Insert the three footnotes. Tap ENTER once between each footnote.

2. Key all three sources on a separate reference page in hanging indent format. Position the title *References* at 2" and apply Title style.

3. Remove the hyperlinks in the footnotes and references.

4. Proofread and check; click Next to continue. (*47-drill1*)

DRILL 2 — DELETE FOOTNOTES

1. Open *47-drill1*, the document you just saved and closed.

2. Delete the second footnote.

3. Proofread and check; click Next to continue. (*47-drill2*)

Payton Devaul set the school record for points in a game—50.[1] He holds six state-wide records. This makes him one of the top ten athletes in the school's history.[2] He expects to receive a basketball scholarship at an outstanding university.[3]

Footnotes

Book → [1]Marshall Baker, *High School Athletic Records* (Seattle: Sports Press, 2011), p. 41.

[2]Lori Guo-Patterson, "Top Ten Athletes," *Sports Journal*, Spring 2011,

Online Journal → www.tsj.edu/athletes/topten.htm (accessed June 25, 2011).

[3]Payton Devaul, pdevaul@mail.com "Basketball Scholarship," January 9, 2011,

E-mail → e-mail to Kirk Stennis (accessed April 15, 2011).

References

Baker, Marshall. *High School Athletic Records*. Seattle: Sports Press, 2011.

Devaul, Payton. pdevaul@mail.com "Basketball Scholarship." January 9, 2011, e-mail to Kirk Stennis (accessed April 15, 2011).

Guo-Patterson, Lori. "Top Ten Athletes." *Sports Journal*. Spring 2011. www.tsj.edu/athletes/topten.htm (accessed June 25, 2011).

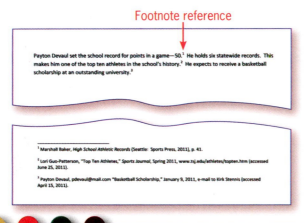

Footnote reference

2"

References ← Title Style

Hanging indent

Lesson 25 | Assessment

WARMUP

Lessons/25a Warmup

Key each line twice.

alphabet 1 My wife helped fix a frozen lock on Jacque's vegetable bins.
figures 2 Sherm moved from 823 West 150th Street to 9472--67th Street.
double letters 3 Will Scotty attempt to sell his accounting books to Elliott?
easy 4 It is a shame he used the endowment for a visit to the city.

| 1 | 2 | 3 | 4 | 5 | 6 | 7 | 8 | 9 | 10 | 11 | 12 |

25b Reach Review
Key each line once; repeat.

TECHNIQUE TIP

Keep arms and hands quiet as you practice the long reaches.

n/y 5 deny many canny tiny nymph puny any puny zany penny pony yen
6 Jenny Nyles saw many, many tiny nymphs flying near her pony.

b/r 7 bran barb brim curb brat garb bray verb brag garb bribe herb
8 Barb Barber can bring a bit of bran and herbs for her bread.

c/e 9 cede neck nice deck dice heck rice peck vice erect mice echo
10 Can Cecil erect a decent cedar deck? He erects nice condos.

n/u 11 nun gnu bun nut pun numb sun nude tuna nub fun null unit gun
12 Eunice had enough ground nuts at lunch; Uncle Launce is fun.

E   ALL LETTERS

25c Timed Writing
Key two 3' writings. Strive for accuracy. **Use wordwrap.**

Goal: 3', 19–27 gwam.

	gwam	3'

    The term careers can mean many different things to   3 | 51
different people. As you know, a career is much more than a   8 | 55
job. It is the kind of work that a person has through life.   12 | 59
It includes the jobs a person has over time. It also involves 16 | 63
how the work life affects the other parts of our life. There   20 | 67
are as many types of careers as there are people.   23 | 71

    Almost all people have a career of some kind. A career   27 | 74
can help us to reach unique goals, such as to make a living   31 | 79
or to help others. The kind of career you have will affect   35 | 83
your life in many ways. For example, it can determine where   39 | 87
you live, the money you make, and how you feel about yourself. 44 | 91
A good choice can thus help you realize the life you want.   47 | 95

3' | 1 | 2 | 3 | 4 |

Lesson 47 | Report with Footnotes and Endnotes

New Commands
- Footnotes
- Endnotes
- Section Breaks
- Show/Hide White Space

New Commands

47b

KEYBOARDING PRO DELUXE 2

*References/Word 2010
Commands/Lesson 47*

FOOTNOTES

AB¹
Insert
Footnote

References cited in a report are often indicated within the text by a superscript number (. . . story.¹) and a corresponding footnote with full information at the bottom of the same page where the reference was cited. Additionally, content or explanatory footnotes supplement the information included in the body of the report.

Word automatically numbers footnotes sequentially with Arabic numerals (1, 2, 3), positions them at the left margin, and applies 10-point type. A footnote is positioned the same as the paragraph of the report. In a single-spaced or 1.15 line spacing report, the paragraphs and the footnotes are not indented. However, if the report is double-spaced and paragraphs indented, tap the TAB key to indent the footnote 0.5" from the left margin.

To insert and edit footnotes:

References/Footnotes/Insert Footnote

1. Switch to Print Layout View if not in it.
2. Position the insertion point in the document where the footnote reference is to be inserted.
3. Follow the path to insert the footnote. The reference number and the insertion point appear at the bottom of the page. Key the footnote **❶**.

   A footnote divider line **❷** is automatically added above the first footnote on each page. Tap ENTER once to add one blank line between footnotes.
4. Click anywhere above the footnote divider line to return to the document.

To edit a footnote, click in the footnote at the bottom of the page and make the revision. To delete a footnote, select the reference number in the text and tap DELETE.

Skill Building

25d Textbook Keying

Key each line once; DS between groups.

Key with precision and without hesitation.

13 is if he do rub ant go and am pan do rut us aid ox ape by is

14 it is | an end | it may | to pay | and so | aid us | he got | or own | to go

15 Did the girl make the ornament with fur, duck down, or hair?

16 us owl rug box bob to man so bit or big pen of jay me age it

17 it | it is | time to go | show them how | plan to go | one of the aims

18 It is a shame they use the autobus for a visit to the field.

| 1 | 2 | 3 | 4 | 5 | 6 | 7 | 8 | 9 | 10 | 11 | 12 |

E ALL LETTERS/FIGURES

25e Figure Check

In the Word Processor, key two 3' writings at a controlled rate. Save the timings as *xx-25e-t1* and *xx-25e-t2*. **Use wordwrap.**

Goal: 3', 16–14 *gwam*.

	gwam	3'
Do I read the stock market pages in the news? Yes; and	4	35
at about 9 or 10 a.m. each morning, I know lots of excited	8	39
people are quick to join me. In fact, many of us zip right	12	43
to the 3rd or 4th part of the paper to see if the prices of	16	47
our stocks have gone up or down. Now, those of us who are	19	51
"speculators" like to "buy at 52 and sell at 60"; while the	23	55
"investors" among us are more interested in a dividend we	27	59
may get, say 7 or 8 percent, than in the price of a stock.	31	62

3' | 1 | 2 | 3 | 4 |

Communication

25f Edited Copy

1. In the Word Processor, key your name, class, and date at the left margin, each on a separate line.
2. Key the paragraphs and make the corrections marked with proofreaders' marks. Use the BACKSPACE key to correct errors.
3. Check all number expressions and correct any mistakes.
4. Save as *xx-25f*.

Last week the healthy heart foundation relased the findings of a study that showed exercise diet and if individuals don't smoke are the major controllable factors that led to a healthy heart. Factors such as heredity can not be controlled. The study included 25 to 65 year-old males as well as females. The study also showed that just taking a walk benefits our health. Those who walked an average of 2 to 3 hours a week were more then 30 percent less likely to have problems than those who did no exercise.

46-d1
Academic Report

1. Key the academic report on pages 186–187. Change line spacing to double spacing and change spacing after paragraph to 0.
2. Tap ENTER to position the main heading at about 2". Key the title in upper- and lowercase letters and bold, and then center it. Bold all side headings.
3. Insert the Plain Number 3 page number at the top right of the page. Click to the left of the page number and key your last name followed by five spaces.
4. Indent the two long quotations 0.5" from the left margin.
5. Check that side headings are not alone at the bottom of the page. Use the Keep with next command if needed.
6. Proofread and check; click Next to continue. (*46-d1*)

46-d2
Reference Page

1. Open *46-d1*.
2. Position the insertion point at the end of the report. Press CTRL + ENTER to begin a new page. Key **References** approximately 2" from the top of the page. Tap ENTER once and change to single spacing.
3. Key the references in hanging indent style. Try the shortcut, CTRL + T.
4. Remove the hyperlink in the second reference.
5. Proofread and check; click Next to continue. (*46-d2*)

Millsaps, John Thomas. *Report Writing Handbook: An Essential Guide.* Columbus, OH: Wellington Books, 2011.

Quattlebaum, Sarah. "Apply Reference Styles Correctly." *The Reference Journal.* November 10, 2011. www.reportmanuscript.com/applystyles.htm (accessed December 15, 2011).

46-d3
Edit Report

TIP

The manuscript style used in this academic report shows the table number and title at the left margin.

1. Open *46-d2*. Convert the unbound report to a leftbound report.
2. Key the table shown below the first paragraph in the section *Well-Cited References*. Select the table and change to single spacing. Use the Table Grid style. Adjust spacing after the table as learned in Module 5.
3. Key the following sentence as sentence that precedes the table: **When sharing this literature in the body of the report, the report writer understands the basic principles of report documentation listed in the table below.**
4. Check and close. (*46-d3*)

Table 1	
Basic Principles of Report Documentation	
✓	Cite all ideas of others so that credit is given appropriately. Follow specific guidelines for citing each type of reference.
✓	Apply correct formatting rules to direct quotations and to paraphrased ideas. If a long quotation, format as a block quote and indent from the left margin.
✓	Provide a thorough list of references so that the reader will be able to locate the material if needed.

Skill Builder 2

KEYBOARDING PRO DELUXE 2	Skill Building	*Technique Builder*

Select the Skill Building tab from the Main menu and then Technique Builder. Select the drill and follow the directions in the book.

DRILL 8

Opposite Hand Reaches

Key each line once and DS between groups of lines. Key at a controlled rate; concentrate on the reaches.

i/e

1 ik is fit it sit laid site like insist still wise coil light
2 ed he ear the fed egg led elf lake jade heat feet hear where
3 lie kite item five aide either quite linear imagine brighter
4 Imagine the aide eating the pears before the grieving tiger.

w/o

5 ws we way was few went wit law with weed were week gnaw when
6 ol on go hot old lot joy odd comb open tool upon money union
7 bow owl word wood worm worse tower brown toward wrote weapon
8 The workers lowered the brown swords toward the wood weapon.

DRILL 9

Proofreaders' Marks

Key each line once and DS after each sentence. Correct the sentence as edited, making all handwritten corrections. Do not key the numbers.

≡ Capitalize
/ Change letter
⌒ Close up space
⌿ Delete
∧ Insert
ℓℭ Lowercase
Space
⋃ Transpose

1. When a writer create the preliminary version of a document, they are concentrating on conveying the intended ideas.
2. This version of a preliminary document is called a rough.
3. After the draft is created the Writer edits refines the copy.
4. Sometimes proofreader's marks are used to edit the draft.
5. The changes will them be make to the original.
6. After the changes have been made then the Writer reads the copy.
7. Edit ing and proofreading requires alot of time and effort.
8. An attitude of excellance is required to produce error free message.

DRILL 10

Proofreading

Compare your sentences in Drill 9 with Drill 10. How did you do? Now key the paragraph for fluency. Concentrate on keying as accurately as possible.

When a writer creates the preliminary version of a document, he or she is concentrating on conveying ideas. This preliminary version is called a rough draft. After the draft is created, the writer edits or refines the copy. Proofreaders' marks are used to edit the rough draft. The editing changes will be made to the original. Then the writer reads the copy again. Editing requires a lot of time and effort. An attitude of excellence is required to produce an error-free message.

carefully reviewing the acceptable formats in the appropriate style manual. Sarah Quattlebaum (2011) writes:

> For example, be sure to correct the reference list as it will not be formatted as a hanging indent.
>
> Simply select the entire list and then apply the hanging indent command. Other items to check
>
> are the correct format for the names of authors (i.e., Quattlebaum, S. or Quattlebaum, Sarah)
>
> and the appropriate capitalization of article and book titles. (159)

Summary

Experienced writers understand the importance of selecting credible resources, documenting references in the report, and applying the exact reference style required for the report. Learning to document your references accurately is an important step toward becoming an experienced writer.

Assess skill growth:

1. Select the Timed Writings tab from the Main menu.

Timed Writings

2. Select the writing number such as Writing 8.
3. Select 3' as the length of the writing. **Use wordwrap.**
4. Repeat the timing if desired.

Word Processor option:

1. Key 1' writings on each paragraph of a timing. Note that paragraphs within a timing increase by two words. **Goal:** to complete each paragraph
2. Key a 3' timing on the entire writing.

gwam
1' | 3'

Writing 8

Any of us whose target is to achieve success in our professional | 13 | 4
lives will understand that we must learn how to work in harmony | 26 | 8
with others whose paths may cross ours daily. | 35 | 12

We will, unquestionably, work for, with, and beside people, just | 13 | 16
as they will work for, with, and beside us. We will judge them, | 26 | 20
as most certainly they are going to be judging us. | 38 | 24

A lot of people realize the need for solid working relations and | 13 | 28
have a rule that treats others as they, themselves, expect to be | 26 | 33
treated. This seems to be a sound, practical idea for them. | 40 | 37

Writing 9

I spoke with one company visitor recently; and she was very much | 13 | 4
impressed, she said, with the large amount of work she had noted | 26 | 9
being finished by one of our front office workers. | 36 | 12

I told her how we had just last week recognized this very person | 13 | 16
for what he had done, for output, naturally, but also because of | 26 | 21
its excellence. We know this person has that "magic touch." | 38 | 25

This "magic touch" is the ability to do a fair amount of work in | 13 | 29
a fair amount of time. It involves a desire to become ever more | 26 | 34
efficient without losing quality--the "touch" all workers should | 39 | 38
have. | 40 | 38

Writing 10

Isn't it great just to untangle and relax after you have keyed a | 13 | 4
completed document? Complete, or just done? No document is | 25 | 8
quite complete until it has left you and passed to the next step. | 38 | 13

There are desirable things that must happen to a document before | 13 | 17
you surrender it. It must be read carefully, first of all, for | 26 | 22
meaning to find words that look right but aren't. Read word for | 39 | 26
word. | 40 | 26

Check all figures and exact data, like a date or time, with your | 13 | 31
principal copy. Make sure format details are right. Only then, | 26 | 35
print or remove the work and scrutinize to see how it might look | 39 | 39
to a recipient. | 42 | 40

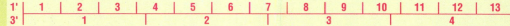

| 1' | 1 | 2 | 3 | 4 | 5 | 6 | 7 | 8 | 9 | 10 | 11 | 12 | 13 |
| 3' | | 1 | | | 2 | | | 3 | | | 4 | | |

2"

Writing a Scholarly Report ←——— Title 11 point

Preparing a thorough and convincing scholarly report requires excellent research, organization, and composition skills as well as extensive knowledge of documenting referenced materials. The purpose of this report is to present the importance of documenting a report with credible references and the techniques for creating accurate citations.

Well-Cited References Bold side headings

For a report to be believable and accepted by its readers, a thorough review of related literature is essential. This background information is an important part of the report and shows integrity of the report.

Good writers must learn quickly how to evaluate the many printed and electronic references that have been located to support the theme of the report being written. Those references judged acceptable are then cited in the report. Writer John Millsaps (2011) shares this simple advice:

Long quotation indented 0.5" ——→

> Today writers can locate a vast number of references in very little time. Electronic databases and Internet Web pages . . . provide a multitude of information. The novice writer will be quick to include all these references in a report without verifying their credibility. Experienced writers check electronic sources as well. (12)

Correct Styles Applied

Three popular style manuals are the *MLA Handbook*, *The Chicago Manual of Style*, and the *Publication Manual of the American Psychological Association*. *Microsoft Word* now offers the ability to generate citations and a reference list automatically using the citations and bibliography commands. After the citations and references are created by the software, be sure to verify the accuracy of each by

Writing 11

Anyone who expects some day to find an excellent job should   4 | 34
begin now to learn the value of accuracy. To be worth anything,   8 | 38
completed work must be correct, without question. Naturally, we   13 | 43
realize that the human aspect of the work equation always raises   17 | 47
the prospect of errors; but we should understand that those same   20 | 51
errors can be found and fixed. Every completed job should carry   26 | 56
at least one stamp; the stamp of pride in work that is exemplary.   30 | 60

Writing 12

No question about it: Many personal problems we face today   4 | 34
arise from the fact that we earthlings have never been very wise   8 | 38
consumers. We haven't consumed our natural resources well; as a   13 | 43
result, we have jeopardized much of our environment. We excused   17 | 47
our behavior because we thought that our stock of most resources   20 | 51
had no limit. So, finally, we are beginning to realize just how   26 | 56
indiscreet we were; and we are taking steps to rebuild our world.   30 | 60

Writing 13

When I see people in top jobs, I know I'm seeing people who   4 | 34
sell. I'm not just referring to employees who labor in a retail   8 | 38
outlet; I mean those people who put extra effort into convincing   13 | 43
others to recognize their best qualities. They, themselves, are   17 | 47
the commodity they sell; and their optimum tools are appearance,   20 | 51
language, and personality. They look great, they talk and write   26 | 56
well; and, with candid self-confidence, they meet you eye to eye.   30 | 60

3' | 1 | 2 | 3 | 4 |

INTERNAL CITATIONS

The last name of the author(s), the publication date, and the page number(s) of the cited material are shown in parentheses within the body of the report (Crawford, 2011, 134). When the author's name is used in the text to introduce the quotation, only the year of publication and the page numbers appear in parentheses: Crawford (2011, 134) said, "Faculty are uploading podcasts lectures to their distance website."

If a portion of the text that is referenced is omitted, use an ellipsis (. . .) to show the omission. An ellipsis is three periods, each preceded and followed by a space. If an ellipsis occurs at the end of a sentence, include the period or other punctuation.

Short, direct quotations of three lines or fewer are enclosed within quotation marks. Long quotations of four lines or more are indented 0.5" from the left margin and DS. The first line is indented an additional 0.5" if the quotation is the beginning of a paragraph. Tap ENTER once before and after the long quotation.

According to Estes (2010, 29), "Successful business executives have long known the importance of good verbal communication."

SHORT QUOTATION

Probably no successful enterprise exists that does not rely for its success upon the ability of its members to communicate.

Make no mistake, both written and verbal communication are the stuff upon which success is built in all types of organizations. . . . Both forms deserve careful study by any business that wants to grow. Successful businesspeople must read, write, speak, and listen with skill. Often professional development in these areas is needed. (Schaefer, 2010, 28)

LONG QUOTATION

REFERENCE PAGE

References cited in the report are listed at the end of the report in alphabetical order by authors' last names. Study the guidelines and the model shown below.

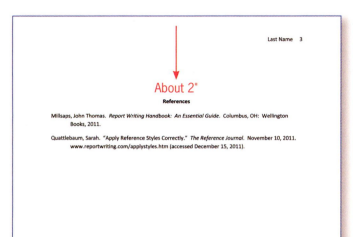

Last Name   3

About 2"

References

Millsaps, John Thomas. *Report Writing Handbook: An Essential Guide.* Columbus, OH: Wellington Books, 2011.

Quattlebaum, Sarah. "Apply Reference Styles Correctly." *The Reference Journal.* November 10, 2011. www.reportwriting.com/applystyles.htm (accessed December 15, 2011).

- Begin the references on a new page (insert manual page break at the end of the report).
- Key the title in upper- and lowercase letters at approximately 2" from the top of the page (same as the first page of the report); center and bold.
- Format references in hanging indent format.
- SS references; DS between each reference.
- Number the reference page at the top right of the page using same format as the report.

Writing 14

What do you expect when you travel to a foreign country? Quite a few people realize that one of the real joys of traveling is to get a brief glimpse of how others think, work, and live.

12	4
23	8
36	12
40	12

The best way to enjoy a different culture is to learn as much about it as you can before you leave home. Then you can concentrate on being a good guest rather than trying to find local people who can meet your needs.

11	16
24	20
36	24
44	27

Writing 15

What do you enjoy doing in your free time? Health experts tell us that far too many people choose to be lazy rather than to be active. The result of that decision shows up in our weight.

12	4
24	8
36	12
37	13

Working to control what we weigh is not easy, and seldom can it be done quickly. However, it is quite important if our weight exceeds what it should be. Part of the problem results from the amount and type of food we eat.

12	16
24	21
37	25
44	27

If we want to look fit, we should include exercise as a substantial part of our weight loss plan. Walking at least thirty minutes each day at a very fast rate can make a big difference both in our appearance and in the way we feel.

11	31
23	35
35	39
47	42

Writing 16

Doing what we like to do is quite important; however, liking what we have to do is equally important. As you ponder both of these concepts, you may feel that they are the same, but they are not the same.

10	4
23	8
36	12
41	14

If we could do only those things that we prefer to do, the chances are that we would do them exceptionally well. Generally, we will take more pride in doing those things we like doing, and we will not quit until we get them done right.

12	18
25	22
37	26
47	29

We realize, though, that we cannot restrict the things that we must do just to those that we want to do. Therefore, we need to build an interest in and an appreciation of all the tasks that we must do in our positions.

11	33
23	37
36	41
44	44

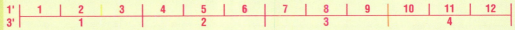

1'	1	2	3	4	5	6	7	8	9	10	11	12
3'		1			2			3			4	

1. Change the line spacing to double spacing.

2. Change the spacing after the paragraph to 0 pt.

3. Key the heading and the three paragraphs related to internal citations shown on the next page. Bold the heading.

4. Proofread and check; click Next to continue. (*46-drill4*)

Document Design

46d

ACADEMIC REPORTS

Academic reports are reports prepared in an academic setting, such as a term paper required for an English class or a manuscript prepared for publication. Specific requirements are established for each. Study the guidelines shown below for a typical academic report and refer to the full-page model on pages 186–187.

- DS paragraphs and indent 0.5".
- Key the report title at approximately 2" in upper- and lowercase letters, center, and bold. Bold all side headings.
- Number pages at the top right of every page. Include the writer's last name and the page number (Last Name   2). Check specific style manual for other requirements in the header.
- Include footnotes, endnotes, or internal citations to document published material that is quoted or closely paraphrased by the writer.
- Include a complete alphabetical listing of all references cited in the report.

Page numbers with Last Name ➝ Last Name 1

Writing a Scholarly Report ⟵ Title

Preparing a thorough and convincing scholarly report requires excellent research, organization, and composition skills as well as extensive knowledge of documenting referenced materials. The purpose of this report is to present the importance of documenting a report with credible references and the techniques for creating accurate citations.

Well-Cited References

For a report to be believable and accepted by its readers, a thorough review of related literature is essential. This background information is an important part of the report and shows integrity of the report.

Good writers must learn quickly how to evaluate the many printed and electronic references that have been located to support the theme of the report being written. Those references judged acceptable are then cited in the report. Writer John Millsaps (2011) shares this simple advice:

Today writers can locate a vast number of references in very little time. Electronic databases and Internet Web pages . . . provide a multitude of information. The novice writer will be quick to include all these references in a report without verifying their credibility. Experienced writers check electronic sources as well. (12)

Correct Styles Applied

Three popular style manuals are the *MLA Handbook*, *The Chicago Manual of Style*, and the *Publication Manual of the American Psychological Association*. Microsoft Word now offers the ability to generate citations and a reference list automatically using the citations and bibliography commands. After the citations and references are created by the software, be sure to verify the accuracy of each by

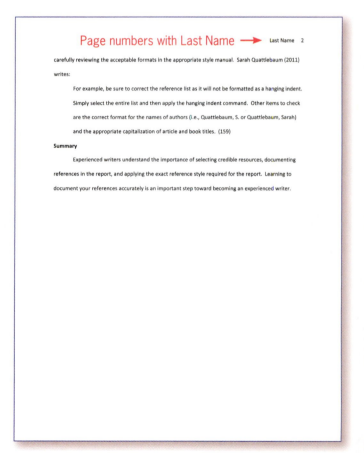

Page numbers with Last Name ➝ Last Name 2

carefully reviewing the acceptable formats in the appropriate style manual. Sarah Quattlebaum (2011) writes:

For example, be sure to correct the reference list as it will not be formatted as a hanging indent. Simply select the entire list and then apply the hanging indent command. Other items to check are the correct format for the names of authors (i.e., Quattlebaum, S. or Quattlebaum, Sarah) and the appropriate capitalization of article and book titles. (159)

Summary

Experienced writers understand the importance of selecting credible resources, documenting references in the report, and applying the exact reference style required for the report. Learning to document your references accurately is an important step toward becoming an experienced writer.

Writing 17

Many people like to say just how lucky a person is when 11 | 4 | 29
he or she succeeds in doing something well.   Does luck play a 24 | 8 | 33
large role in success?   In some cases, it might have a small 36 | 12 | 37
effect. 37 | 13 | 38

Being in the right place at the right time may help, but 11 | 16 | 41
hard work may help far more than luck.   Those who just wait for 24 | 20 | 46
luck should not expect quick results and should realize luck 36 | 24 | 50
may never come. 39 | 26 | 51

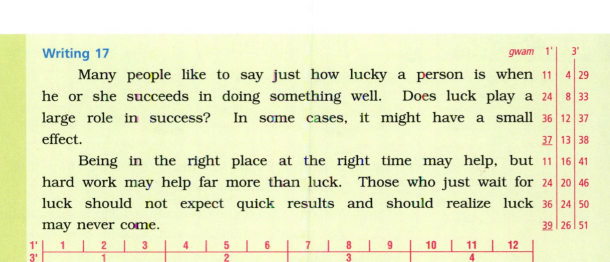

Writing 18

New golfers must learn to zero in on just a few social 11 | 4 | 39
rules.   Do not talk, stand close, or move around when another 23 | 8 | 44
person is hitting.   Be ready to play when it is your turn. 35 | 12 | 47

Take practice swings in an area away from other people. 11 | 15 | 51
Let the group behind you play through if your group is slow. 24 | 20 | 55
Do not rest on your club on the green when waiting your turn. 36 | 23 | 59

Set your other clubs down off the green.   Leave the green 12 | 27 | 63
quickly when done; update your card on the next tee.   Be sure 24 | 31 | 67
to leave the course in good condition.   Always have a good time. 37 | 36 | 72

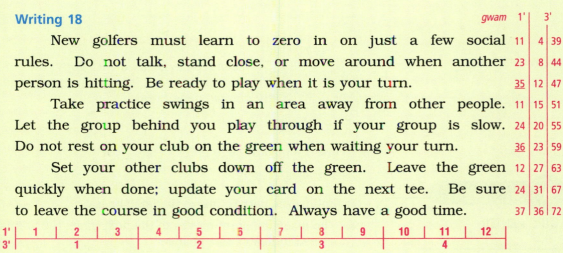

Writing 19

Do you know how to use time wisely?   If you do, then its 11 | 4 | 51
proper use can help you organize and run a business better. 24 | 8 | 55
If you find that your daily problems tend to keep you from 35 | 12 | 59
planning properly, then perhaps you are not using time well. 48 | 16 | 63
You may find that you spend too much time on tasks that are 60 | 20 | 67
not important. Plan your work to save valuable time. 70 | 24 | 70

A firm that does not plan is liable to run into trouble. 12 | 27 | 74
A small firm may have trouble planning.   It is important 23 | 31 | 78
to know just where the firm is headed.   A firm may have a 35 | 35 | 82
fear of learning things it would rather not know.   To say 46 | 39 | 86
that planning is easy would be absurd.   It requires lots of 58 | 43 | 90
thinking and planning to meet the expected needs of the firm. 70 | 47 | 94

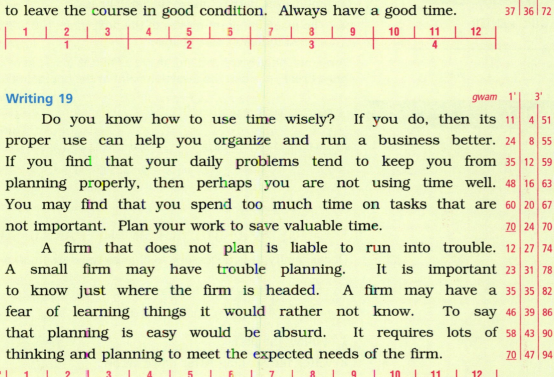

1. Drag the Hanging Indent marker to 0.5" to the right; then key the references below.

2. Tap ENTER after keying the last entry. Turn Hanging Indent off by dragging the Hanging indent marker back to the left margin.

3. Proofread and check; click Next to continue. (*46-drill2*)

Godo, Eiko and Krystol McCurdy. *The Style Manual.* 6th ed. Boston: Blackwell and Johnson Publishers, 2010.

Osaji, Allison. "Know the Credibility of Electronic Citations." *Graduate Education Journal.* November 2011, 93–97.

Walters, Daniel S. dswalters2@umt.edu "Final Report Available on Intranet." August 11, 2010, e-mail to Stephen P. Cobb (accessed September 14, 2010).

INSERT AND DELETE PAGE BREAKS

When a page is filled with copy, the software automatically inserts a soft page break. To begin a new page before it is full, insert a manual page break.

To insert a manual page break:

Insert/Pages/Page Break

SHORTCUT

CTRL + ENTER

1. Follow the path to insert the page break.
2. The insertion point moves to the next page; the status line at the bottom of the screen indicates this change.

A manual page break will not move as text is inserted or deleted. To remove a manual page break, position the insertion point at the beginning of the page and tap BACKSPACE.

1. In the open document, place the Insertion point at the beginning of Goal 2.

2. Insert a manual page break.

3. Proofread and check; click Next to continue. (*46-drill3*)

CHANGE SPACING AFTER THE PARAGRAPH

Occasionally, it is necessary to change the default 10 point after the paragraph.

To change spacing after the paragraph:

Page Layout/Paragraph/Spacing Before or After

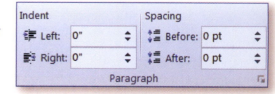

1. Follow the path.
2. Click the Spacing After down arrow until 0 pt displays.

Writing 20

If asked, most people will agree that some people have far more creative skills than others, and they will also say that these skills are in great demand by most organizations. A follow-up question is in order. Are you born with creative skills or can you develop them? No easy answer to that question exists, but it is worth spending a bit of time pondering.

If creative skills can be developed, then the next issue is how can you develop these skills. One way is to approach each task with a determination to solve the problem and a refusal to accept failure. If the normal way of doing a job does not work, just keep trying things never tried before until you reach a good solution. This is called thinking outside the box.

Writing 21

Figures are not as easy to key as many of the words we use. Balanced-hand figures such as 16, 27, 38, 49, and 50, although fairly easy, are slower to key because each one requires longer reaches and uses more time per stroke.

Figures such as 12, 45, 67, and 90 are even more difficult because they are next to one another and each uses just a single hand to key. Because of their size, bigger numbers such as 178, 349, and 1,220 create extra speed losses.

Writing 22

Skill Transfer

1. Set the Timer for 2'. Take a 2' writing on paragraph 1.

2. Set the Timer for 2'. Take a 2' writing on paragraph 2.

3. Take 2 or more 2' writings on the slower paragraph.

Few people attain financial success without some kind of planning. People who realize the value of prudent spending and saving are those who set up a budget. A budget helps individuals determine just how much they can spend and how much they can save so that they will not squander their money recklessly.

Keeping records is a ~~crucial~~ vital part of a budget. Complete records of income and expenses over a period of ~~a number of~~ several months ~~can~~ will help ~~to~~ determine what bills, ~~as~~ like utilities water or rent, are ~~static~~ fixed and which are flexible. To get the most out of your income, ~~pay~~ focus attention ~~to~~ on the items that ~~you~~ can ~~modify~~ be changed.

Lesson 46 | Academic Report with Reference Page

New Commands
- Hanging Indent
- Page Breaks
- Change Paragraph Spacing

KEYBOARDING PRO DELUXE 2

WARMUP

Lessons/46a Warmup

Skill Building

46b Textbook Keying

1. Key each line, concentrating on using good keying techniques. Tap ENTER twice after each 3-line group.
2. Repeat the drill if time permits.

caps
1 James Carswell plans to visit Austin and New Orleans in December.
2 Will Peter and Betsy go with Mark when he goes to Alaska in June?
3 John Kenny wrote the book *Innovation and Timing—Keys to Success*.

double letters
4 Jeanne arranges meeting room space in Massey Hall for committees.
5 Russell will attend to the bookkeeping issues tomorrow afternoon.
6 Todd offered a free book with all assessment tools Lynette sells.

balanced hand
7 Jane, a neighbor and a proficient auditor, may amend their audit.
8 Blanche and a neighbor may make an ornament for an antique chair.
9 Claudia may visit the big island when they go to Orlando with us.

New Commands

46c

KEYBOARDING PRO DELUXE 2

*References/Word 2010
Commands/Lesson 46*

SHORTCUT

CTRL + T; then key the paragraph; or select the paragraphs to be formatted as hanging indents and press CTRL + T.

HANGING INDENT

Hanging indent places the first line of a paragraph at the left margin and indents all other lines to the first tab. It is commonly used to format bibliography entries, glossaries, and lists. Hanging indent can be applied before or after text is keyed.

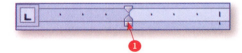 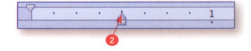

To create a hanging indent:

1. From the Horizontal Ruler, click on the Hanging Indent marker ❶.
2. Drag the Hanging Indent marker ❷ to the position where the indent is to begin.
3. Key the paragraph. The second and subsequent lines are indented beginning at the marker.

DRILL 1   **HANGING INDENT**   glossary

1. In the open document, select all the glossary entries and format them with a hanging indent. *Hint:* Use the shortcut CTRL + T.

2. Proofread and check; click Next to continue. (*46-drill1*)

LESSON A

KEYBOARDING PRO DELUXE 2 | **Skill Building** | *Accuracy Emphasis*

1. Select the Skill Building tab, Accuracy Emphasis, and then Assessment 1.

2. Key the timing from the screen for 3'; work for control.

3. Complete Lesson A or the first lesson you have not completed in either Speed Emphasis or Accuracy Emphasis as suggested by the software.

4. Your results will be summarized in the Skill Building Report.

KEYBOARDING PRO DELUXE 2 | **Timed Writings**

Writing 23

1. Key a 1' writing on each paragraph. (Remember to change the source in the Timed Writing Settings dialog box.) Compare your *gwam* on the two paragraphs.

2. Key additional 1' writings on the slower paragraph.

	gwam	1'	3'
There are many qualities which cause good employees to stand		12	6
out in a group. In the first place, they keep their minds on the		25	13
task at hand. Also, they often think about the work they do and		38	19
how it relates to the total efforts of the project. They keep		52	26
their eyes, ears, and minds open to new ideas.		60	30
Second, good workers may be classed as those who work at a		13	6
steady pace. Far too many people work by bits and pieces. They		25	13
begin one thing, but then they allow themselves to be easily taken		39	19
away from the work at hand. A lot of people are good starters,		52	26
but many less of them are also good finishers.		60	30

```
1' |  1  |  2  |  3  |  4  |  5  |  6  |  7  |  8  |  9  |  10  |  11  |  12  |  13  |
3' |        1        |        2        |        3        |        4        |
```

✓ Invoke the Widow/Orphan control feature to ensure that no lines display alone at the bottom or top of a page, and use the Keep with next command to keep side headings from appearing alone at the bottom of the page.

✓ Take advantage of the following features essential in report writing: table of contents, table of figures, index, captioning, and citations. The usefulness of these features becomes apparent during the revision process. Citations are easily moved and updated; the table of contents is updated in a click, and the caption moves with the chart or table.

✓ Master the design of attractive tables and charts as these elements increase the readability and attractiveness of long and complex reports.

1.5" Writers also take advantage of the online thesaurus for choosing the most appropriate word and 1" the spelling and grammar features for ensuring spelling and grammar correctness. Additionally, electronic desk references and style manuals are just a click away.

These simple steps will assist you in your goal to create well-written and attractive reports. The next step is to practice, practice, practice.

LESSON B

1. Select the Skill Building tab and choose either Speed Emphasis or Accuracy Emphasis as recommended in Assessment 1. Complete Lesson B.
2. Your results will be summarized in the Skill Building Report.

KEYBOARDING PRO DELUXE 2 | **Skill Building** | Technique Builder

DRILL 11

Balanced-Hand Combinations

Key each line once, working for fluency. DS between groups.

1 to today stocks into ti times sitting until ur urges further tour
2 en entire trend dozen or order support editor nd and mandate land
3 he healthy check ache th these brother both an annual change plan
4 nt into continue want of office softer roof is issue poison basis

5 My brother urged the editor to have an annual health check today.
6 The manager will support the change to order our stock annually.
7 The time for the land tour will not change until further notice.
8 Did the letter mention her position or performance in the office?

KEYBOARDING PRO DELUXE 2 | **Timed Writings**

1. Key a 1' writing on each paragraph. Compare your gwam.
2. Key additional 1' writings on the slower paragraph.

Writing 24

	gwam	1'	3'
Most of us, at some time, have had a valid reason to complain—		12	6
about a defective product, poor service, or perhaps being tired of		26	13
talking to voice mail. Many of us feel that complaining, however,		39	20
to a firm is an exercise in futility and don't bother to express		52	26
our dissatisfaction. We just write it off to experience and		64	32
continue to be ripped off.		70	35
Today, more than at anytime in the past consumers are taking some		12	6
steps to let their feelings be known—and with a great amount of		25	13
success. As a result, firms are becoming more responsive to		38	19
the needs of the consumer. complaints from customers alert firms		51	26
to produce or service defect and there by cause action to be taken		65	33
for their benefit.		70	35

| 1' | 1 | 2 | 3 | 4 | 5 | 6 | 7 | 8 | 9 | 10 | 11 | 12 | 13 |
| 3' | | 1 | | | 2 | | | 3 | | | 4 | | |

2"

Title # Report Writing and Technology

Being able to communicate effectively in a clear, concise, and logical manner continues to be one of the most demanded work skills. Employees who practice effective revision skills are far ahead of their counterparts who have had the mind-set that the first draft is the final draft. This report details effective revision skills as it relates to report writing.

Heading 1 ## Revising the Draft

After a first draft of a report is completed, the writer is ready to refine or polish the report. The writer must be objective when revising the report draft and cultivate a mind-set for improving the report by always considering the draft as a draft.

1.5"   First, read the draft for content. This might mean rewriting sections of the report or adding information to areas that appear weak in this review. In this evaluative review, the writer may   1" realize that one section would fit more logically after another section.

When the writer is satisfied with the content, it is time to verify that all style rules have been followed. For example, check all headings to ensure they are "talking" headings. Do the headings describe the content of the section? Also, be sure all headings are parallel. If the writer chooses the side heading *Know Your Audience*, other side headings must also begin with a verb. Note that the side headings in this report are parallel, with both beginning with a gerund.

Ensuring Correct and Attractive Format

The effective writer understands the importance of using technology to create an attractive document that adheres to correct style rules. Review the list below to determine your use of technology in the report writing process.

- ✓ Number preliminary pages of the report with small Roman numerals at the bottom center of the page. Number the pages of the report with Arabic numbers in the upper-right corner.
- ✓ Browse the excellent built-in design galleries provided in the word processing software to select attractive headers or footers that contain helpful information for the reader.
- ✓ Suppress headers, footers, and page numbering on the title page and on the first page of the report.

LESSON C

Select the Skill Building tab, the appropriate emphasis, and then Lesson C. Your results will be summarized in the Skill Building Report.

KEYBOARDING PRO DELUXE 2 | Skill Building | *Technique Builder*

DRILL 12

Balanced-Hand

Key each line once for fluency; DS between groups.

1 an anyone brand spans th their father eighth he head sheets niche
2 en enters depends been nd end handle fund or original sport color
3 ur urban turns assure to took factory photo ti titles satin still
4 ic ice bicycle chic it item position profit ng angle danger doing

5 I want the info in the file on the profits from the chic bicycle.
6 The original of the color photo she took of the factory is there.
7 Assure them that anyone can turn onto the road to the urban area.
8 The color of the title sheet depends on the photos and the funds.

KEYBOARDING PRO DELUXE 2 | **Timed Writings**

1. Take a 1' writing on each paragraph.
2. Take a 3' writing on both paragraphs.

Writing 25

	gwam	1'	3'
Practicing basic health rules will result in good body condition.		14	5
Proper diet is a way to achieve good health. Eat a variety of foods each		28	9
day, including some fruit, vegetables, cereal products, and foods rich		42	14
in protein, to be sure that you keep a balance. Another part of a good		57	19
health plan is physical activity, such as running.		67	22
Running has become popular in this country. A long run is a big		13	27
challenge to many males and females to determine just how far they		26	31
can go in a given time, or the time they require to cover a measured		40	36
distance. Long runs of fifty or one hundred miles are on measured		53	40
courses with refreshments available every few miles. Daily training is		67	45
necessary in order to maximize endurance.		76	48

1' | 1 | 2 | 3 | 4 | 5 | 6 | 7 | 8 | 9 | 10 | 11 | 12 | 13 |
3' | | 1 | | 2 | | 3 | | 4 |

Applications

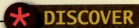

45-d1

Multiple-Page Report

1. Key the leftbound two-page report on pages 180–181. Use the Office document theme and apply the appropriate styles for the title and side headings.

2. Use the Page Number command to number the pages at the top right. Select the Accent Bar 2 page number style. Click Different First Page to suppress the page number on the first page.

3. Format the bulleted list using the check mark ✓.

4. Preview the document to verify page numbers and that side headings are not left alone at the bottom of the page.

5. Proofread and check; click Next to continue. (*45-d1*)

45-d2

Revise Report

 writing

1. Open *45-d1* and change the leftbound report to an unbound report. Apply the Executive document theme.

✱ 2. Insert the data file *writing* below the first paragraph. **Note:** Be sure to position the insertion point where you want the text to appear before inserting the file. Format the side headings appropriately.

3. Position the insertion point on page 2 of the report. Change the page number style to Rounded Rectangle 3.

4. Check and close. (*45-d2*)

✱ DISCOVER

Insert a File—To insert a file, click the insertion point where the new file is to be inserted. On the Insert tab, in the Text group, click the drop-list arrow on the Object button. Then choose Text from File. Select the file to be inserted and click Insert.

ANDERSEN ROSS/BRAND X PICTURES/JUPITER IMAGES

! WORKPLACE SUCCESS

Integrity

Integrity is synonymous with the word *honesty* and is confronted by employees in the workplace daily. Think about these rather common situations where integrity is clearly a choice:

- Arriving at work ten minutes late and then drinking coffee and chatting with coworkers for ten more minutes
- Talking with relatives and friends throughout the day
- Leaving work early regularly for personal reasons
- Presenting a report to the supervisor as original work without crediting the proper individuals for thoughts and ideas in the report
- Presenting a report that was completed at the last minute and that includes facts and figures that have not been verified as accurate

In all situations, ask the question, "Am I being honest?"

LESSON D

KEYBOARDING PRO DELUXE 2 | **Skill Building** | *Accuracy Emphasis*

Select the Skill Building tab; choose the appropriate emphasis and then Lesson D.

KEYBOARDING PRO DELUXE 2 | **Skill Building** | *Technique Builder*

DRILL 13

Adjacent Key Review

Key each line once; strive for accuracy. DS between groups.

1 nm many enmity solemn kl inkling weekly pickle oi oil invoice join
2 iu stadium medium genius lk milk talk walks uy buy buyer soliloquy
3 mn alumni hymn number column sd Thursday wisdom df mindful handful
4 me mention comment same fo found perform info le letter flew files

5 The buyer sent his weekly invoices for oil to the group on Thursday.
6 Mindful of the alumni, the choirs sang a hymn prior to my soliloquy.
7 An inmate, a fogger, and a genius joined the weekly talks on Monday.
8 They were to join in the talk shows to assess regions of the Yukon.

KEYBOARDING PRO DELUXE 2 | **Timed Writings**

1. Take a 1' writing on each paragraph.
2. Take a 3' writing on both paragraphs.

Writing 26

gwam 1' | 3'

	1'	3'
All people, in spite of their eating habits, have two major needs	13	4
that must be met by their food. They need food that provides a	26	9
source of energy, and they need food that will fill the skeletal and	40	13
operating needs of their bodies. Carbohydrates, fats, and protein	53	18
form a major portion of the diet. Vitamins and minerals are also	66	22
necessary for excellent health.	72	24
Carbohydrates make up a major source of our energy needs.	12	28
Fats also serve as a source of energy and act as defense against	25	32
cold and trauma. Proteins are changed to amino acids, which are	38	37
the building units of the body. These, in turn, are utilized to make	52	41
most body tissue. Minerals are required to control many body	64	45
functions, and vitamins are used for normal growth and aid against	77	50
disease.	84	52

1' | 1 | 2 | 3 | 4 | 5 | 6 | 7 | 8 | 9 | 10 | 11 | 12 | 13
3' | | 1 | | 2 | | 3 | | 4

MULTIPLE-PAGE REPORT

Because reports are often longer than one page, page numbers are required for ease in reading the report. Can you picture an executive reading a business report without page numbers? Always remember when formatting any multiple-page document, insert page numbers on all pages except the first page.

Traditionally, page numbers are positioned at the top right of the page. However, in lengthy and more formal documents such as annual reports or manuals, attractive headers and footers are designed. The applications that follow will include the Simple gallery of page number designs. Advanced headers and footers will be presented in Book 2 of this series.

Study the illustration below, noting specifically the position of page numbers. Review the callouts to reinforce your understanding of report formats.

To format a multiple-page report with page numbers at the top right:

1. Insert page numbers at the upper-right corner in the header position (0.5").

2. Suppress the page number on the first page.

3. Protect side headings that may be separated from the related paragraph with the Keep with next command. **Note:** When styles are applied to side headings, the Keep with next command is automatically applied and side headings will not display alone at the bottom of a page.

Report Writing and Technology

Being able to communicate effectively in a clear, concise, and logical manner continues to be one of the most demanded work skills. Employees who practice effective revision skills are far ahead of their counterparts who have had the mind-set that the first draft is the final draft. This report details effective revision skills as it relates to report writing.

Revising the Draft

After a first draft of a report is completed, the writer is ready to refine or polish the report. The writer must be objective when revising the report draft and cultivate a mind-set for improving the report by always considering the draft as a draft.

First, read the draft for content. This might mean rewriting sections of the report or adding information to areas that appear weak in this review. In this evaluative review, the writer may realize that one section would fit more logically after another section.

When the writer is satisfied with the content, it is time to verify that all style rules have been followed. For example, check all headings to ensure they are "talking" headings. Do the headings describe the content of the section? Also, be sure all headings are parallel. If the writer chooses the side heading *Know Your Audience*, other side headings must also begin with a verb. Note that the side headings in this report are parallel, with both beginning with a gerund.

Ensuring Correct and Attractive Format

The effective writer understands the importance of using technology to create an attractive document that adheres to correct style rules. Review the list below to determine your use of technology in the report writing process.

✓ Number preliminary pages of the report with small Roman numerals at the bottom center of the page. Number the pages of the report with Arabic numbers in the upper-right corner.

✓ Browse the excellent built-in design galleries provided in the word processing software to select attractive headers or footers that contain helpful information for the reader.

✓ Suppress headers, footers, and page numbering on the title page and on the first page of the report.

Page | 2

✓ Invoke the Widow/Orphan control feature to ensure that no lines display alone at the bottom or top of a page, and use the Keep with next command to keep side headings from appearing alone at the bottom of the page.

✓ Take advantage of the following features essential in report writing: table of contents, table of figures, index, captioning, and citations. The usefulness of these features becomes apparent during the revision process. Citations are easily moved and updated; the table of contents is updated in a click, and the caption moves with the chart or table.

✓ Master the design of attractive tables and charts as these elements increase the readability and attractiveness of long and complex reports.

Writers also take advantage of the online thesaurus for choosing the most appropriate word and the spelling and grammar features for ensuring spelling and grammar correctness. Additionally, electronic desk references and style manuals are just a click away.

These simple steps will assist you in your goal to create well-written and attractive reports. The next step is to practice, practice, practice.

Page 1   **Page 2**

LESSON E

Select the Skill Building tab; choose the appropriate emphasis and then Lesson E.

KEYBOARDING PRO DELUXE 2 | **Skill Building** | *Technique Builder*

DRILL 14

Word Beginnings

Key each line once, working for accuracy. DS between groups.

br
1 bright brown bramble bread breath breezes brought brother broiler
2 In February my brother brought brown bread and beans from Boston.

exe
3 exercises exert executives exemplify exemption executed exemplary
4 They exert extreme effort executing exercises in exemplary style.

bt
5 doubt subtle obtains obtrusion subtracts indebtedness undoubtedly
6 Extreme debt will cause more than subtle doubt among my creditors.

ny
7 tiny funny company nymph penny nylon many anyone phony any brainy
8 Anyone as brainy and funny as Penny is an asset to their company.

KEYBOARDING PRO DELUXE 2 | **Timed Writings**

1. Take a 1' writing on each paragraph.
2. Take a 3' writing on both paragraphs.

Writing 27

	gwam	1'	3'
Many people believe that an ounce of prevention is worth a pound		13	4
of cure. Care of your heart can help you prevent serious physical		26	9
problems. The human heart is the most important pump ever		38	13
developed. It constantly pushes blood through the body tissues. But		51	17
the layers of muscle that make up the heart must be kept in proper		65	22
working order. Exercise can help this muscle to remain in good		77	26
condition.		80	27
Another important way of keeping a healthy heart is just to avoid		13	31
habits which are considered detrimental to the body. Food that is high		27	36
in cholesterol is not a good choice. Also, use of tobacco has quite a		41	40
bad effect on the function of the heart. You can minimize your chances		56	45
of heart trouble by avoiding these bad health habits.		66	49

1' | 1 | 2 | 3 | 4 | 5 | 6 | 7 | 8 | 9 | 10 | 11 | 12 | 13 |
3' | 1 | 2 | 3 | 4 |

LINE AND PAGE BREAKS

Pagination or breaking pages at the appropriate location can easily be controlled using two features: Widow/Orphan control and Keep with next.

Widow/Orphan control prevents a single line of a paragraph from printing at the bottom or top of a page. A check mark displays in this option box indicating that Widow/Orphan control is "on" (the default).

Keep with next prevents a page break from occurring between two paragraphs. Use this feature to keep a side heading from being left alone at the bottom of a page.

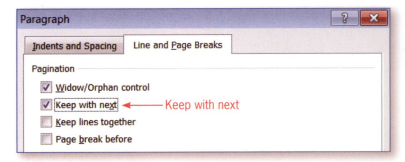

To use Keep with next:

Home/Paragraph/Dialog Box Launcher

1. Select the side heading and at least two lines of the paragraph that follows it.
2. Follow the path to display the Paragraph dialog box.
3. From the Line and Page Breaks tab, select Keep with next.

DRILL 1	PAGE NUMBERS	keep with next

1. In the open document, add page numbers positioned at the top of page at the right. Do not print a page number on the first page.

2. Select the side heading at the bottom of the page along with the entire address and the first line with a time note.

3. Apply the Keep with next command so the side heading moves to page 2.

4. Preview to verify that the page number appears on page 2 only and that the side heading appears on page 2.

5. Proofread and check; click Next to continue. (*45-drill1*)

QUICK ✔

Check to see if a page number appears on page 2 and that the side heading appears at the top of page 2. A page number should not appear on page 1.

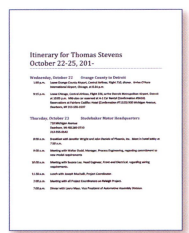

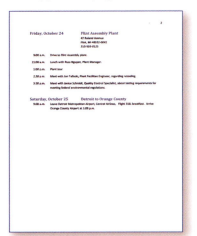

WORD PROCESSING DOCUMENT DESIGN

Level **+2**

Learning Outcomes

Keyboarding

+ To key fluently using good keying techniques.

+ To key about 40 words per minute with good accuracy.

Document Design Skills

+ To format memos, letters, tables, and reports appropriately.

+ To apply basic design skills to announcements, invitations, and newsletters.

+ To enhance documents with basic graphics.

Word Processing Skills

+ To learn word processing commands.

+ To create, edit, and format documents effectively.

Communication Skills

+ To review and improve basic communication skills.

+ To compose simple documents.

+ To use proofing tools effectively.

+ To proofread and edit text effectively.

Lesson 45 | Multiple-Page Report

New Commands
- Page Numbers
- Line and Page Breaks
- Insert File

New Commands

45b

KEYBOARDING PRO DELUXE 2

*References/Word 2010
Commands/Lesson 45*

PAGE NUMBERS

Multiple-page documents such as reports require page numbers. The Page Number command automatically inserts the correct page number on each page. Page numbers may be positioned automatically in the header position (0.5" at top of page) or in the footer position (0.5" from bottom of the page). To prevent the number from printing on the first page, you will modify the page layout on the first page.

To insert page numbers:

Insert/Header & Footer/Page Number

1. Follow the path to display a list of page number positions and formatting options.

2. Click an option such as Top of Page ❶ to display a gallery of page number styles.

3. Click the down scroll arrow to browse the various styles ❷. **Note:** To remove page numbers, click Remove Page Numbers ❸.

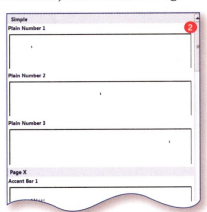

Double-click in the body of the document to close the header. Double-click in the header or footer area to open the header/footer.

To remove the page number from the first page:

Header & Footer Tools Design/Options/Different First Page

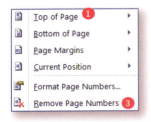

When the page number is inserted, the Header and Footer Design Tools contextual tab displays. On the Design tab from the Options group, click Different First Page ❹. The page number does not display on the first page.

Note: You may also select Different First Page from the Layout tab of the Page Setup dialog box (Page Layout/Page Setup/Dialog Box Launcher).

Word 2010 Basics

LEARNING OUTCOMES

- Learn basic *Word 2010* commands.
- Create, save, and print documents.
- Apply text, paragraph, and page formats.
- Navigate, review, and edit documents.
- Build keyboarding skills.

Lesson 26 | *Getting Started*

New Commands

- Format Text
- Error-Check
- Open
- Close
- New
- Mini Toolbar
- Print
- Exit

KEYBOARDING PRO DELUXE 2

WARMUP

Lessons/26a Warmup

LA ALL LETTERS

Skill Building

26b Timed Writing

1. Key a 1' writing on each paragraph; work to increase speed. Use wordwrap.
2. Key a 3' timing on all paragraphs.

	gwam	1'	3'

Learning new software can be fun, but it often requires much | 12 | 4
hard work. However, if you are willing to work hard, in a short period | 26 | 9
of time, you can learn important skills. | 35 | 12

If you accept change easily, you are more likely to learn new | 12 | 16
things quickly. A person who avoids change has just about the | 25 | 20
same chance of learning new software as a lazy person. | 36 | 24

Working smart might be just as important as working hard. | 12 | 28
Help is easy to use if you will take the time to explore the resources | 26 | 32
that are provided in your software. | 33 | 35

1' | 1 | 2 | 3 | 4 | 5 | 6 | 7 | 8 | 9 | 10 | 11 | 12 | 13
3' | | 1 | | | 2 | | | 3 | | | 4 | |

New Commands

26c Getting Started

LEARNING THE BASICS

Most of you have used *Keyboarding Pro DELUXE 2* to complete the skill-building activities in Modules 1 and 2. In Module 3, you will use *KPD2* with *Word 2010*. *Word* will enable you to create and format professional-looking documents that are easy to read.

44-d1
Leftbound Report

1. Key the model report on the previous page. Tap ENTER three times to position the title at about 2". Change the left margin to 1.5".
2. Apply the Flow document theme. Apply appropriate styles to the title and side headings.
3. Format the bulleted list with square bullets.
4. Proofread and check; click Next to continue. (44-d1)

44-d2
Cover Page

1. Open *44-d1*. Insert a cover page using the Sideline cover page.
2. Key the following information:
   Company name: **Swartsfager, Inc.**
   Document title: Key the report title.
   Subtitle: **For John E. Swartsfager, Marketing Director**
   Author: Key your name.
   Date: Select the current date.
3. Proofread and check; click Next to continue. (44-d2)

44-d3
Edit Report

1. Open *43-d3* and format the document as a leftbound report.
2. Apply the Elemental document theme.
3. Add the last paragraph shown below. Apply Heading 1 style to the side heading.
4. Search for the word *photos* and replace with **photographs**.
5. Search for all occurrences of italic formatting and replace all occurrences with no italic.
6. Search for all occurrences of bold formatting and replace all occurrences with no bold except the side headings. *Hint:* Click No Formatting before you begin the new search. Click Find Next and review each replacement.
7. Use the Navigation pane to find the Summary heading. Proofread carefully.
8. Use the Go To command to locate page 2. Then use the Navigation pane to locate page 2.
9. Preview, check, and close the document. (44-d3)

Summary Apply Heading 1 style

Remember to plan your page layout with the three basic elements of effective page design. Always include sufficient white space to give an uncluttered appearance. Learn to add bold when emphasis is needed, and do consider your audience when choosing typestyles. Finally, use typestyles to add variety to your layout, but remember, no more than two typestyles in a document.

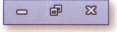
LAUNCH WORD

Keyboarding Pro DELUXE 2 will launch or open *Microsoft Word* automatically when you choose the first activity to be done in *Word*. For example, if you select 26-Drill 1, the Document Options menu screen shown below will display. Select Begin new document and then click OK to open *Word*.

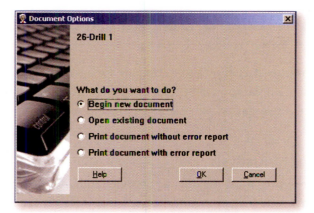

WORD SCREEN

You will notice immediately that the *Word* screen has three different segments. The first segment at the top of the screen is the Microsoft Office Fluent Interface—often called the Ribbon. The Ribbon contains all of the word processing commands that you will use. The Ribbon on your computer may display slightly differently from the one shown below. The way the Ribbon displays is determined by the size and resolution of your screen.

The center portion of the *Word* screen is the New Document screen on which you will key your documents. It resembles a blank sheet of paper. The insertion point indicates the position at which you will begin to key.

The third segment of the screen is the status bar located at the bottom of the screen. The left side of the status bar provides information about the document. The right side provides different ways to view a document.

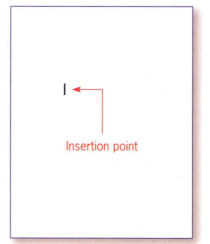

Insertion point

Left side of status bar

Right side of status bar

2" (Tap ENTER three times.)

Title
Planning a Successful Presentation Title style

Presenters realize the need to prepare for a successful presentation. Two areas of extensive preparation are the development of a thorough audience analysis and a well-defined presentation purpose.

Side heading
Audience Analysis Heading 1 style

The presenter must conduct a thorough audience analysis before developing the presentation. The profile of the audience includes the following demographics.

- Age
- Gender
- Education
- Ethnic group
- Marital status
- Geographic location
- Group membership

Given sufficient time, the presenter will research each of these areas carefully. Additionally, interviews with program planners and organization leaders will provide insight into the needs, desires, and expectations of the specific audience. Many successful presenters find it useful to arrive early to the presentation and meet participants as they enter the meeting room. Carefully planned questions can provide pertinent information needed to ensure a relevant presentation for the audience. Often presenters may begin the presentation with one or two directed questions to understand the profile of the audience. Knowing the audience is an important first step in preparing a successful presentation.

1.5"

1"

Purpose of the Presentation

After analyzing the audience profile, the presenter has a clear focus on the needs of the audience and then writes a well-defined purpose of the presentation. With a clear focus, the presenter confidently conducts research and organizes a presentation that is on target. The presenter remembers to state the purpose in the introduction of the presentation to assist the audience in understanding the well-defined direction of the presentation.

SELECT AND FORMAT TEXT

You entered text using the keyboard and wordwrap in Modules 1 and 2. Remember that when text reaches the end of the line, it automatically wraps to the next line and continues to do this until you tap ENTER to begin a new paragraph.

In this module, you will learn to format text. To format or edit text, you must move the insertion point around with the mouse or use the arrow keys on the keyboard. To use the mouse, move the I-beam pointer to the desired position and click the left mouse button.

To select text:

- Click at the beginning of the text and drag the mouse over the text to highlight it. The selected text is highlighted in blue.
- Double-clicking within a word will select that word.

Home   To format text, you will use the commands on the Home tab of the Ribbon. The Ribbon contains three basic components:

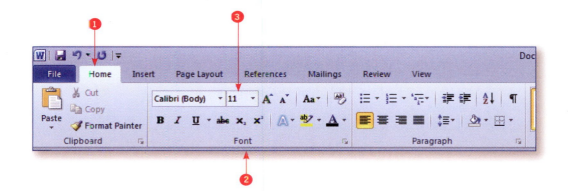

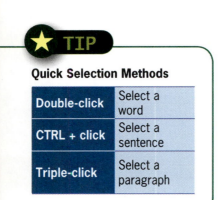
❶ **Tabs**—located at the top of the Ribbon. Home, the first tab, is shown above.

Note that when you click a different tab, the Ribbon shows options and features that relate to that tab. The *Word* tabs are Home, Insert, Page Layout, References, Mailings, Review, and View. The File tab shown in blue displays a menu of options that you will learn in later lessons. Try clicking the Insert tab and the Page Layout tab. Note the types of activities that are included below each of these tabs. Click the Home tab again.

❷ **Groups**—contain a number of related items. The names are positioned at the bottom of the Ribbon below each group. The group indicated above is the Font group, which you will use to format text in this lesson.

On the Home tab, the groups are Clipboard, Font, Paragraph, Styles, and Editing. These functions are commonly used while you are keying, formatting, and editing text.

❸ **Commands**—the buttons, the boxes for entering information, and the menus that provide a choice of options. The command indicated above is the Font Size command. Clicking the arrow next to a command will display additional options.

DOCUMENT THEMES

Built-In document themes incorporate colors, fonts, effects, and styles that can be applied to a *Word* document or to documents in other *Microsoft Office* applications. The default theme is Office. In addition to the Built-In themes, users can customize themes to meet specific needs.

To apply a document theme:

Page Layout/Themes/Themes

1. Follow the path to display the gallery of Built-In themes.
2. Click the document theme you wish to use.

DRILL 4   **DOCUMENT THEMES**   document themes

1. Review the open document; note the information about the headings and Live Preview.

2. Display the Document Theme gallery and use Live Preview to view at least six of the theme options. Note changes in color and font styles.

3. Apply Aspect document theme.

4. Proofread and check; click Next to continue (*44-drill4*)

Document Design

44d

KEYBOARDING PRO DELUXE 2

References/Document Formats/Reports

LEFTBOUND REPORT

Reports prepared with binders are called leftbound reports. The binding takes 0.5" of space. Study the illustration below and the full model on page 174 and note the 1.5" left margin required for leftbound reports. Review the other report formats that are the same for unbound and leftbound reports.

Left margin: 1.5"

Right margin: 1"

Bottom margin: Approximately 1"; last page may be deeper

Font: 11 point for body of report

Title: ❶

- Position at about 2".
- Capitalize the first letter of all main words and apply Title style.

Side headings: ❷

- Capitalize the first letter of all main words and apply Heading 1 style.

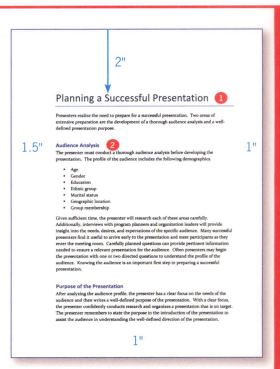

FORMAT TEXT, CONTINUED

Home tab/Font group/Font commands

Note that the path shown above (Home tab/Font group/Font commands) guides you in the location of commands. To follow the path: Click on the tab (Home); then look for the group label (Font) at the bottom of the Ribbon, and finally select the desired command (such as Font Size or Bold). The path will be provided for most commands throughout this textbook to assist you in locating commands quickly and easily. In this lesson, you will apply the format commands from the Font group to text that you have selected.

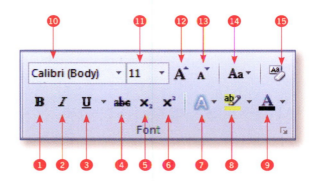

❶ Bold ❷ Italic ❸ Underline ❹ Strikethrough ❺ Subscript ❻ Superscript

❼ Text Effects ❽ Text Highlight Color ❾ Font Color ❿ Font ⓫ Font Size

⓬ Grow Font ⓭ Shrink Font ⓮ Change Case ⓯ Clear Formatting

DRILL 1   FORMAT TEXT

1. In a new document, key your name in the New Document screen and tap ENTER.

2. Click the Home tab and move the mouse pointer over each of the 15 commands (6 in top row; 9 in bottom row) in the Font group to identify the command and note the short description of the function it performs.

3. Note that some of the commands such as Font and Underline have drop-list arrows on the side of the command. Click the drop-list arrow to see the gallery of options that can be selected.

4. Key the names of the commands listed above from 1 to 15; tap ENTER after each command.

5. Select each of the first four commands you keyed and apply the format to the name of the command.

6. Key the number **1** at the end of *Subscript* and **2** at the end of *Superscript*; select and apply the format to the numbers.

7. Select *Text Effects* and apply the Gradient Fill – Orange, Accent 6, Inner Shadow text effect in the last line.

8. Select *Text Highlight Color* and apply yellow highlight.

9. Select *Font Color* and change the color to Blue from the Standard Colors palette.

10. Select *Font* and change to Cambria; select *Font Size* and change to 14 point.

11. Select *Grow Font* and click the Grow Font command twice.

12. Select *Shrink Font* and click the Shrink Font command once.

13. Select *Change Case* and change to UPPERCASE.

14. Select *Clear Formatting* and apply Bold and Italic; then click the drop-list arrow next to Underline and select a double underline.

15. With *Clear Formatting* selected, click the Clear Formatting command to clear the formatting.

16. Leave the document open – keep it on your screen.

1. In the open document, click the Find button to display the Navigation pane.

2. Display all occurrences of the word *speeches* and replace with **presentations**.

3. Display all occurrences of the word *objective*. Click on the last occurrence and replace with **goal**.

4. Display all occurrences of the word *confident*. Click Options and select Find whole words only. Replace the one occurrence with **assured**.

5. Find *audience* and highlight each occurrence in yellow. *Hint:* Be sure to set the Highlight button to yellow.

6. Click to browse all pages of the document.

7. Click to browse all report headings. Click on the second heading and then the third heading to move in the report.

8. Click the Magnifying Glass button and click Footnotes/Endnotes to display the footnote on page 1. Click the x to end the search; the Magnifying Glass button displays.

9. Click the Magnifying Glass button and click Tables to go to the table in the report.

10. Proofread and check; click Next to continue. (*44-drill2*)

GO TO

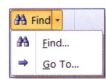

The Go To command can also be used to navigate a document. A variety of document segments can be located with the Go To command, such as pages, footnotes, tables, or headings.

To use the Go To command:

SHORTCUT

CTRL + G

1. Click the drop-list arrow on the Find command; then click Go To.

2. Click on the item you wish to find, such as Page or Heading. Then key the number in the text box.

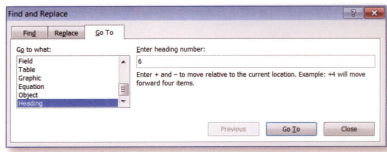

Note: You may also click the Magnifying Glass button and click Go To.

DRILL 3   GO TO

1. Open *44-drill2*. Use the Go To command to go to page 2.

2. Go to page 1.

3. Go to footnote 1.

4. Go to Heading 2.

5. Go to Table 1.

6. Proofread and check; click Next to continue. (*44-drill3*)

SAVE AND CHECK DOCUMENTS USING *KEYBOARDING PRO DELUXE 2*

 Click Back to save the document without checking it. This option is normally used for work in progress.

Click Check to error-check a document and save it.

DRILL 1 CONTINUED   SAVE DOCUMENT USING *KEYBOARDING PRO DELUXE 2*

1. Click the Back button and save the document without checking it.   2. You will open it again for the next activity.

OPEN AN EXISTING DOCUMENT

To open and edit a document previously prepared, select Open existing document from the Document Options screen. *Word* launches.

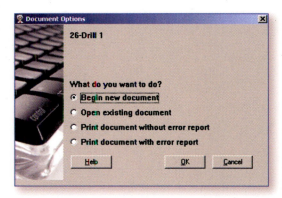

The Document Toolbar displays in the upper-right corner of the open document. Click Back to save the open document without checking it. Click Check after proofreading for mistakes and previewing the placement. The Document Toolbar then changes. Generally click Next to move to the next application; click Close after the last application in a lesson.

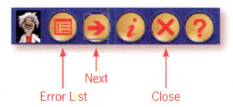

Error List   Next   Close

Error List displays the type of mistakes made. The error number correlates to the numbered errors on the document.

Next returns you to the Document Option menu for the next application; *Word* remains open.

Close closes *Word* and returns you to the Document Option menu for the next application.

DRILL 1 CONTINUED   CHECK DOCUMENT

1. Open the existing document completed earlier in Drill 1.   3. Click Continue to move to the next exercise. (*26-drill1*)

2. Check the document and review the report.

To browse for pages in a document:

1. Click Browse the pages in your document button ❶.
2. Click the desired page ❷ to go to that page in the document.

Note: For other searches, click the Magnifying Glass button to search for Graphics, Tables, Equations, Footnotes/Endnotes, or Reviewers.

To replace text:

<mark>Home/Editing/Replace</mark>

1. Follow the path to display the Find and Replace dialog box.
2. Key the text you wish to locate in the Find what box.
3. Key the replacement text in the Replace with box.
4. Click Find Next to find the next occurrence of the text. Click Replace to replace one occurrence or Replace All to replace all occurences of the text.

To find text and apply a format such as highlight:

<mark>Home/Editing/Replace</mark>

1. Follow the path to display the Find and Replace dialog box.
2. Key the text you wish to locate in the Find what box.
3. Click More to display additional options.
4. Click in Replace with and then click Format ❸ and select Highlight.

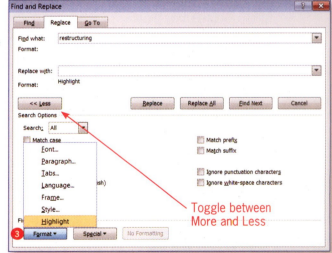

Toggle between More and Less

Note the search options available when you click More, such as Match case or Find whole words only. Finding whole words only prevents you from finding letters within a word.

MINI TOOLBAR

The Mini toolbar provides a shortcut to apply frequently used formatting commands. When you select text, the Mini toolbar appears in a very light or faded view. You may have noticed the toolbar when you selected text to format

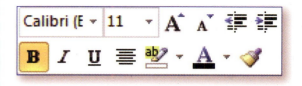

in Drill 1. To darken the Mini toolbar, move the mouse pointer toward it. You can click a button from this toolbar to apply a format. This toolbar simplifies editing text by positioning frequently used commands at the point at which they are needed. You have not yet learned some of the commands on the Mini toolbar; you will learn these commands later in this module.

To use the Mini toolbar:

1. Select text to which you want to apply a commonly used format.

2. Move the mouse pointer toward the Mini toolbar when it appears in a faded view.

3. Click the command(s) that you want to apply when the Mini toolbar darkens.

DRILL 2 — OPEN NEW DOCUMENT

1. On the menu, click the next activity, *26-Drill 2*.

2. Key your name at the top of the document and tap ENTER.

3. Key the document name **26-drill2** and tap ENTER.

4. Key the following sentence:
   This is a new document I have created.

5. Select the document name and use the Mini toolbar to change the font to Cambria and the font size to 14 point.

6. Select *new document* in the sentence you keyed and use the Mini toolbar to highlight it in Bright Green.

7. Proofread and check; click Next to continue. (*26-drill2*)

PRINT A DOCUMENT USING *KEYBOARDING PRO DELUXE 2*

Click Print on the screen that displays the document.

-or-

1. Reopen a completed document.

2. Choose Print from the Document Options dialog box.

DRILL 3 — PREVIEW AND PRINT DOCUMENT

1. On the menu, click *26-Drill 3* to open the activity completed in Drill 1.

2. Position the insertion point at the end of your name and tap ENTER. Then key **Drill 3** on the line below your name.

3. Use *Keyboarding Pro DELUXE 2* to print the document.

4. Proofread and check; click Next to continue. (*26-drill3*)

EXIT *KEYBOARDING PRO DELUXE 2*

1. From Main menu, click the Send button to send file to the Web Reporter or to send file to your instructor.

2. Click the Logout button to return to the logout page and exit *Keyboarding Pro DELUXE 2*.

Page Layout/Page Setup/Margins/Custom Margins

2. Proofread and check; click Next to continue. (*44-drill1*)

1. In the open document, change the left, right, and top margins to 1.5". Apply margin settings to the whole document.

FIND AND REPLACE

Locating text, headings, footnotes, graphics, page breaks, comments, formatting, and other items within a document quickly is an essential skill when working with long documents such as reports.

To find text:

Home/Editing/Find

1. Follow the path to display the Navigation pane on the left side of the screen.

2. Key the text you wish to locate in the search box ❶. The matches display below the search box. Click each match ❷ to go to the location in the document.

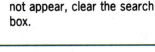
To display other find options:

Click the Magnifying Glass button ❸. Click Options. The Find Options dialog box displays. Review the various find options to determine its usefulness in a search.

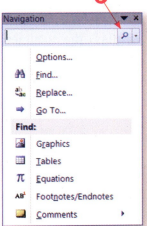

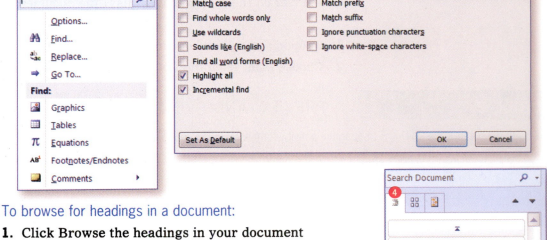

To browse for headings in a document:

1. Click Browse the headings in your document button ❹.

2. Click the desired heading ❺ to go that heading in the document.

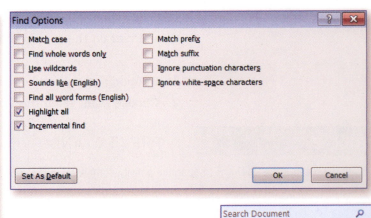

STANDARD OPERATING PROCEDURES

To complete *Word* documents, follow these procedures:

1. Key and format documents as directed in the textbook.

2. Proofread for keying or formatting errors. Check your document against the exercise in the textbook. Preview for placement.

3. When you are satisfied with the document, click the Check button. The software will check your document and display a checked version on screen. Mistakes will be counted above each paragraph and errors will be highlighted.

4. Select Display Error List for an explanation of each error.

5. Scroll to the bottom of the screen to view the report of errors, *gwam*, number of errors, etc.

6. Print the document using the *Word* Print command if desired.

7. Click Next to continue to the next application or Close if it is the last application in a lesson.

Applications

26-d1

Create a New Document

1. In a new document, key your name on the first line and then key **26-d1** on the next line.

2. Key the following sentences. Do not key the letters used to identify the sentences. Tap ENTER after each sentence.

   a. The default for Heading 1 is Cambria 16-point font.

   b. I use red font color, yellow highlighting, or purple text effects for emphasis.

   c. This sentence illustrates bold text, italic text, and underline formats.

   d. Is H2O the chemical symbol for water? The second formula was a2 + b2.

   e. He said, "Revert back to the previous form."

   f. Use text formats to emphasize text in documents, but do not overuse them.

3. In sentence a, apply Cambria font and 16-point font size to *Heading 1*.

4. In sentence b, apply Red font color to the word *red*, Yellow highlight to the word *yellow*, and Gradient Fill – Purple, Accent 4, Reflection to the word *purple*.

5. In sentence c, apply bold format to the word *bold*, italic format to the word *italic*, and underline format to the word *underline*.

6. In sentence d, apply subscript format to *2* in H2O and superscript format to *2* in both a2 and b2.

7. In sentence e, apply strikethrough to the word *back*.

8. In sentence f, apply bold, italic, and Red font color to the words *emphasize text*.

9. In sentence f, use clear formatting to remove all formats from the words *emphasize text*.

10. Check and close the document. (*26-d1*)

11. Exit *Keyboarding Pro DELUXE 2*.

Lesson 44 | *Leftbound Report*

New Commands

- Custom Margins
- Go To
- Find and Replace
- Document Themes

Skill Building

44b   Textbook Keying

1. Key each drill, concentrating on using good keying techniques. Tap ENTER twice after each 3-line group.
2. Repeat the drill if time permits.

first row

1 Take the Paz exit; make a right turn; then the street veers left.
2 Stop by and see the amateur videos of Zoe at six o'clock tonight.
3 I made an excellent pizza with leftover bread, cheese, and beef.

home row

4 Dallas shall ask Sal to sell fake flash fads; Sal sells all fads.
5 A small fast salad is all Kallas had; Dallas adds a dash of salt.
6 Dallas saw all flasks fall; alas Dad adds a fast fake hall flask.

third row

7 We used thirty pails of yellow powder; Wesley threw the rest out.
8 I should go to the store with Paul to get eggs for the apple pie.
9 Did you see the request for Sy to take the test with your sister?

New Commands

44c

KEYBOARDING PRO DELUXE 2

*References/Word 2010
Commands/Lesson 44*

CUSTOM MARGINS

At this point you have used the Normal margin setting or have selected from the built-in gallery of margin settings (Narrow, Moderate, Wide, or Mirrored). To set specific margin settings, use the Custom Margins command. The last custom setting will then display at the top of the built-in margins gallery.

Office 2003 Default			
Top:	1"	Bottom:	1"
Left:	1.25"	Right:	1.25"

Custom Margins...

To set custom margins not listed in the gallery:

Page Layout/Page Setup/Margins/Custom Margins

1. Follow the path to display the Page Setup dialog box.
2. From the Margins tab ❶, click the up or down arrows to increase or decrease the default settings ❷.
3. Apply margins to the Whole document ❸ unless directed otherwise. Click OK.

Lesson 27 | *Word 2010 Basics*

New Commands

- Start Word
- Save
- Save As
- New Folder

- Close
- Open
- Recent

- New
- Print
- Exit

KEYBOARDING PRO DELUXE 2   **WARMUP**   *Lessons/27a Warmup*

LA   **ALL LETTERS**

Skill Building

27b   Timed Writing

1. Key a 1' writing on each paragraph; work to increase speed. Use wordwrap.
2. Key a 3' timing on all paragraphs.

	gwam	1'	3'
Many students find it quite difficult to juggle the things		12	4
they want to do with the things they ought to do. Too often the		25	8
things that they find the most tempting and desirable to do are just		39	13
distractions from doing things that need to be given priority.		51	17
The key is to set priorities and stick with them. Those who		12	21
organize their work and do the critical things first not only		25	25
accomplish more, they are the most likely to have sufficient time		38	30
to do the things that they enjoy doing as well.		47	33
Choosing friends wisely also helps you to stay on target.		12	37
Students who have friends with the same type of expectations as		25	41
they do usually help each other to meet their goals. They value		38	45
their time and try to use it well.		44	48

1'	1	2	3	4	5	6	7	8	9	10	11	12	13
3'		1			2			3			4		

New Commands

27c   Getting Started with Word

KEYBOARDING PRO DELUXE 2

References/Word 2010 Commands/Lesson 27

LEARNING THE BASICS

Exit *Keyboarding Pro DELUXE 2* at this point.

You will complete the next activities using *Word 2010* software without the use of *Keyboarding Pro DELUXE 2*. In Lesson 26, you used *Keyboarding Pro DELUXE 2* to launch *Word* and learned that *Keyboarding Pro DELUXE 2* performs a number of commands automatically for you. You opened documents from the Lesson menu and saved, checked, and printed them. In addition, *Keyboarding Pro DELUXE 2* managed all of your files automatically.

When you are using *Word* to prepare papers for your other classes, documents for a part-time job, or personal business documents, you will need to learn how to use these commands without the assistance of *Keyboarding Pro DELUXE 2*. You will also need to learn how to manage your files so that you can locate and access them easily.

43-d3

continued

Using a small size type (or font) is not recommended. In most cases, a font that is 11 point or larger makes the document easy to read. Copy that is arranged in more than one column is also more attractive. Preferably break the page into smaller columns of copy and intersperse with photos or illustrations.

Choosing a typeface

Typeface refers to the style of printing on the page. Matching the style or "feeling" of the type with the purpose of the finished product is very important. For example, a layout would not include use of a gothic or "old style" typeface to promote a modern, high tech product. Consider the boldness or lightness of the style, the readability factor, and the decorativeness or simplicity. Mixing more than three different typefaces on a page should also be avoided. Vary the type sizes to give the effect of different type styles. *Bold* and *italics* can also be added for emphasis and variety, especially when only one type style is being used.

43-d4

Cover Page

1. Open *43-d3*. Create a cover page using the Tiles cover page. Use the information that follows:

   Company name: **Bartlett Communications, Inc.**
   Document title: Report title from *43-d3*
   Document subtitle: **Basic Design Rules**
   Author: Student's Name
   Date: Select the current year.
   Address: **2119 Earhart Boulevard, New Orleans, LA 70112-2119**

2. Check and close. (*43-d4*)

LAUNCH WORD

Word can be launched in several different ways. The first time you launch *Word*, you will probably have to click the Start button on the taskbar. The illustration below shows how to launch *Word* using *Windows* 7 as the operating system.

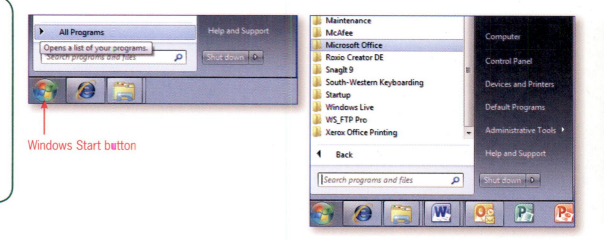

Windows Start button

To launch *Word*:

Start/All Programs/Microsoft Office/Microsoft Word 2010

1. Follow the path shown above by:
   a. Clicking the Start button.
   b. Clicking All Programs.
   c. Clicking Microsoft Office to display the list of applications and then selecting *Word 2010*.
2. Note that when *Word* opens, the *Word* icon will appear in the taskbar.

To make it easier to launch *Word* in the future, you can pin *Word* to the taskbar in *Windows* 7. When a program is pinned to the taskbar, you can open it by simply clicking the icon on the taskbar.

To pin *Word* to the taskbar in *Windows 7*:

1. Right-click the *Word* icon.
2. Click Pin this program to taskbar.

43-d1
Unbound Report

1. Key the model report on the previous page. Tap ENTER three times to position the title at about 2". Use default side margins.
2. Capitalize the first letter of all main words in the title; tap ENTER once after the title. Then select the title and apply Title style.
3. Select each side heading and apply Heading 1 style. Tap ENTER once after each side heading.
4. Apply square bullets to the list.
5. Proofread and check; click Next to continue. (*43-d1*)

43-d2
Cover Page

1. Open *43-d1*. Create a cover page using the Cover Page feature. From the Built-In category, select the Alphabet cover page.
2. Key the following information:
   Document title: Report title from *43-d1*
   Document subtitle: **For All Division Staff**
   Date: Select the current date.
   Author: **Dana Olmstead, Division Manager**
3. Proofread and check; click Next to continue. (*43-d2*)

43-d3
Edit Unbound Report

 brochure

1. In the open document, position the title at approximately 2". Apply Title style.
2. Correct the capitalization of the side headings; apply Heading 1 style.
3. Make other edits shown in the report. Refer to proofreaders' marks on page 55.
4. Proofread and check; click Next to continue. (*43-d3*)

Who Can Design a Better Brochure?

Producing a brochure with a professional appearance requires careful creativity and planning. Not every one is an accomplished paste-up artist who is capable of creating a complex piece of printed art, but most skilled computer users can create an attractive layout for a basic brochure.
Working with blocks

Work with copy and illustrations in blocks. Key body of text copy, leaving plenty of space for illustrations and headlines. The blocks should then be arranged in an orderly and eye appealing manner.

(continued)

FILE MANAGEMENT

File management refers to saving documents in an organized manner so that they can be easily located and used again. Any students not using *Keyboarding Pro DELUXE 2* in this class should create a new folder for each module of the textbook. Documents for this module should be saved in a folder named *Module 3*. The name you should use for each drill or application is provided in parentheses at the end of the directions.

All students need to learn how to store files on removable media such as a flash drive or a CD. If you do not complete a lesson in class, you may wish to store the file so that you can continue working on it in a computer lab or at home.

FILE MENU

File/command

The File tab located in the upper-left corner of the Ribbon provides you with all of the commands that you need to work with files. When you click the File tab with only a blank document open, a menu drops down with the commands shown on the left and the most recently opened documents on the right.

★ DISCOVER

Note the pin is engaged on the first file shown in the illustration at right. Pinned files remain on the Recent Documents list; other files rotate off as new files are added. You can pin a document by clicking the pin symbol next to any file.

Take a few minutes to review some of the options on the menu shown at the right. For example, you can create a new document, open an existing document, save a document, or print a document from this menu.

Note: The path for the File tab (File/command) is used for working with files on the File drop-down menu. The normal path (tab/group/command) is not used because the File menu is available for all tabs on the Ribbon. Remember to click the File tab any time you want to use a command to work with files—New, Open, Close, Save, Save As, or Print.

SAVE AND CREATE NEW FOLDER

The Save and Save As commands are used to preserve documents for future use. Save is used to save a document with the same name. Save As is used to save a document with a name for the first time or to save a document with a different name or to a different location. The first time you save a document, clicking either Save or Save As will display the Save As dialog box. The Save As dialog box also gives you an opportunity to create a new folder in which to save the document.

2" (Tap ENTER three times.)

Title →

Electronic Mail Guidelines   Title style

Electronic mail, a widely used communication channel in the business environment, clearly has three major advantages—time effectiveness, distance effectiveness, and cost effectiveness. To reap full benefit from this common and convenient communication medium, follow the basic guidelines regarding the creation and use of e-mail when used for business purposes.

Side heading →

Message Content   Heading 1 style

Although perceived as informal documents, e-mail messages are business records. Therefore, follow these effective communication guidelines.

1"

Bulleted list →

- Write clear, concise sentences, avoiding clichés, slang, redundancies, and wordiness.
- Avoid emoticons and text message jargon or acronyms.
- Break the message into logical paragraphs, sequencing in an appropriate order. White space is   1"   important in e-mail messages as well as printed documents, so be sure to add extra space between paragraphs.
- Limit e-mail messages to one idea per message, and preferably limit to one screen.
- Always include a subject line that clearly defines the e-mail message.
- Consider carefully the recipients of the e-mail; do not waste your colleagues' valuable time by sending or copying unnecessary e-mails.
- Spell-check e-mail messages carefully; verify punctuation and content accuracy.
- Check the tone of the message carefully. If angry, wait at least one hour before clicking the Send button. Review the message, modify if needed, and then send the message.

Preferences

Although e-mail is a common means of communication, other methods include face-to-face communication, telephone, voice mail, and instant messaging. It is important to realize that each person has preferred methods of communication, and the method will vary depending upon the message content. To accomplish tasks more effectively, be aware of individuals' preferred channels of communication and use those channels if appropriate for the business purpose.

Remember that effective communication is essential to be successful in today's business world. Apply these important guidelines as you prepare e-mail messages.

To save a document in a new folder:

File/Save or Save As

1. With the document open, click Save or Save As to display the Save As dialog box. Note that the dialog box opens to the Documents library where documents are stored.

2. Click the New folder button to create a new folder in which to store the document. The new folder displays in blue.

3. Click in the name box and key the name of the folder, such as *Module 3*.

4. Click Open or double-click the new folder (Module 3) to open it.

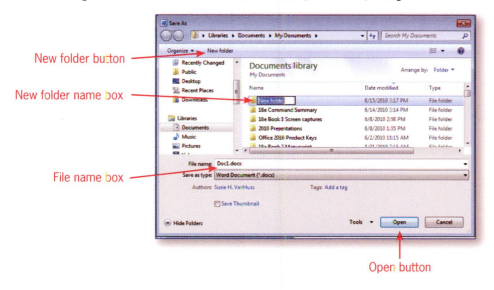

New folder button

New folder name box

File name box

Open button

5. In the File name box, select Doc1 and key the name of the file, such as *27-drill1*.

6. Click Save.

DRILL 1

SAVE IN NEW FOLDER

1. Launch *Word*.

2. In the new document, key your name; then tap ENTER.

3. Key the text below.

4. Create a new folder named **Module 3**.

5. Save and name the document **27-drill1**. Leave the document open.

An effective way to manage files is to create folders to store related documents. An important part of file management is naming files and folders logically. For example, it is more effective to store all documents that relate to your History class in one folder named History and to your Economics class in a different folder named Economics than to store them all in one folder. Note filenames are typically formatted using lowercase.

Insert/Pages/Cover Page

1. Create a cover page using the Cover Page feature. Select the Alphabet style in the Built-In category.

2. Click [Type the document title] and key **Updates for Document Processing**.

3. Key **Word 2010** as the document subtitle.

4. Key **Jun Yoshino** as the author name.

5. Click [Pick the date], select the drop-list arrow, and select the current date.

6. Proofread and check; click Next to continue. (43-drill3)

Document Design   UNBOUND REPORT FORMAT

43d

Report Format Guides

KEYBOARDING PRO DELUXE 2

References/Document Formats/Reports

Reports prepared without binders are called **unbound reports**. Unbound reports may be attached with a staple or paper clip in the upper-left corner. Study the illustration below to learn to format a one-page unbound report. A full-page model is shown on page 166.

Margins: Use the preset default top, side, and bottom margins.

Font size: Use the 11-point default font size.

Spacing: Use the default 1.15 line spacing for all reports.

Title:

- Position at about 2". (Tap ENTER three times.)
- Capitalize the first letter of all main words.
- Tap ENTER once after title.
- Apply Title style; this style is 26-point Cambria font with a bottom border.
- If the title is long, shrink the font so the title fits on one line.

Side heading:

- Key side headings at the left margin.
- Capitalize the first letter of all main words.
- Apply Heading 1 style; this style is 14-point Cambria font.
- Tap ENTER once after heading.

Enumerated or bulleted items:

- Use the default 0.25" indention of bulleted and numbered items.
- Tap ENTER once after each item.

Electronic Mail Guidelines

Electronic mail, a widely used communication channel in the business environment, clearly has three major advantages—time effectiveness, distance effectiveness, and cost effectiveness. To reap full benefit from this common and convenient communication medium, follow the basic guidelines regarding the creation and use of e-mail when used for business purposes.

Message Content

Although perceived as informal documents, e-mail messages are business records. Therefore, follow these effective communication guidelines.

- Write clear, concise sentences, avoiding clichés, slang, redundancies, and wordiness.
- Avoid emoticons and text message jargon or acronyms.
- Break the message into logical paragraphs, sequencing in an appropriate order. White space is important in e-mail messages as well as printed documents, so be sure to add extra space between paragraphs.
- Limit e-mail messages to one idea per message, and preferably limit to one screen.
- Always include a subject line that clearly defines the e-mail message.
- Consider carefully the recipients of the e-mail; do not waste your colleagues' valuable time by sending or copying unnecessary e-mails.
- Spell-check e-mail messages carefully; verify punctuation and content accuracy.
- Check the tone of the message carefully. If angry, wait at least one hour before clicking the Send button. Review the message, modify if needed, and then send the message.

Preferences

Although e-mail is a common means of communication, other methods include face-to-face communication, telephone, voice mail, and instant messaging. It is important to realize that each person has preferred methods of communication, and the method will vary depending upon the message content. To accomplish tasks more effectively, be aware of individuals' preferred channels of communication and use those channels if appropriate for the business purpose.

Remember that effective communication is essential to be successful in today's business world. Apply these important guidelines as you prepare e-mail messages.

SAVE TO USB MEMORY DEVICE (FLASH DRIVE)

To save a document in a new folder on another drive:

File/Save As/Computer/Removable Disk

1. With the document open, click Save As to display the Save As dialog box.

2. Insert your USB memory device (flash drive) into a USB port.

3. Click Computer, find the Removable Disk (Flash Drive) on your computer, and double-click it to open it. It displays in the location box. Note that you can create a new folder on the flash drive by clicking New folder if you wish to do so.

4. Select or key the filename.

5. Click Save.

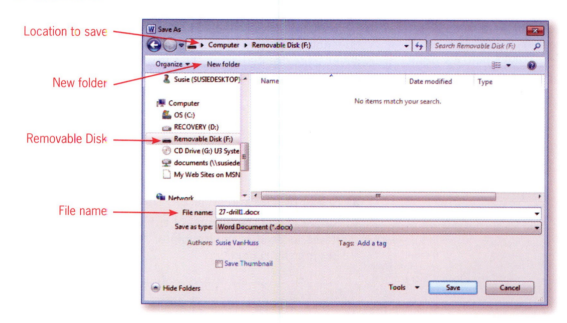

CLOSE DOCUMENT

You can close a document and leave *Word* open, or you can close a document and exit *Word*. If you have only one document open, and you click the Close button at the upper-right side of the screen, you will close the document and exit *Word*. If you have more than one document open, the Close button will close the document only.

Close If you click the Close command on the File menu, you can close the document and keep *Word* open.

To close a document and leave *Word* open:

File/Close

1. Click the File tab.

2. Click the Close command on the drop-down list.

Traditional Title Page

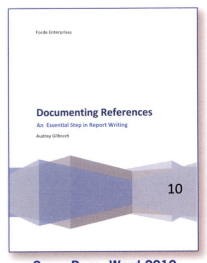

Forde Enterprises

Documenting References

An Essential Step in Report Writing

Audrey Gilbrech

10

Cover Page, Word 2010

COVER PAGE

Reports often include a cover or title page that identifies the report to the reader. As the name implies, the cover page is positioned on top of the report and provides an attractive cover for the report. Traditionally a title page includes the title of the report, the name and title of the individual or the organization for which the report was prepared, the name and title of the writer, and the date the report was completed.

For your information, the illustration at the left shows a title page created without the built-in cover pages. Each line is center-aligned, text is bold 14 point, and the page is center-aligned. Allow near equal space between parts of the page (tap ENTER about five times).

Word offers the Cover Page feature, which inserts a fully formatted cover page. You may choose from a variety of attractively formatted covers. Study the illustration of a cover page created using the Cover Page feature below. Remember this only illustrates one specific style; you have many others from which to choose.

To create a cover page:

Insert/Pages/Cover Page

1. Follow the path to display a gallery of cover pages.
2. Click the scroll arrows in the gallery to determine the desired style.
3. Select the desired style ❶. The cover page opens as a *Word* document.
4. Select [Type the document title] ❷ and key the report title. Repeat for all other items located in the template. **Note:** A blank page follows the cover page for keying the report.

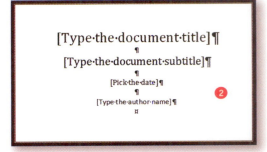

[Type·the·document·title]¶
¶
[Type·the·document·subtitle]¶
¶
[Pick·the·date]¶
¶
[Type·the·author·name]¶
¤

OPEN EXISTING DOCUMENT

 You can open an existing document by using the Open command or the Recent Documents list.

To open an existing document:

File/Open

1. Follow the path to display the Open dialog box.
2. Select the location where you saved the file. Click on the appropriate folder, select the filename, and click Open. You may also double-click the filename to open it.

-or-

If you have recently worked with the document, double-click it on the list of Recent Documents.

 TIP

Clicking Recent also displays a list of Recent Places, allowing you to quickly open folders you have visited recently.

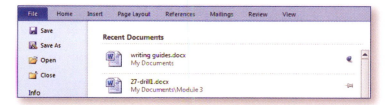

Note: These same procedures can be used to open a document stored on your flash drive. Insert the USB device in the USB port and double-click its name in the Computer dialog box to open it. Then select the file to open.

DRILL 2   OPEN AND CLOSE

1. Close the open document. (*27-drill1*)
2. Open *27-drill1* and on the line below your name, key: **27-drill2**.
3. Save as *27-drill2* and close; do not exit *Word*. (*27-drill2*)

4. Open *27-drill2* and save it to a flash drive.
5. Close the file.

NEW DOCUMENT

New   The New command on the File menu displays the new document options. Note the options that are available.

To create a new *Word* document:

File/New

1. Follow the path to display the new document options.
2. Double-click the Blank document option or click Create near the right side of the screen.

BULLETS AND NUMBERING

Bullets are used for lists of unordered items, whereas numbering is used for items that are in a sequence. Bullets can be converted to numbers, and numbers can be converted to bullets. The drop-list arrow on bullets and numbering display a library of styles for each command. If you have recently used bullets or numbering, the style used will display at the top of the library. Bullets and numbering are easier to apply after text has been keyed.

To apply Bullets and Numbering:

Home/Paragraph/Bullets or Numbering

1. Key the list.
2. Select the list and click either the Bullets or the Numbering command.

To select a different format for Bullets and Numbering:

1. Click the drop-list arrow on either the Bullets or the Numbering button to display the library of styles.
2. Select the desired style.

DRILL 2   **BULLETS AND NUMBERING** bullets

1. In the open document, apply bullets to the first list below the heading, *Procedures for Completing an Activity*.

2. Apply numbering to the second list below the heading, *Things to Do This Weekend*.

3. Convert the first list with bullets to numbering using the number with right parentheses format.

4. Convert the second list with numbering to square bullets.

5. Proofread and check; click Next to continue. (*43-drill2*)

! WORKPLACE SUCCESS

TETRA IMAGES/JUPITER IMAGES

Copyright Law

With the ease of copying text, graphics, Web page codes, sound, and video files, technology users find it very tempting to "steal" another's copyrighted materials. Consider these important points regarding copyright:

✓ **Understand the copyright law.** According to copyright law, copyright is in place when an original work is first placed in tangible form. Copyright law would include original documents saved to a hard drive; photographs, video, or sound files, e-mails, and other original works. Referencing the properties of each electronic file reveals quickly and accurately the date of creation of the work and the date of any modification.

✓ **Key copyright notice on printed documents.** Key the copyright notice on a printed document. Copyright © 2011 Austin Brantley

✓ **Seek permission to use copyrighted materials.** To use copyrighted materials lawfully, seek the permission of the originator and follow his or her specific instructions on how the materials can be used.

PRINT

The Print command is located on the File menu. Print displays the printing options on the left side of the screen and a preview of the document on the right side. Print options display information about the printer, settings, and page setup.

To print a document:

File/Print/Print

1. Follow the path to display the Print options.
2. Preview the document.
3. Select the printing options desired.
4. Click Print.

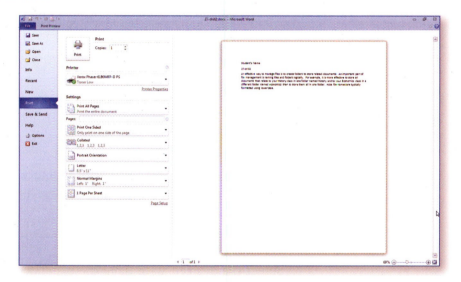

DRILL 3   PRINT AND CREATE A NEW DOCUMENT

1. Open *27-drill2*.
2. Preview and print one copy of the document.
3. Close the document.
4. Open a new document.

5. Key your name on the first line and **27-drill3** on the line below it.
6. Save and close the document. (*27-drill3*)
7. Exit *Word*.

Applications

27-d1

Create, Save, and Print a Document

1. In a new document, key your name on the first line, and then key **27-d1** on the next line.
2. Save the document as **27-d1** in a new folder named **Applications**. Keep the document open.
3. Save the document with the same name on a flash drive.
4. Preview and print the document.
5. Close the document and exit *Word*. (*27-d1*)

⭐ **TIP**

Remember to proofread and
preview each document SOP.
You will not be reminded to
do this.

STYLES

The **Styles** feature enables you to apply a group of formats automatically to a document. A new *Word* document opens with approximately 18 styles attached to it. These styles include Normal, Heading 1, Heading 2, Heading 3, Heading 4, and Title. Normal is the default style of 11-point Calibri, left alignment, 1.15 spacing, and no indent. Text that you key is formatted in the Normal style unless you apply another style.

Styles include both character and paragraph styles. The attributes listed in the Font group on the Home ribbon and in the Font dialog box make up the character styles. **Character styles** apply to a single character or characters that are selected. To apply character styles using the Font group, select the characters to be formatted and apply the desired font.

Paragraph styles include both the character style and other formats that affect paragraph appearance such as line spacing, bullets, numbering, and tab stops.

To apply paragraph styles:
Home/Styles

1. Select the text to which you want to apply a style.

2. Follow the path and choose a desired style from those displayed in the Quick Styles Gallery.

3. If the desired tab does not display, click the More button ➊ to expand the Quick Styles Gallery.

4. Select the desired style from the expanded list of styles ➋.

DRILL 1   STYLES   📄 schedule

1. In the open document, select the title on the first line. Apply Title style. Click the More button to select this style if it is not visible.

2. Select the subtitle on the second line. Apply Subtitle style.

3. Select *Monday*; apply Heading 1 style. *Hint:* Click the scroll buttons to the right of the Styles buttons to move in the Styles list.

4. Repeat step 3 for remaining days of the week and the heading *Extracurricular Activities*.

5. Proofread and check; click Next to continue. (*43-drill1*)

Lesson 28 | Paragraph Formats

New Commands

- Alignment
- Indent
- Show/Hide
- Line Spacing
- Quick Access Toolbar

WARMUP

KEYBOARDING PRO DELUXE 2

Lessons/28a Warmup

Skill Building

28b Textbook Keying

1. Key each line once, concentrating on using good keying techniques. Tap ENTER twice after each 2-line group.
2. Repeat the drill if time permits.

one-hand

1 A few treats were served as reserve seats were set up on a stage.
2 In my opinion, a few trees on a hilly acre created a vast estate.

balanced hand

3 Pam and Jake did go to visit the big island and may fish for cod.
4 Ken may visit the men he met at the ancient chapel on the island.

1/2 fingers

5 Kimberly tried to grab the bar, but she missed and hurt her hand.
6 My name is Frankie, but I prefer to be called Fran by my friends.

3/4 fingers

7 Zola and Polly saw us play polo at Maxwell Plaza; we won a prize.
8 Zack quickly swam past all six boys at a zoo pool on Saxony Land.

New Commands

28c

References/Word 2010 Commands/Lesson 28

⭐ **TIP**

From this point forward, *Keyboarding Pro DELUXE 2* will launch *Word* for all activities unless you are specifically directed otherwise.

PARAGRAPH FORMATS

Home/Paragraph/Command

Some paragraph commands are positioned together in subgroups separated from one another by divider bars. The following overview presents the commands by the subgroups. Some paragraph commands will be applied in this lesson; others will be taught in later lessons.

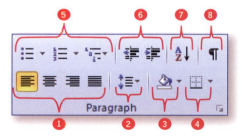

❶ **Alignment commands**—Align Text Left, Center, Align Text Right, and Justify—specify how text lines up.

❷ **Line and Paragraph Spacing**—determines the amount of space between lines of text and before and after paragraphs.

❸ **Shading**—applies color as a background for text and paragraphs.

❹ **Border**—applies and removes inside and outside borders and horizontal lines.

❺ **Bullets, Numbering, and Multilevel List**—apply formats to lists of information. Bullets and Numbering present information on one level, whereas Multilevel List presents information in a hierarchy.

❻ **Decrease and Increase Indent**—move all lines of a paragraph to the right or left.

❼ **Sort**—alphabetizes selected text or arranges numerical data in ascending or descending order.

❽ **Show/Hide**—displays paragraph markings and other nonprinting characters.

Reports

LEARNING OUTCOMES

- Format two-page reports with styles.
- Insert cover page and number report pages with section breaks.
- Format academic report with citations and reference page.
- Insert and edit footnotes and endnotes.
- Insert file.

Lesson 43 | *Unbound Report with Cover Page*

New Commands

- Styles
- Bullets and Numbering
- Cover Page

KEYBOARDING PRO DELUXE 2

WARMUP

Lessons/43a Warmup

LA   ALL LETTERS

Skill Building

43b   **Timed Writing**

1. Key a 1' timed writing, working for speed.
2. Key a 3' timed writing, working for control.

	gwam	3'
The most important element of a business is its clientele. It is	4	61
for this reason that most organizations adopt the slogan that the	9	65
customer is always right. The saying is not to be taken literally, but	13	70
in spirit.	14	71
Patrons will continuously use your business if you provide a	18	75
quality product and good customer service. The product you sell must	23	79
be high quality and long lasting. The product must perform as you	27	84
claim. The environment and surroundings must be safe and clean.	32	88
Customers expect you to be well groomed and neatly dressed.	36	92
They expect you to know your products and services and to be	40	96
dependable. When you tell a customer you will do something, you must	44	101
perform. Patrons expect you to help them willingly and quickly. Add	49	105
a personal touch by greeting clientele by name, but be cautious about	54	110
conducting business on a first-name basis.	56	113

3'   1   2   3   4

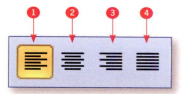

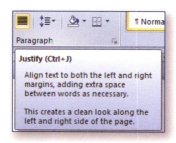

❶ Align Text Left—all lines begin at left margin.

❷ Center—all lines are centered.

❸ Align Text Right—all lines are aligned at the right margin.

❹ Justify—all lines are aligned at both the left and right margins.

> Right-aligned text
>
> Centered Text
>
> Left-aligned text is the most frequently used alignment. All lines begin at the left margin. The right margin is uneven when text is aligned at the left side.
>
> Justify aligns text at both the left and the right margins. All lines are even on both sides except that the last line of a paragraph may be shorter and will not end at the right margin. The system allocates additional space as needed to force the right margin to align evenly.

To apply alignment formats:

Home/Paragraph/Align Text Left, Center, Align Text Right, or Justify

1. Click in a single paragraph or select multiple paragraphs to which a format is to be applied.

2. Click the format to be applied.

DRILL 1   ALIGNMENT

1. In a new document, move the mouse pointer over each command to view the Enhanced ScreenTips for the format paragraph commands. Click the drop-list arrow on those commands that have a drop-list arrow to view the options.

2. Key the document shown above; do not format as you key.

3. Apply the alignment formats shown above.

4. Proofread and check; click Next to continue. (*28-drill1*)

42-d3

Table with Shading

1. Create a 4-column, 12-row table. Key the table below.
2. Change the height of row 1 to 0.6". Change the height of row 2 to 0.3".
3. Adjust column width so that the text does not wrap in columns B and C.
4. Merge the cells in column A for each day. Center the text in column A vertically and horizontally. Bold the text.
5. Shading will be used to separate each day. Apply shading as follows:
   a. Row 1 and cell A5: Olive Green, Accent 3 – Lighter 40%.
   b. Row 2 and cell A4: Orange, Accent 6 – Lighter 40%.
   c. Cell A3 (Monday): Aqua, Accent 5 – Lighter 40%.
   d. Shade the remainder of row 3 Aqua, Accent 5 – Lighter 80%.
   e. Shade the remainder of row 4 Orange, Accent 6 – Lighter 80%.
   f. Shade the remainder of row 5 Olive Green, Accent 3 – Lighter 80%.
6. Check test and close. (42-d3)

WEALTH PROTECTION STRATEGIES			
Day	**Time**	**Room**	**Breakout Session**
Monday **To Tax or Not to Tax the Estate**	9:30 a.m.	Harvard	Protect your estate for the family.
	10:30 a.m.	Princeton	The why, what, and how of a Revocable Living Trust.
	1:30 p.m.	Harvard	Resolve probate and conservatorship problems.
	3:30 p.m.	Yale	Solutions to eliminate 37%–45% estate taxes.
Tuesday **Using Trust Accounts to Minimize Estate Taxes**	9:30 a.m.	Princeton	Dynasty Trusts are used to protect family wealth, real estate, and business interests.
	10:30 a.m.	Duke	Use Irrevocable Life Insurance Trusts to protect life insurance from estate taxes.
	1:30 p.m.	Harvard	Wealth Accumulation Trusts and Income Savings Trusts can be used to minimize federal and state taxes.
	3:30 p.m.	Yale	Qualified Personal Residence Trusts can be used to safely transfer your home.
Wednesday **Wealth Preservation**	9:30 a.m.	Duke	Protect your family, business, and assets from the risks of lawsuits.
	10:30 a.m.	Yale	Use limited partnerships and limited liability companies to hold real estate and other investments.

BOOKMARK

www.collegekeyboarding.com
Module 5 Practice Quiz

INCREASE INDENT AND DECREASE INDENT

 The Indent commands indent all lines in the paragraph to the same point. The Indent commands are used to indent text on the left side of the paragraph. Remember that the TAB key indents only the first line.

To indent text:

Home/Paragraph/Increase Indent or Decrease Indent

- Click the Increase Indent command to increase the indent to 0.5".
- Click the Decrease Indent command to decrease the indent 0.5".

DRILL 2	INDENT TEXT

1. In a new document, change the font to Times New Roman, 12 point, key your name on the first line, and right-align it.

2. Tap ENTER three times and key the title, **EFFECTIVE FORMATTING**. Center it and tap ENTER.

3. Click Justify and key all text shown below. Do not make any other format changes until all text has been keyed.

4. Apply 14-point font size and bold to the title.

5. Click in the second paragraph and click Increase Indent twice to indent it 1" on the left side.

6. With the Insertion point in the second paragraph, click Decrease Indent once to reduce the indent to 0.5" on the left side.

7. Proofread and check; click Next to continue. (28-drill2)

Good formatting produces a document with a professional image. However, appearance is only one of many reasons to format documents effectively. My instructor said:

Indent   Effective formatting improves the readability of a document. It also adds structure and makes the document easier to understand. In addition, the format can be used to indicate which ideas are more important than other ideas.

My textbook makes the same points that my instructor made and emphasizes formatting documents appropriately.

! WORKPLACE SUCCESS

Social Networks

Social networks are websites designed to foster social interaction among a group of people with common interests. *Facebook* and *MySpace* popularized the idea of social networks and initially appealed to teenagers and college students. Today, many other networks and social media tools have been created, and the profiles of those who use them have changed significantly. Many businesses as well as nonprofit organizations are using social media tools to promote their organizations and enhance their businesses. However, these organizations tend to move cautiously because they realize that the benefits of rapid and inexpensive communication are offset by the lack of control of information once it has been posted on a social network.

42-d1

Create Table, Apply Table Style, Adjust Cell Sizes

1. Key the heading in 14-point bold font, centered. Key the table; adjust column width so that text does not wrap to a second line.
2. Center columns B and D. Right-align the values in column C.
3. Apply Light Shading – Accent 5 style to the table.
4. Adjust Cell Size height to 0.25" for the entire table. Center the text vertically in the cells. Center the table horizontally.
5. Proofread and finalize the document. Continue to the next document. (*42-d1*)

OXFORD LEARNING SYSTEMS

Book Title	Publication	Sales	Unit Price
Computer Crimes	2010	$478,769.00	$49.50
Digital Data Forensics	2010	$91,236.00	$63.75
Computer Criminology	2011	$89,412.50	$75.95
Law and Ethics in Computer Crimes	2010	$104,511.95	$85.99
Role of Operating Systems in Computer Forensics	2012	$194,137.50	$73.50

42-d2

Insert and Delete Columns and Rows

1. Open *42-d1*.
2. Delete column D (*Unit Price*). Insert a new column between columns A and B.
3. Key the text below in the new column. Center the column head and align the remainder of the column with Align Center Left.

Publisher
Bodwin
American
TWSS
Bodwin
TWSS

4. Insert a new row above *Law and Ethics in Computer Crimes* and add the following information:

   Digital Data Analysis Tools | American | 2009 | $9,675.95

5. Insert a blank row above row 1; merge the cells in the row. Cut the main heading and paste it in the new row 1. Change the row height to 0.3" and center the text vertically in the cell.
6. Proofread and finalize the document. Continue to the next document. (*42-d2*)

SHOW/HIDE

Home/Paragraph/Show/Hide

¶ Paragraph formats apply to an entire paragraph. Each time you tap ENTER, *Word* inserts a paragraph mark and starts a new paragraph. Thus, a paragraph may consist of a partial line or of several lines. You must be able to see where paragraphs begin and end to format them. Turning on the Show/Hide button displays all nonprinting characters such as paragraph markers (¶) or spaces (..). The Show/Hide button appears highlighted when it is active. Nonprinting characters can be turned off by clicking the Show/Hide button again.

DRILL 3   SHOW/HIDE

1. In a new document, turn on Show/Hide. Tap ENTER three times.

2. Key the text shown below; then apply both the text formats and the alignment formats listed in the following steps.

3. Apply bold format to your name; right-align it.

4. Apply Cambria 14-point font and bold to the centered text.

5. Add italic to *personal assistant* in the last line.

6. Proofread and check; click Next to continue. (*28-drill3*)

Student's Name

Why Use Show/Hide?

Using Show/Hide will help you format your documents correctly. It can also help you earn better scores on your work as it will display symbols to indicate spacing and other errors before the checker on *Keyboarding Pro DELUXE* finds them.

Think of Show/Hide as a personal assistant when you key documents!

LINE SPACING OPTIONS

The default line spacing for *Word 2010* is 1.15. Note the options that are displayed by clicking the drop-list arrow on the Line and Paragraph Spacing button. Earlier *Word* versions used 1.0 as single spacing (SS) and 2.0 as double spacing (DS). The 1.15 default is treated the same as single spacing; it just allows a little more space between lines of type. The default amount of space after each paragraph is 10 points.

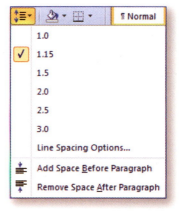

To change line spacing:

Home/Paragraph/Line and Paragraph Spacing

1. Position the insertion point in the paragraph whose spacing you wish to change.

2. Click the Line and Paragraph Spacing button and select the desired spacing.

Lesson 42 | Assessment

Skill Building

42b Timed Writing
Take two 5' timed writings.

gwam 3' | 5'

Whether any company can succeed depends on how well it fits	4	2
into the economic system. Success rests on certain key factors	8	5
that are put in line by a management team that has set goals for	13	8
the company and has enough good judgment to recognize how best to	17	10
reach these goals. Because of competition, only the best-organized	21	13
companies get to the top.	23	14
A commercial enterprise is formed for a specific purpose:	27	16
that purpose is usually to equip others, or consumers, with	31	19
whatever they cannot equip themselves. Unless there is only one	36	21
provider, a consumer will search for a company that returns the	40	24
most value in terms of price; and a relationship with such a	43	27
company, once set up, can endure for many years.	47	28
Thus our system assures that the businesses that manage to	51	31
survive are those that have been able to combine successfully an	56	33
excellent product with a low price and the best service—all in a	60	36
place that is convenient for the buyers. With no intrusion from	64	39
outside forces, the buyer and the seller benefit both themselves	69	41
and each other.	70	42

```
3'  |        1        |        2        |        3        |        4        |
5'  |          1          |          2          |          3          |
```

Applications

42c

Assessment

 Continue

 Check

When you complete a document, proofread it, check the spelling, and preview for placement. When you are completely satisfied, click the Continue button to move to the next document. Click the Check button when you are ready to error-check the test. Review and/or print the document analysis results.

Paragraph 1 is keyed using the *Word 2010* default line spacing of 1.15. This line spacing provides slightly more space than traditional single spacing, but less than the amount of space for double spacing.

Default (1.15) spacing ⟶

Single (1.0) spacing ⟶

Paragraph 2 is keyed with traditional single spacing (1.0). Note that the lines of type are closer together than they are in Paragraph 1.

Paragraph 3 is keyed using double spacing (2.0). Note that when

Double (2.0) spacing ⟶

double spacing is used, paragraphs are indented. Use of double spacing is

declining since the default spacing provides enough space to enhance

reading.

Note the differences between 1.15 spacing, 1.0 spacing, and 2.0 spacing shown above. Also note the amount of space (10 points) between paragraphs.

DRILL 4	LINE SPACING

Home/Paragraph/Line and Paragraph Spacing

1. In a new document, key the three paragraphs illustrated above; then apply the formatting shown in each paragraph.

2. Proofread and check; click Next to continue. (*28-drill4*)

TIP

The Quick Access Toolbar is available from all tabs on the Ribbon.

QUICK ACCESS TOOLBAR

The Quick Access Toolbar is located in the upper-left corner of the screen above the File and Home tabs. It contains icons for three frequently used commands: Save, Undo, and Redo. In the last lesson, you used the Save command, but you accessed it by clicking File tab. The Quick Access Toolbar provides a shortcut or one-click option for these frequently used commands.

❶ **Save** preserves the current version of a document or displays the Save As dialog box to save a new document.

❷ **Undo** reverses the most recent action you have taken (such as inserting or deleting text or removing formats). The drop-list arrow displays a list of the commands that you can undo. Selecting an item on the list will undo all items above it on the list.

❸ **Redo** reverses the last undo; it can be used several times to redo the past several actions. Before you use Undo, this command has a different appearance and can be used to repeat actions.

41-d2

Memo with Table

 REVIEW

Don't forget to insert space before the paragraph that follows the table.

Home/Paragraph/Line and Paragraph Spacing/Add Space Before Paragraph

1. Key the memo below to **Roberto Perez** from **Marcia Lewis**. The subject is **Purchase Order 5122**. Insert the current date.

2. Apply the Colorful List – Accent 1 table style. Center the data in columns A and C. Adjust column width to remove extra space in each column; center table horizontally.

3. Proofread and check; click Next to continue. (*41-d2*)

The items you requested on Purchase Order 5122 are in stock and will be shipped from our warehouse today. The shipment will be transported via Romulus Delivery System and is expected to arrive at your location in five days.

Item Number	Description	Unit Price
329-8741	Lordusky locking cabinet	$265.00
336-1285	Anchorage heavy duty locking cabinet	$465.00
387-6509	Lordusky locking cabinet (unassembled)	$195.00

Please call us if we can assist you any further.

41-d3

Block Letter with Table

1. Key the block letter below with open punctuation. The letter is from **Veejah Patel, Collections Manager**. Supply necessary letter parts.

2. Center the data in column A; right-align the amounts in column D. Apply the table style Light Grid – Accent 2.

3. Adjust column width and center table horizontally on the page.

4. Check and close. (*41-d3*)

Ms. Beatrice Snow | Collections Manager | Precision Office Products |
2679 Orchard Lake Road | Farmington Hills, MI 48333-5534

Thank you for allowing International Financial Systems to assist you in managing your delinquent accounts. We provide you with the fastest interface to International Systems Collection Services. The activity report for last month is shown below.

Client Number	Last Name	First Name	Current Balance
1487	Rodriguez	Delia	$1,576.00
1679	Kim	Lisa	$954.35
1822	Batavia	Kirsten	$1,034.21
1905	Vokavich	Kramer	$832.09

Please verify the accuracy of the names transmitted by your billing office. If you find any transmission errors, please contact Joseph Kerning at 888-555-0134 immediately.

CUSTOMIZE QUICK ACCESS TOOLBAR

You can customize or add commands that you use frequently to the Quick Access Toolbar.

To customize the Quick Access Toolbar:

1. On the Quick Access Toolbar, click the Customize Quick Access Toolbar button to display the gallery.

2. Click the desired command that you wish to add to the Quick Access Toolbar. Note that the default commands Save, Undo, and Redo are already on the toolbar.

3. If you click Print Preview and Quick Print, the toolbar would appear as shown in the illustration at the right.

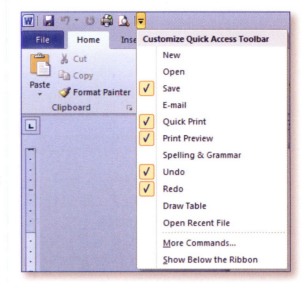

DRILL 5 — QUICK ACCESS TOOLBAR

1. In a new document, key the first sentence below; then apply bold and underline to *Undo/Redo*.

2. Undo the underline in sentence 1.

3. Key sentences 2 and 3; then apply bold to *Undo* in sentence 2 and *Redo* in sentence 3. Then apply italic to both.

4. Remove italic in both sentences 2 and 3.

5. Key sentence 4 and apply bold to *use*.

6. Use Undo to remove the bold from *use*. Then use Redo to reapply bold to *use*.

✱ 7. Select *You can* and then click the Bold Repeat command to apply bold.

8. Key your name on the line below the last sentence and then right-align it.

9. Use Undo to remove the right-align; then use Redo to go back to right-align.

10. Add Quick Print and Print Preview to your Quick Access Toolbar.

11. Preview your document using Print Preview on the Quick Access Toolbar.

12. Proofread and check; click Next to continue. (*28-drill5*)

Keying and formatting changes can be reversed easily by using the Undo/Redo commands.

If you make a change, one click of the Undo command can reverse the change.

If you undo a change and decide that you want to keep the change as it was originally made, you can go back to the original change by clicking the Redo command.

You can use the Redo command as a Repeat command.

CHRISTINA L. ZAMPICH
583 Post Oak Road
Savannah, GA 31418-0583
912-555-0171
E-mail: clz@cable.net

CAREER OBJECTIVE
To obtain a position as an Office Support Assistant in a general business, educational, or medical environment that allows me to utilize my skills and previous work experience.

SUMMARY OF ACHIEVEMENTS
Acquired several years of work experience in educational and medical environments. Interact well with people at all levels including professionals, patients, children, and students. Excellent oral and written communication skills.

EDUCATION
A.A., Administrative Office Management and Computer Applications (double major), Cypress College, Cypress, California. May 201-. GPA: 3.9/3.7.

SPECIAL SKILLS

Environments:	Windows 7, Vista, and Windows XP
Software:	Microsoft Office 2010, Adobe Photoshop, Microsoft Project
Certifications:	Microsoft Certified Application Specialist (MCAS) Certified Nursing Assistant
Languages:	Fluent in English and Spanish
Keyboarding skills:	70 words per minute

EXPERIENCE
Cypress College Learning Resource Center, Cypress, California. Clerical Assistant, 2009 to present. Answer telephone, perform mailing, create information brochures. Help students locate books, periodicals, and online materials.

Costa Mesa General Hospital, Costa Mesa, California. Certified Nursing Assistant. 2005-2008.

HONORS AND ACTIVITIES
Dean's List (3.5 GPA or higher); Cypress College
President of the Student Association, Cypress College, 2009-2010.
Recipient of the *Employee of the Year Award* in 2008 from Costa Mesa General Hospital.

REFERENCES
Available upon request.

28-d1

Format Title, Headings, and Paragraphs

1. In a new document, key all paragraphs below using default font, size, and spacing. Turn on Show/Hide.
2. Position the insertion point at the beginning of the title, *Standard Operating Procedures*, and tap ENTER three times; apply bold, 16-point Arial font to the title, and center it.
3. Apply bold and 14-point Arial font to the three side headings.
4. Key your name on the line below the last line of the document and right-align it. Key the document number, **28-d1**, on the line below your name.
5. Proofread and check; click Next to continue. (*28-d1*)

Standard Operating Procedures

Many companies develop standard operating procedures (SOPs) for virtually every phase of their business. When standard operating procedures are mentioned, most people think of a manufacturing or service business and are surprised to learn that standard operating procedures apply to management and office administration as well. Most companies have SOPs for producing documents in their offices for several reasons.

Quality Control

SOPs ensure that company image is consistent throughout the organization. Guides are presented for using and protecting the logo, standard colors may be specified, and document formats are standardized.

Training Tools

New and experienced employees both want to do a good job. SOPs provide an excellent training tool to ensure that all employees do their work accurately and meet company expectations consistently. Most employees do not like to be told repeatedly what to do. Having a set of guides to follow enables them to work independently and still meet quality standards.

Productivity Enhancement and Cost Reduction

Documents are very expensive to produce. SOPs are designed to be efficient, and efficiency translates to cost savings.

28-d2

Apply Font and Paragraph Format

1. Open *28-d1*; turn on Show/Hide; use the Mini toolbar to shrink the title to 14 point.
2. Select the paragraph below the centered title and change the line spacing to double spacing. Also change the font to Times New Roman 11 point and TAB to indent the first line of the paragraph.
3. Select the paragraph below each side heading and change the line spacing to double spacing. Then change the font to Times New Roman 11 point and TAB to indent the first line of each paragraph.
4. Indent the paragraph below the heading, *Quality Control*, 0.5" from the left side.
5. Change the document number below your name to **28-d2**. Change your name and the document number to Times New Roman font.
6. Turn off Show/Hide.
7. Check and close. (*28-d2*).

The items you requested on Purchase Order 5122 are in stock and will be shipped from our warehouse today.

Item Number	Description	Unit Price
329-8741	Base cabinet	265.00
336-1285	Hutch	465.00
387-6509	Shelf unit	195.00

Please call us if we can assist you any further.

xx

USE A TABLE TO CREATE A RESUME

Using a table to create a resume helps you keep the text neatly aligned; the table saves you from having to tab each line of the resume. The resume on the next page shows the name and address centered at the top of the page. A table was created below the name and address for the body of the resume. The left column contains the headings, and the right column contains the content. Each heading and its content are keyed in one row.

Applications

Resume

To remove all borders:
Table Tools Design/Table
Styles/Borders/No Border

1. Key the resume on the next page. Center the name using 18-point, bold font; then tap ENTER.
2. Center the address, telephone number, and e-mail address in 12-point bold font.
3. Tap ENTER. Insert a 2-column, 13-row table.
4. Key **CAREER OBJECTIVE** in cell A1 and adjust column width to 1.5". Tap TAB to key the text in the second column; text will wrap to the next line.
5. Leave a blank row; then key **SUMMARY OF ACHIEVEMENTS**. Continue keying the remainder of the resume in the same format. Leave a blank row between each section.
6. *Special Skills* row: Set a tab at 3" in column B. Key the skill (**Environments:**); then press CTRL + TAB to move to the 3" tab and key the skill name. Key the remainder of the skills using the same format.
7. Select the left column of the table and apply bold, caps, and 14-point font.
8. Remove all the borders from the table.
9. Proofread and check; click Next to continue. (*41-d1*)

Lesson 29 | Navigate and Review Documents

New Commands

- Scroll Bars
- Views
- AutoCorrect

- Spelling and Grammar
- Thesaurus
- Translate

- Help

WARMUP

Lessons/29a Warmup

Skill Building

29b Textbook Keying

1. Key each line once, concentrating on using good keying techniques. Tap ENTER twice after each 2-line group.
2. Repeat the drill if time permits.

Balanced-hand words, phrases, and sentences

1 if me to so he is us do go or sod fir for pen may big dig got fix
2 dog jam sit men lap pay cut nap tug lake worn make torn turn dock

3 he is | it is | of it | is it | go to | to go | is he | he is it | for it | she can
4 did he | pay them | she may | is it torn | it is worn | he may go | the lake

5 He may also go with them to the dock or down to the lake with us.
6 Did she go with Keith to the lake, or can she go to town with us?

New Commands

29c

KEYBOARDING PRO DELUXE 2

References/Word 2010
Commands/Lesson 29

NAVIGATE AND VIEW A DOCUMENT

The document window displays only a portion of a page at one time. The keyboard, mouse, and scroll bars can be used to move quickly through a document to view it.

Keyboard options—press CTRL + HOME to go to the beginning of a document and CTRL + END to move to the end of the document. The Page Up and Page Down keys can also be used to move through a document.

Mouse and scroll bar—use the scroll bar located on the right side of the screen to move through the document. Scrolling does not change the position of the insertion point; it only changes your view of the document. You must click in the text to change the position of the insertion point.

Slider—can be used to view document with enlarged or reduced displays of text. Zoom on the View menu provides another alternative to view portions of the document.

Views—document views are available from both the status bar and the View menu.

Note that in Module 6, you will learn to navigate documents with Heading Styles using the Navigation pane.

Lesson 41 | *Tables within Documents*

KEYBOARDING PRO DELUXE 2

WARMUP

Lessons/41a Warmup

Skill Building

41b Textbook Keying

1. Key each line once, concentrating on using good keying techniques. Tap ENTER twice after each 3-line group.
2. Repeat the drill if time permits.

d 1   do did dad sad faded daddy madder diddle deduced hydrated dredged

k 2   keys sake kicked karat kayak karate knock knuckle knick kilometer

d/k 3   The ten tired and dizzy kids thought the doorknob was the donkey.

w 4   we were who away whew snow windward waterway window webworm award

o 5   on to too onto solo oleo soil cook looked location emotion hollow

w/o 6   Those who know their own power and are committed will follow through.

b 7   be bib sub bear book bribe fiber bombard blueberry babble baboons

v 8   vet vat van viva have over avoid vapor valve seven vanish vanilla

b/v 9   Bo gave a very big beverage and seven coins to everybody bowling.

r 10   or rear rare roar saturate reassure rather northern surge quarrel

u 11   yours undue unity useful unique unusual value wound youth succumb

r/u 12   The truth of the matter is that only Ruth can run a rummage sale.

| 1 | 2 | 3 | 4 | 5 | 6 | 7 | 8 | 9 | 10 | 11 | 12 | 13 |

Application Review

41c

POSITION A TABLE IN A DOCUMENT

In previous lessons, you have worked with stand-alone tables, or tables that are introduced by a simple heading and/or subheading. In the business world, however, tables are frequently inserted in documents to provide additional information about the document's text. A table showing sales by quarter may be inserted in a memo on annual sales, for example, or a table showing items ordered may be included with a purchase confirmation.

When inserting a table into a document, care must be taken to provide the same amount of space below the table as above the table. Word's default Normal style inserts a 10-point space after a paragraph and uses 1.15 line spacing. However, Word defaults to single spacing in a table with no spacing after a paragraph. Therefore, when a table is keyed within a document, extra spacing needs to be inserted below the table to match the spacing above the table. The extra space can easily be inserted by clicking on the paragraph below the table, clicking the Line and Paragraph Spacing drop-list arrow, and choosing Add Space Before Paragraph.

Tables in documents may be formatted with the same design and layout options as stand-alone tables. A table that is less than the full-page width should be centered horizontally.

SCROLL BAR

The scroll bar on the right side of the screen provides four options for moving through a document.

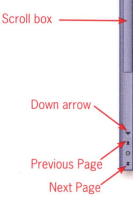

Scroll box

Down arrow

Previous Page

Next Page

To move through a document:

- Click above or below the scroll box. -or-
- Click the box and drag it to the desired position. -or-
- Click the up and down arrows. -or-
- Click the Previous Page or Next Page double arrows.

SLIDER AND ZOOM

The Slider, located in the status bar at the lower-right of the *Word* window, is used to zoom in and out on a document. Note that the Slider is positioned in the center of the bar, which shows text at 100% of its actual size.

Slider

To view smaller or larger versions of text:

1. To view a larger version of a segment of text, move the Slider toward the right or positive (+) side. The text will be larger, but you see a smaller segment of it.

2. To see more of the document at one time, move the Slider toward the left or the negative (–) side. If you move the Slider to about 50%, you can see two full pages.

To view documents using Zoom options:

View/Zoom/Zoom or Page Options

1. To view smaller or larger portions of text, click Zoom and select percentage.

2. To view a full page, two pages, or page width, click the appropriate alternative.

DRILL 1   NAVIGATE AND VIEW

1. Open *28-d2* and move to the last line of the document; select the document name, and replace it with **29-drill1**.

2. Use the keyboard to move up and down through the document. Press CTRL + HOME to go to the beginning of the document; then press CTRL + END to move to the end of it.

3. Use the mouse, the scroll box, and the up and down arrows to move in the document.

4. Move the Slider to the left to 50% and view the document; then move it to 200% and view the document.

5. Move the Slider back to the center at 100%.

6. Use the View tab to change the document view to Page Width.

7. Leave the document open. (*29-drill1*)

FORMS OF DIABETES

Type	Characteristics	Treatment
Type 1 Diabetes—Juvenile Diabetes **Insulin-dependent diabetes mellitus (IDDM)**	Usually develops before age 30 Patient cannot produce the hormone insulin Patient is usually within the weight guidelines or is underweight	Diet Exercise Insulin injections
Type 2 Diabetes—Adult-onset Diabetes **Noninsulin-dependent diabetes (NIDDM)**	Usually develops gradually after age 40 Insulin production may be decreased, increased, or normal, but the body is not able to utilize it Patient is often overweight, has high blood pressure, or has a family history of diabetes	Diet Exercise Weight control Oral hypoglycemics
Gestational Diabetes	Develops only during pregnancy Overweight women are more susceptible Older women may also be more susceptible	Diet Insulin Usually disappears after pregnancy, but Type 1 or Type 2 diabetes may appear later in life

VIEW

Document views display a document in different formats. The view that is selected when you save and close a document will be the view that displays when that document is opened again. Document views can be accessed by clicking the view on the View tab or the status bar. With some views, the Close option must be clicked to exit the view.

To view documents using Document Views:

View/Document Views/Print Layout or other options

1. Click the desired document view.

2. Click the view's Close button if necessary.

Print Layout—shows the document as it will look when it is printed.

Full Screen Reading—uses the full screen to display the document. To return to the Print Layout view, click Close at the upper-right corner of the screen.

Web Layout—shows the document as it will appear on the Web.

Outline—displays the document in outline format.

Draft—displays the document without graphics and formatting.

To access document views from the status bar:

1. Click the desired document view.

2. Click the view's Close button if necessary.

DRILL 1 CONTINUED   NAVIGATE AND VIEW

1. With *29-drill1* open, hover the mouse pointer over each document view on the status bar to display the ScreenTip.

2. Click each of the document views on the View tab. Close the view as required.

3. Return to Print Layout view.

4. Proofread and check; click Next to continue. (*29-drill1*)

Check your table against the illustration below.

REGENTS MEMORIAL MEDICAL CENTER February Seminars		
Seminar Title	**Description**	**Registration**
Surgical Weight Loss	Methods of losing weight, including healthy diet, exercise, and medication, will be discussed in detail. Surgical weight loss is an option for those who are motivated and willing to commit to lifestyle changes.	Classes will be held at the Outpatient Surgery Center 75 Pacific Crest Laguna Niguel, CA 92677-5773. Call 949-555-0111 to register.
Life in Motion with Osteoarthritis	Osteoarthritis no longer means that you need to live with a painful disability. Modern medicine, diet, exercise, and surgery can help you enjoy life more fully. Intricate surgical procedures including joint replacement and spinal fusion will be covered.	Register online at www.regents.org/calendar. Materials fee $10.00.
Experts' Cancer Updates	The cancer experts of Regents Medical Center will unveil the results of the latest cancer studies. They will discuss breakthrough treatments. They will explain what you should know about cancer screenings. They will also provide tips on preventing various types of cancers.	Call 949-555-0100 or register online at www.regents.org/calendar.

40-d2

Table with Applied Borders and Shading

 REVIEW

To change font color:

Home/Font/Font Color

Click the Font Color drop-list arrow and select the desired color from the color palette.

1. Key the main heading shown on the next page centered at 2" in bold, 14-point font. Then create a 3-column, 4-row table and key the text, double-spacing between paragraphs.

2. Select row 1 and apply Red, Accent 2 shading. Change the font color in row 1 to white, and bold and center headings.

3. Select cells A2–A4 and apply Red, Accent 2, Lighter 40% shading. Bold cells A2–A4.

4. Select cells B2–B4 and apply Red, Accent 2, Lighter 80% shading.

5. Select cells C2–C4 and apply Red, Accent 2, Lighter 60% shading.

6. Select row 2. Change line style to a single, solid line (if necessary). Change line weight to 4½ pt. Change Pen Color to Red, Accent 2. Click the Borders drop-list arrow and select Bottom Border.

7. Select row 3; then click the Borders button to add the colored solid line to separate rows 3 and 4.

8. Adjust column widths as needed. Your columns will wrap differently than those in the table shown on the next page.

9. Preview, check, and close the document. (40-d2)

AUTOCORRECT

TIP

You can also use AutoCorrect to have *Word* automatically correct keying or spelling errors you make frequently by keying the incorrect version in the Replace box and the correct version in the With box.

Your instructor may ask that you remove these changes if you are using a classroom or laboratory computer. To remove the entry, select it and tap DELETE.

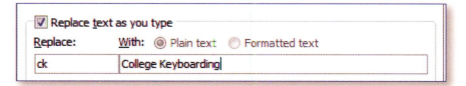

AutoCorrect Options...

AutoCorrect is the feature that corrects many errors while you are keying. You can add or change things that AutoCorrect will correct as you key.

To change AutoCorrect options:

File/Options/Proofing/AutoCorrect Options

1. Click AutoCorrect Options to display the AutoCorrect dialog box.

2. Key a shortcut for a longer phrase or a word you often misspell in the Replace box and the correct version of the word(s) in the With box.

3. Click Add and then OK.

☑ Replace text as you type

Replace: With: ◉ Plain text   ○ Formatted text

ck   College Keyboarding

DRILL 2   AUTOCORRECT

1. In a new document, key and right-align your name; then return to left alignment.

2. Make the AutoCorrect entries shown at the right; then key the sentence shown below the entries. Check to see that the shortcuts are replaced.

3. Proofread and check; click Next to continue. (*29-drill2*)

Replace: **ck**   With: **College Keyboarding**
Replace: **kpd**   With: **Keyboarding Pro DELUXE**
I use ck with kpd.

SPELLING AND GRAMMAR

Review/Proofing/Spelling & Grammar

Three options are available for detecting errors in your documents.

TIP

The Spelling & Grammar feature on the Review tab is generally used to check the entire document at once. Note that many errors you make keying are corrected automatically by AutoCorrect.

1. Check spelling and grammar using the proofing tools on the Review tab.

   a. Click Spelling & Grammar to display the Spelling and Grammar dialog box.

   b. Click Change to accept the suggested change. You can also ignore errors if you choose to do so. If the word marked as an error is actually correct, you can add it to the dictionary.

ABC ✓ Spelling & Grammar   Research   Thesaurus   ABC 123 Word Count

Proofing

1. Key the main heading using 14-point font, uppercase, and bold. Key the secondary heading in 12-point bold, capitalizing each word. Key the table, double-spacing between paragraphs as shown below.

2. Change the height of row 1 to 0.75"; change the height of row 2 to 0.3".

3. Apply Medium Shading 1 – Accent 1 table style. Adjust column widths to display information attractively.

4. Bold and center the text vertically and horizontally in rows 1 and 2.

5. Use the Quick Check on the next page to compare your table.

6. Proofread and check; click Next to continue. (40-d1)

REGENTS MEMORIAL MEDICAL CENTER February Seminars		
Seminar Title	**Description**	**Registration**
Surgical Weight Loss	Methods of losing weight, including healthy diet, exercise, and medication, will be discussed in detail. Surgical weight loss is an option for those who are motivated and willing to commit to lifestyle changes.	Classes will be held at the Outpatient Surgery Center 75 Pacific Crest Laguna Niguel, CA 92677-5773. Call 949-555-0111 to register.
Life in Motion with Osteoarthritis	Osteoarthritis no longer means that you need to live with a painful disability. Modern medicine, diet, exercise, and surgery can help you enjoy life more fully. Intricate surgical procedures including joint replacement and spinal fusion will be covered.	Register online at www.regents.org/ calendar. Materials fee $10.00.
Experts' Cancer Updates	The cancer experts of Regents Medical Center will unveil the results of the latest cancer studies. They will discuss breakthrough treatments. They will explain what you should know about cancer screenings. They will also provide tips on preventing various types of cancers.	Call 949-555-0100 or register online at www.regents.org/ calendar.

To correct the errors identified by the color-coded lines, right-click the error and select the correct alternative.

2. Color-coded squiggly lines appear in your text as you key. Red indicates spelling or keying errors, green indicates grammar errors, and blue indicates contextual errors such as using *to* for *two* or *too*. You can correct these errors as you key.

axtual   (Spelling)

It are to late.   (Grammar and contextual)

3. The grammar and spelling status is shown in the status bar at the bottom of the screen. The ✏ (pencil) shows it is still checking. The × indicates the document has errors. The ✓ indicates the document is error free.

PROOFING TOOLS

In addition to Spelling & Grammar, the other proofing tools are also helpful in reviewing documents. Hover the mouse pointer over Research, Thesaurus, and Word Count to view the tips describing each command.

The Thesaurus is a tool that enables you to look up words and replace them with synonyms, antonyms, or related words. It is important to select the appropriate meaning before replacing a word.

To use the Thesaurus:

Review/Proofing/Thesaurus

1. Position the insertion point in the word you wish to replace and click Thesaurus.

2. Scroll down to locate a replacement with the appropriate meaning, hover the mouse pointer over it to display a drop-list arrow, click the arrow, and then click Insert.

An alternate way to use the Thesaurus is to position the insertion point in a word and right-click the mouse. Select Synonyms and then the desired word or Thesaurus to display the Research pane.

DRILL 3   PROOFING TOOLS

1. In a new document, key your name on the first line and right-align it.

2. Key the first paragraph on the right exactly as it is shown.

3. Correct the three errors in the paragraph.

4. Key the words below the paragraph on separate lines; then use the Thesaurus to replace the words as follows.

   a. For *cheap*, use the first alternative meaning inexpensive.

   b. For *smart*, use the second alternative meaning elegant.

   c. For *fact*, use an antonym.

   d. For *delightful*, use the fifth alternative meaning pleasant.

5. Proofread and check; click Next to continue. (*29-drill3*)

Spelling errors are ofen corrected automatically. If an error are not detected by the software, you should proofread and correct it. To often writers skip the proofreading step.

Cheap
Smart
Fact
Delightful

TABLE STYLES

Microsoft Word has preformatted table styles that you can use to make your tables more attractive. The styles contain a combination of font attributes, color, shading, and borders to enhance the appearance of the table.

Table styles are located in the Table Styles group on the Design tab. As you move the mouse over each style, you will also see your table formatted in that style. A ToolTip also displays with the name of the style. Additional styles display when you click the More button.

Table styles can be modified by selecting and deselecting options in the Table Style Options group of the Table Tools Design tab. For example, if you choose a table style that places extra emphasis on the header row and you do not want the first row emphasized, you can deselect Header Row to remove the formatting.

To apply table styles:

Table Tools Design/Table Styles

1. Click in the table to display the Table Tools tabs.
2. Follow the path to Table Styles. Click the More button to display the Table Styles gallery.
3. Move the mouse pointer over each table style until you find the desired one. Use the scroll bar, if needed, to view all available styles.
4. Click a style to apply it to the table ❶.
5. Adjust table style options, if necessary ❷.
6. Recenter the table horizontally after applying a style.

DRILL 3   **TABLE STYLES AND STYLE OPTIONS** styles

1. Click in the table and display the Table Styles gallery.
2. Apply Medium Shading 2 – Accent 4 style to the table.
3. Insert a row at the end of the table. Key **Total** in cell A8. Key **$581,700** in cell C8.
4. Click the Total Row checkbox in the Table Styles Options group; additional formatting has been applied to the total row.
5. Remove the check mark from the First Column checkbox to change the look of the first column.
6. Center the table horizontally on the page.
7. Proofread and check; click Next to continue. (*40-drill3*)

TRANSLATE

The Translate command is a very useful, quick tool for checking the translation for a word, phrase, or sentence. Individuals choose from a pair of languages available such as English to Spanish or English to French. The Mini Translator brings up a bilingual dictionary. You can also use the Translate Selected Text option that displays in the Research pane.

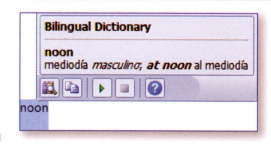

To use the Bilingual Dictionary:
Review/Language/Translate

1. Follow the path and then click Mini Translator to turn it on.

2. Point at the word (such as *noon*) or select the phrase or sentence you wish to translate; then point at the Bilingual Dictionary to darken it.

3. Turn the Mini Translator off after you finish translating.

HELP

Help provides information on how to do most word processing functions. Help can be accessed in several ways.

To access *Word* Help:

1. Tap the F1 key. -or-

2. Click the Help button at the upper-right side of the screen.

3. Click the See all link to browse *Word* Help and select a topic. -or-

4. In the *Word* Help search box, key the topic on which you need help.

TIP

The first time you use the Mini Translator, you must select the language pair you want to use.

TIP

If you highlight a single word, the Bilingual Dictionary translates it. If you select a phrase or sentence, the WorldLingo feature translates the entire phrase or sentence. The translation may take a few seconds to display.

CHANGE TABLE BORDERS

 In a plain, unformatted table, each cell has a top, left, right, and bottom border. You can see the borders for a cell on the Borders drop list.

Removing some borders can give the table a more "open" look. Many documents, including web pages, are created using a table structure; afterwards, the table borders are removed so that the document or web page does not appear to be "boxed in."

To change table borders:

<mark>Table Tools Design/Table Styles/Borders</mark>

	Bottom Border
	Top Border
	Left Border
	Right Border
	No Border
	All Borders
	Outside Borders
	Inside Borders
	Inside Horizontal Border
	Inside Vertical Border
	Diagonal Down Border
	Diagonal Up Border
	Horizontal Line
	Draw Table
	View Gridlines
	Borders and Shading...

1. Select the portion of the table where the borders will be changed, or click the Table Move handle to select the entire table.

2. Follow the path and click the Borders drop-list arrow.

3. Deselect an existing border option to remove that border. -or-
Click another border option to apply it. -or-
Click No Border to remove the cell or table borders.

DRILL 1   APPLY SHADING AND REMOVE BORDERS   noborder

1. In the open document, turn on Show/Hide. Click the mouse pointer on the ¶ above the table. Tap ENTER two times to place the first row of the table at 2".

2. Select row 1 and apply White, Background 1, Darker 25% shading.

3. Select the entire table; then click the Borders drop-list arrow and choose No Border.

4. Proofread and check; click Next to continue. (40-drill1)

CHANGE LINE STYLE AND WEIGHT

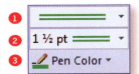 The Line Style ❶ and Line Weight ❷ features used in combination with the Borders option can be used to enhance the appearance and readability of the table. The Draw Borders group contains a Line Style drop list and a Line Weight drop list.

To change the line style, simply click the Line Style drop-list arrow to display a variety of line styles. You can choose a line that is solid, dotted, wavy, single, double, triple, or other variations. Click the Line Weight drop-list arrow to select from a variety of line weights or thicknesses. The color of the line can be changed by clicking the Pen Color drop-list arrow ❸ and selecting a color.

Once the line style and line weight have been selected (and a different color, if desired), select the cells to be changed and then click the appropriate border option.

DRILL 2   CHANGE LINE STYLE, WEIGHT, AND BORDER

1. Open 39-drill1.

2. Select the table. Change the Line Style to a single line, if necessary. Change the Line Weight to ½ pt if necessary.

3. Deselect Inside Borders from the Borders drop list.

4. Change the Line Style to a double line.

5. Select Outside Borders from the Borders drop list. A double-line border now displays around the outside of the table.

6. Proofread and check; click Next to continue. (40-drill2)

29-d1

Edit and Proofread

1. In a new document, key the ten sentences (tap ENTER after each sentence). Make the edits indicated by the proofreaders' marks.

2. Proofread and correct errors.

3. Use Spelling and Grammar and Help as needed.

4. Proofread and check; click Next to continue. (*29-d1*)

★ **TIP**

Review proofreaders' marks in Lesson 23, page 55

Do you assess you writing skills as average, great, or mediocre?

You should also ask your instructor about *to assess* your writing skills.

Your instructor will know *may teach you* how to greatly improve your writing skills.

Do you always *take the time to* edit and proofread carefully things that you write?

few people who donot bother to edit there work are good writers.

Learning to edit effective *ly* may be just as important as writing well.

Another question to ask *answer* is: how important are writing skills?

Good *reat* writing skills are needed to be successful in most *many* careers.

You can improve your writing skills by making it a priority *to do so*.

Judge your writing only if *after* you have proofread and edited your work.

✱ **DISCOVER**

Insert/Delete—To insert text, click in the document at the point you wish to insert text and key the text.

To delete text, select the text and tap DELETE.

29-d2

Compose and Edit

1. In a new document, key the paragraph, filling in the information indicated. Use Undo and Redo as you compose and edit. Use Translate, Thesaurus, and Help as needed.

2. Use the Quick Access Toolbar to print the document; proofread it and mark any corrections needed using proofreaders' marks.

3. Correct the document; recheck it using proofing tools. Check and close. (*29-d2*)

My name is (*student's name*). The reason I enrolled in this course is (*complete sentence*). What I like most about this course is (*complete sentence*). What I like least about this course is (*complete sentence*).

Lesson 40 | *Table Tools—Design*

New Commands
- Apply Shading
- Table Borders
- Line Style and Weight
- Table Styles

Skill Building

40b   Timed Writing
Key two 3' timed writings.

	gwam	3'
I have an interesting story or two that will transport you to	4	53
faraway places, to meet people you have never known, to see	8	57
things you have never seen, to experience things available only to	13	61
a select few. I can help you master appropriate skills you desire	17	66
and need; I can inspire you, excite you, instruct you, challenge	22	70
you, and entertain you. I answer your questions. I work with you	26	75
to realize a talent, to express a thought, and to determine just who	31	79
and what you really are and want to be. I help you to understand	35	84
words, to write, and to read. I help you to discover the mysteries	40	88
of the past and the secrets of the future. I am your library. I hope	44	93
I shall see you regularly. You are very likely to find me online.	49	97

3' | 1 | 2 | 3 | 4 |

New Commands

40c

KEYBOARDING PRO DELUXE 2

References/Word 2010
Commands/Lesson 40

DESIGN TAB

After a table is created, it needs to be formatted to make it more attractive and enhance its readability. Table design features can be accessed by clicking in the table and then clicking the Design tab. The Design tab is divided into three groups: Table Style Options, Table Styles, and Draw Borders.

APPLY SHADING

The Shading tool in the Table Styles group on the Design tab is used to add color or degrees of shading to portions of the table.

To apply shading to cell(s):

Table Tools Design/Table Styles/Shading

1. Select the cell or cells to be shaded.
2. Follow the path and click the drop-list arrow on the Shading command to display the Theme Colors palette.
3. Move the mouse pointer over each color to see its name and then click the color desired.

★ **TIP**

You can also apply shading to paragraphs, using the Shading command in the Paragraph group on the Home tab.

Lesson 30 | Clipboard Commands and Page Formats

New Commands
- Clipboard
- Cut, Copy, Paste
- Format Painter
- Margins
- Orientation
- Center Page

Skill Building

30b Textbook Keying

1. Key each line once, concentrating on using good keying techniques. Tap ENTER twice after each 3-line group.
2. Repeat the drill if time permits.

Direct reach words, phrases, and sentences

1 hung deck jump cent slope decide hunt serve polo brave cedar pump

2 no way | in tune | many times | jump in | funny times | gold plated | in sync

3 June and Cecil browsed in craft shops and found many funny gifts.

Adjacent reach words, phrases, and sentences

4 were pop safe sad quick column tree drew opinion excite guy point

5 we are | boil over | are we | few rewards | short trek | where are we going

6 Bert said he tries to shop where we can buy gas, oil, and treats.

New Commands

30c

KEYBOARDING PRO DELUXE 2

*References/Word 2010
Commands/Lesson 30*

CLIPBOARD GROUP

The commands on the Clipboard group (located on the Home tab) are very useful editing tools. An overview of the four editing commands it contains is provided below. The Clipboard is used to store up to 24 items of text or graphics that have been cut or copied so they can be used in other locations. The Office Clipboard task pane is illustrated below on the right. It is accessed by clicking the small arrow (called the Dialog Box Launcher) located at the lower-right corner of the Clipboard group. Items can be pasted by using the Paste button or from the Clipboard. Note that you can paste items individually or all at one time.

Cut—removes the selected text from its current location.

Paste—positions the text that was cut in another location.

Copy—makes an additional copy of the selected text.

Format Painter—enables you to copy the format of one paragraph to another.

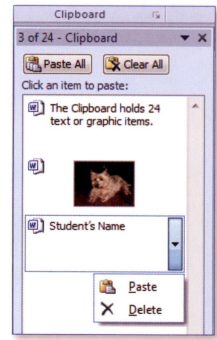

39-d2

Insert Column, Insert Row, and Merge

1. Open *39-d1*. Insert the following column between columns B and C.

   Division
   Commercial
   Space Shuttle
   Military
   Commercial

2. Insert a blank row above row 1. Merge the cells in the new row 1.

3. Cut the title *SAFETY AWARDS* and paste it in row 1. Change the row height to 0.4" and use Align Center to center the text in the cell.

4. Proofread and check; click Next to continue. (*39-d2*)

39-d3

Insert and Delete Rows

1. Open *39-d2*. Insert a row after Lorianna Mendez and add the following information:

   Robert Ruiz | Research | Military | $2,250

2. Insert a row at the end of the table and add the following information:

   Franklin Cousins | Security | Space Shuttle | $500

3. Delete the row for William Mohammed.

4. Proofread and check; click Next to continue. (*39-d3*)

39-d4

Table with Indented Lines

⭐ **DISCOVER**

To indent lines, press CTRL + TAB. Use this key combination to move to a tab set within a table column.

1. Key the first line of the table at approximately 2". Format the heading in bold, 14-point font, adjust row height to 0.4", and use Align Center alignment.

⭐2. Key the table text, indenting lines as shown.

3. Adjust column width so that each entry fits on one line. Center-align the table.

4. Bold and center the column heads in row 2.

5. Check and close. (*39-d4*)

EFFECTS OF NYMOXIFIN ON PATIENTS		
Body Systems	**Nymoxifin + Aspirin**	**Placebo + Aspirin**
Central nervous system		
Headache	867	402
Dizziness	1,084	839
Gastrointestinal system disorders		
Abdominal pain	317	130
Dyspepsia	62	1,017
Diarrhea	64	9

CUT, COPY, AND PASTE

To cut, paste, and copy text:

Home/Clipboard/Cut, Paste, or Copy

Copy

Cut

Paste

1. To cut text, select the text; click the Cut command to remove the text from its current location and place it on the Clipboard.

2. To paste the text, place the insertion point where the text is to be pasted and click either the Paste command or the drop-list arrow on the Paste command.

   a. If you click the drop-list arrow, the Paste Options buttons display. These buttons provide a live preview of what the text will look like when it is pasted in the copy. Position the mouse over each button to view the text as it will appear when it is pasted. Then select the desired option.

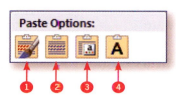

Paste Options:

1. Keep Source Formatting
2. Merge Formatting
3. Use Destination Theme
4. Keep Text Only

   b. If you click the Paste command, the text will paste and at the end of the text the Paste Options button will display as shown at the right. Click the drop-list arrow and the Paste Options will display as shown below. Note that the Paste options are identical to the ones shown above.

   📋 (Ctrl) ▾

   📋 (Ctrl) ▾
   Paste Options:

   Set Default Paste...

3. To copy text, select the text to be copied and click the Copy button to leave the text in its current position and make a copy of it.

4. Position the insertion point where the text is to be pasted and click the Paste button. Use the appropriate Paste option.

⭐ **TIP**

To use the following Clipboard shortcuts, select the text and then apply the shortcut:

Cut:	CTRL + X
Copy:	CTRL + C
Paste:	CTRL + V

DRILL 1   CUT, COPY, AND PASTE

1. In a new document, key only the first two sentences below.

2. Select *carefully* in the first sentence, cut it, and paste it after *packing*. Use the Merge Formatting option.

3. Select *enclosed* in the second sentence; cut and paste it before *diagram*. Use the Keep Text Only option.

4. Copy the second sentence. Paste it below the second sentence and then key the additional text shown in the third sentence below. Use the Keep Source Formatting option.

5. Use Show/Hide and delete paragraph symbols at the end of the document if any exist.

6. Proofread and check; click Next to continue. (*30-drill1*)

Please try to carefully remove the packing before taking the computer out of the box.

The diagram enclosed provides step-by-step instructions for assembling the computer.

The enclosed diagram provides step-by-step instructions for assembling the computer. A Help number to call for assistance is provided on the diagram.

1. Create a 2-column, 5-row table.

2. Merge the cells in row 1; key the main heading in uppercase 14-point bold font. Change the height of row 1 to 0.4".

3. Key **Course Name** in cell A2 and **Enrollment Figures** in cell B2.

4. Select cells B3–B5; split these cells into two columns and three rows. Key **Undergraduates** in cell B3 and **Graduates** in cell C3. Key the rest of the table as shown.

5. Select cells A2 and A3; merge the cells. Align the headings vertically and horizontally. Bold all column heads.

6. Proofread and check; click Next to continue. (*39-drill3*)

FINAL SEAT COUNT		
Course Name	**Enrollment Figures**	
	Undergraduates	**Graduates**
English Reading and Composition	12,875	97
Medical Microbiology	782	1,052

Communication

39d

KEYBOARDING PRO DELUXE 2

References/Communication Skills/Abbreviations

abbreviations

ABBREVIATIONS

1. Review the guidelines on abbreviations in the *abbreviations* data file.

2. In the *Corrected* column, apply the abbreviation guidelines to key a corrected copy of the text in the *Original* column.

3. Add a row above row 1 of the Application table and merge the cells. Key the main heading, **USING ABBREVIATIONS CORRECTLY**, in 14-point bold font. Change the height of row 1 to 0.4". Center the main heading vertically and horizontally in the row.

4. Change the height of row 2 to 0.25" and boldface the headings. Center the text vertically and horizontally in the row.

5. Proofread and check; click Next to continue. (*39d*)

Applications

39–d1

Create Table

1. Key the table; adjust column width and center the table horizontally.

2. Proofread and check; click Next to continue. (*39-d1*)

SAFETY AWARDS

Award Winners	Department	Amount
Lorianna Mendez	Accounting	$2,000
William Mohammed	Marketing	$800
Cynthia Khek	Engineering	$1,500
Charles Pham	Purchasing	$1,000

FORMAT PAINTER

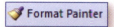 The Format Painter can be used to copy a format from one paragraph to another paragraph or to multiple paragraphs.

To copy a paragraph format to a single paragraph:

Home/Clipboard/Format Painter

1. Click in the paragraph that has the desired format.
2. Click the Format Painter.
3. Drag the Format Painter across each paragraph to copy the desired format.

To copy a paragraph format to multiple paragraphs:

1. Click in the paragraph that has the desired format.
2. Double-click the Format Painter to keep it turned on.
3. Drag the Format Painter across each paragraph to copy the desired format to it.
4. Click Format Painter to turn it off or tap ESC.

DRILL 2   FORMAT PAINTER

Home/Paragraph/Show/Hide

1. In a new document, turn on Show/Hide, tap ENTER three times, and key the document below.

2. Apply 14-point Arial font and bold to the title, **HOW MUCH IS TOO MUCH?**, and center it.

3. Use the Format Painter to copy the title format to the subtitle directly below the title.

4. Format the paragraph below the subtitle using 12-point Times New Roman font, and justify.

5. Use the Format Painter to copy the same format to the last two paragraphs.

6. Proofread and check; click Next to continue. (*30-drill2*)

 TIP

When you key two hyphens with no spaces before or after, *Word* automatically converts them to an em dash.

HOW MUCH IS TOO MUCH?

Executive Compensation—A Hot Topic!

Many people question the huge salaries paid to top executives. Employees earning less than $50,000 a year do not understand how their company can pay one person millions of dollars each year. The gap between executive pay and employee pay creates problems.

Shareholders clearly want to reward and retain executives who increase shareholder value, but they expect pay to be linked to performance. In many cases, executive compensation has increased at the same time that performance has decreased significantly.

Media coverage about mega-bonuses has caused an outrage among investors. In response, the SEC now requires public companies to disclose the amount and source of all compensation paid to their top executives. This information is readily available to the public and to employees.

To delete rows or columns in a table:

Table Tools Layout/Rows & Columns/Delete

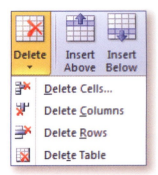

1. Position the insertion point in the row or column to be deleted. If more than one row or column is to be deleted, select them first.

2. Follow the path to display the Delete options. Select the appropriate item to be deleted.

DRILL 2   INSERT ROWS AND COLUMNS

 insert

1. In the open document, insert the following rows so that the items are in correct alphabetical order.

Connors, Margaret	South	$87,560
Roberts, George	East	$97,850
Zales, Laura	West	$93,500

2. Delete the row containing Hoang, Thomas.

3. Insert a column between columns B and C and key the following entries in the column.

Office
Wilshire

Toledo
Lake Forest
Tampa
Las Vegas
Boston
Chicago
San Francisco

4. Left-align cells C2–C9. Click in column C and change the cell width to 1.3" so that *San Francisco* does not wrap.

5. Proofread and check; click Next to continue. (*39-drill2*)

MERGE AND SPLIT CELLS

Merging is the process of combining two or more table cells located in the same row or column into a single cell. Cells can be joined horizontally or vertically. For example, you can merge several cells horizontally to create a table heading row that spans several columns. A cell or several selected cells can be divided into multiple cells and columns by using the Split Cells feature.

To merge cells:

Table Tools Layout/Merge/Merge Cells

1. Select the cells that are to be merged.
2. Follow the path to merge the selected cells.

To split cells:

Table Tools Layout/Merge/Split Cells

1. Click in the cell that is to be divided into multiple cells. If multiple cells are to be split, select them.
2. Follow the path to display the Split Cells dialog box.
3. Key the number of columns or rows that the selected cells are to be split into.

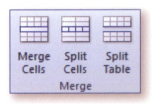

MARGINS

Margins are the distance between the edge of the paper and the text of a document. The default margins for *Word 2010* are 1" at the top, bottom, right, and left. On the gallery of preset margin options, the default margins are called Normal. The space between the left and right margins is called the line of writing. If you want to fit more information on a page, you might select Narrow margins. Or if you have a limited amount of information, you might select Wide margins. If you prefer a traditional style, you could select Office 2003 default. You can also set a custom style to format leftbound reports or other documents.

To change margin settings:

Page Layout/Page Setup/Margins

1. Follow the path to display the gallery of margins options.
2. Click the desired margins option.

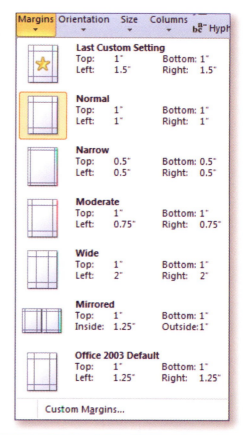

ORIENTATION

The size of standard paper is 8.5" × 11". Page Orientation provides another way of positioning information on a page. Two options are available:

Portrait—positions text so that the top edge of the paper is 8.5" wide. This is the default or most frequently used position.

Landscape—positions text so that the top edge of the paper is 11" wide. This position is often used to accommodate wide tables or graphics.

To change page orientation:

Page Layout/Page Setup/Orientation

1. Follow the path and click the drop-list arrow on the Orientation command.
2. Select desired orientation (Portrait or Landscape).

DRILL 3   CHANGE ORIENTATION AND MARGINS

1. Open *30-drill2* that you just completed.
2. Key your name below the last line and right-align it.
3. Key **30-drill3** on the line below your name.

4. Apply Landscape orientation and then apply Wide margins.
5. Proofread and check; click Next to continue. *(30-drill3)*

To change cell width or height:

Table Tools Layout/Cell Size

- Click in the cell or column and then key the dimension in the Width box or use the spin arrows to set the width dimension.
- Select the cell or row and then key the dimension in the Height box or use the spin arrows to set the height dimension.

CHANGE TEXT ALIGNMENT IN CELL

Table Tools Layout/Alignment

 By default, text displays left-aligned at the top of the cell. After the cell height is increased, the text may need to be centered vertically in the cell to make the table more attractive.

The Alignment option buttons allow text to be aligned at the top, middle, or bottom of the cell. You can also align text at the left, middle, or right of the cell. Select the button that provides the best combination of vertical and horizontal alignment.

To change the alignment of the text in the cell, select the cell(s) and click the appropriate alignment button.

DRILL 1   CHANGE CELL SIZE AND TEXT ALIGNMENT cellsize

1. In the open document, click in the table.

   Table Tools Layout/Cell Size/AutoFit

2. Click AutoFit Contents. Click AutoFit Window to restore the table to full size.

3. Use the mouse to adjust the column borders to leave approximately 0.5" of blank space between the longest line in the column and the right border.

4. Select row 1. Change the row height to 0.3".

5. Click Align Center to center the text horizontally and vertically in the cells.

6. Center the table horizontally on the page.

7. Proofread and check; click Next to continue. (*39-drill1*)

INSERT AND DELETE COLUMNS AND ROWS

Columns can be added to the left or right of existing columns. Rows can be added above or below existing rows.

To insert rows or columns in a table:

Table Tools Layout/Rows & Columns

 TIP

A row can also be added at the end of the table by positioning the insertion point in the last cell and tapping TAB.

1. Position the insertion point where the new row or column is to be inserted. If several rows or columns are to be inserted, select the number you want to insert.

2. Follow the path to the Rows & Columns group. Click the appropriate command.

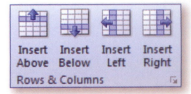

CENTER PAGE

The Center Page command centers a document vertically on the page. Should extra hard returns (¶) appear at the beginning or end of a document, these blank lines are also considered to be part of the document. Therefore, it is important to turn on Show/Hide and delete extra hard returns at the beginning and end of the document before centering a page.

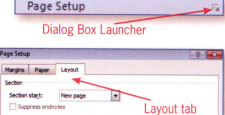

Dialog Box Launcher

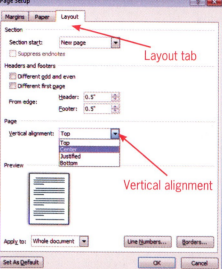

Layout tab

Vertical alignment

To center a page vertically:

Page Layout/Page Setup/Dialog Box Launcher

1. Position the insertion point on the page to be centered.

2. Turn on Show/Hide and remove any extra hard returns.

3. Follow the path to display the Page Setup dialog box.

4. Click the Layout tab.

5. Click the Vertical alignment drop-list arrow and select Center.

DRILL 4 — CENTER PAGE

1. Open *30-drill2* and remove the three hard returns at the top of the page.

2. After the last line, key your name and right-align it.

3. Key **30-drill4** below your name.

4. Apply Wide margins and center the page.

5. Proofread and check; click Next to continue. (*30-drill4*)

Communication

30d

KEYBOARDING PRO DELUXE 2

References/Communication Skills/Proofreading

1. In a new document, key your name on the first line and right-align it.

2. Proofread each sentence on the right and then key the sentence correcting the error in it. Do not key the number.

3. Proofread and check; click Next to continue. (*30d*)

PROOFREADING

1. The only way to proofread numbers effectively is too compare the keyed copy to the original source.

2. Concentration is an important proofreading skill, especially it you proofread on screen.

3. May people skip over the small words when they proofread; yet the small words often contain errors.

4. They sole 15 baskets at $30 each for a total of $450. Always check the math when you proofread.

5. Names are often spelled in different ways; there fore, you must verify the spelling to ensure that you use the correct version.

6. Reading copy on a word-bye-word basis is necessary to locate all errors.

7. Checking for words that my have been left out is also important.

8. Of course, you should also check to make sure the content in correct.

To adjust column widths using the mouse:

1. Point to the column border that needs adjusting.
2. When the pointer changes to ◀‖▶, hold down the left mouse button and drag the border to the left to make the column narrower or to the right to make it wider.
3. Adjust the column widths appropriately. Leave approximately 0.5" to 0.75" between the longest line and the border. Use the Horizontal Ruler as a guide.
4. The widths of the columns can be displayed by pointing to the column marker on the Ruler, holding down the ALT key, and clicking the left mouse button.

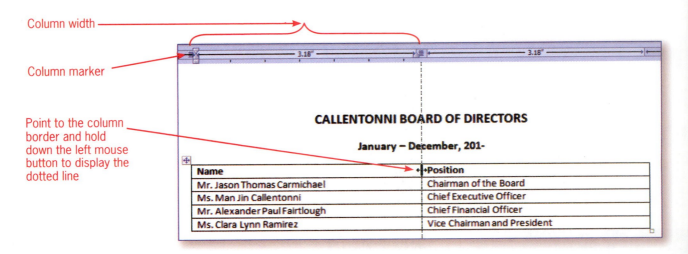

Column width

Column marker

Point to the column border and hold down the left mouse button to display the dotted line

CALLENTONNI BOARD OF DIRECTORS

January – December, 201-

Name	Position
Mr. Jason Thomas Carmichael	Chairman of the Board
Ms. Man Jin Callentonni	Chief Executive Officer
Mr. Alexander Paul Fairtlough	Chief Financial Officer
Ms. Clara Lynn Ramirez	Vice Chairman and President

CENTER TABLE HORIZONTALLY

TIP

Another method of centering a table horizontally is to click the Table Move handle to select the table and then click the Center button on the Home tab.

Once column widths have been adjusted, a table will no longer be full-page width. A table that is not full-page width is usually centered horizontally in the page. Use the Table Properties dialog box to center a table horizontally.

To center table horizontally on page:

Table Tools Layout/Table/Properties

1. Click in a table cell.
2. Follow the path to open the Table Properties dialog box.
3. On the Table tab, select Center.

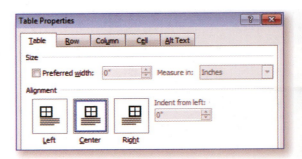

CHANGE CELL SIZE

The Cell Size group on the Layout tab allows you to set cell height and width to exact dimensions. The height of a row is often increased to provide some blank space above and below the text. This usually makes the contents in the cell easier to read.

1. In a new document, key the text shown below. Apply Lucida Calligraphy 14-point font. Center all lines except the last one, which should be left-aligned. Shrink the font on the last line to 11 point. Replace 201- with the current year.
2. Apply 3.0 line spacing.
3. Center the page.
4. Proofread and check; click Next to continue. (*30-d1*)

> You are cordially invited to attend a reception
> Honoring Dr. Fritz H. Schmohe
> Honorary Degree Recipient
> September 28, 201- at 7:30 in the evening
> Koger International Center
> Black Tie Optional

RSVP by September 20, 803-555-0174

1. In a new document, tap ENTER three times, and then key the document below.
2. Apply Verdana 16-point font and bold to the title, *Weekly Report*, and center it.
3. Use the Format Painter to copy the title format to the date shown below the title.
4. In the first sentence, cut *with reporters* and paste it after *spoke*. The sentence should read: *The head football coach spoke with reporters at his weekly news conference.*
5. Apply Verdana 12-point font to the first paragraph below the date. Justify the text.
6. Use Format Painter to copy the first paragraph's format to the last two paragraphs.
7. Indent the second paragraph 0.5" from the left side.
8. Apply Landscape orientation and Wide margins.
9. Proofread and check; click Next to continue. (*30-d2*)

WEEKLY REPORT

June 20, 201-

The head football coach spoke at his weekly news conference with reporters. He was asked about the summer workout program and seemed to be very frustrated with some of his student-athletes. The coach said:

Summer workouts are voluntary programs, and it is against the rules to require student-athletes to participate. However, the workouts are a good way to judge the commitment level of your players. Some of our players are very committed and are very likely to get playing time. Others are lazy, and it is doubtful they will be ready to play when the season begins.

In response to a reporter's question, he indicated only about a dozen of the 85 scholarship players did not show up regularly. The goal of the program is to improve conditioning and lessen the likelihood of injuries.

1. Open *30-d2* and reformat using Portrait orientation and Normal margins.
2. Check and close. (*30-d3*)

Lesson 39 | Table Tools—Layout

New Commands
- Adjust Column Width
- Center Table in Page
- Change Cell Size
- Text Alignment in Cells
- Insert and Delete Columns and Rows
- Merge and Split Cells

KEYBOARDING PRO DELUXE 2

WARMUP

Lessons/39a Warmup

Skill Building

39b Textbook Keying

1. Key each line, concentrating on good keying techniques. Tap ENTER twice after each 3-line group.
2. Repeat the drill if time permits.

t 1 it cat pat to top thin at tilt jolt tuft mitt flat test tent felt

r 2 fur bur try roar soar ram trap rare ripe true rear tort corral

t/r 3 The track star was triumphant in both the third and fourth heats.

m 4 me mine memo mimic named clam month maximum mummy summer remember

n 5 no snow ton none nine ninety noun mini mind minnow kennel evening

m/n 6 Men and women in management roles maximize time during commuting.

New Commands

39c

KEYBOARDING PRO DELUXE 2

References/Word 2010 Commands/Lesson 39

LAYOUT TAB

When you click in a table, additional tabs are added to the Ribbon. The Table Tools tab displays with two tabs under it: the Design tab and the Layout tab. The Design tab contains features that allow you to make changes to the appearance of the table. The Layout tab contains features that allow you to alter the table structure.

ADJUST COLUMN WIDTH

A new *Word* table extends from margin to margin when first created, with all columns the same width regardless of the width of the data in the columns. Some tables, however, would be more attractive and easier to read if the columns were narrower or adjusted to fit the data in the cells.

Use the AutoFit option on the Layout tab to adjust the width of a column to fit the widest entry in each column.

To adjust column width using AutoFit:
Table Tools Layout/Cell Size/AutoFit

1. Click in a table cell.
2. Follow the path to display the AutoFit options.
3. Select the desired option.

Or you can change column widths manually using the mouse. Using the mouse enables you to adjust the widths as you like. Columns look best when approximately 0.5" of blank space is left between the longest line and the column border.

Lesson 31 | Assessment

Skill Building

LA ALL LETTERS

gwam 3'

31b Timed Writing

Key two 3' timed writings.

Click fraud is a recent concern for small businesses that want to   4 | 51
place an advertisement on a website and pay for it by the number of   9 | 56
hits on it. They often think they are getting the most for their money   14 | 61
because they only pay for those who read their ad. The problem,   18 | 65
however, is that someone may be paid to click on the advertisement   22 | 69
many times just to increase the revenue from it.   26 | 73

While a business is working hard to maximize its impact,   30 | 76
frequently it is losing money because some people are trying to scam   34 | 81
them. Many people try to do the right thing, but many others just   39 | 85
are not honest. Often it is difficult to determine if you are working   43 | 90
with an honest person or not when you use the Internet.   47 | 94

1'	1	2	3	4	5	6	7	8	9	10	11	12	13
3'		1			2			3			4		

Applications

31c

Assessment

  Continue

Check

When you complete a document, proofread it, check the spelling, and preview for placement. When you are completely satisfied, click the Continue button to move to the next document. Click the Check button when you are ready to error-check the test. Review and/or print the document analysis results.

1. At approximately 2", key the main heading in uppercase, bold, 14-point font, centered.
2. Create a 2-column, 4-row table. Key the table text using wordwrap; your line endings will not be the same as in the table shown below.
3. Select the cells in column A and apply bold.
4. Check and close. (*38-d3*)

THE COMPUTER FORENSIC PROCESS

Stage 1: Collection or Acquisition	The initial stage is when the examiner identifies the evidence, secures it, and documents the scene.
Stage 2: Analysis	The examiner uses a computer forensic software tool to perform a technical analysis.
Stage 3: Evaluation	Results of the analysis stage are given to the instructing party to determine whether further analysis is needed or whether to seek an alternate path to obtain more clarifying evidence.
Stage 4: Presentation	The examiner provides a formal written report containing the findings. Examiners may also be asked to testify in court.

! WORKPLACE SUCCESS

High-Tech Etiquette

CREATAS IMAGES/JUPITER IMAGES

In today's day and age, high-tech manners can be just as crucial as dining etiquette in developing your professional image. Knowing the difference between Bluetooth and houndstooth is just as important as knowing how to host a business luncheon.

Improper or ill-timed use of new high-tech devices can destroy your professional image rather than enhance it. Using a PDA (also known as a personal digital assistant or a handheld computer) may make you appear technically savvy; however, continually glancing at your device during a meeting is like checking your watch. It is considered rude and inappropriate behavior.

Cell phone usage should be limited during work hours. Some companies require that employees keep their cell phones in their car. If your company allows you to bring your cell phone to your desk, set it on vibrate. Do not walk around the office building talking on a cell phone; this annoys others and is not professional. If you work in a cubicle environment, be mindful that others can hear your conversation and that what you say may not be appropriate for coworkers to hear.

31-d1

Rough Draft

1. In a new document, tap ENTER three times; apply double-spacing; apply Wide margins.
2. Key the title **YOU ARE WHAT YOU EAT**, and apply Arial 14-point bold font, and center-align. Use Times New Roman 12-point font and left alignment for the remainder of the document.
3. Key the document, making all edits indicated by the proofreaders' marks.
4. Right-align your name on the line below the last line.
5. Proofread; use Spelling and Grammar; correct all errors. (*31-d1*).
6. Continue to the next document.

A speaker said, "you are what you eat", the speaker didnot mean to imply that fast food make fast people, or that an hearty meal makes a person heart, or even that good food makes a person good? On the other hand, though, a healthfull diet does indeed make person healthier; and good health effects many things including performance, energy level, and attitude. Learning what to include in a healthful diet is the 1st step. The 2nd step is developing the discipline to apply that knowledge. The results are wellworth the effort. IN fact, good health may be one of the most often over looked treasures within human existance.

31-d2

Font Formats and Landscape Orientation

1. In a new document, apply Narrow margins and Landscape orientation.
2. Key the title centered; apply Cambria 72-point font, apply Gradient Fill – Black, Outline – White, Outer Shadow text effect.
3. Key the remainder of text. Apply Cambria 48-point font and bold.
4. Preview, proofread, and correct errors. (*31-d2*)
5. Check test and close. (*31-d2*)

Room Change Notice

All classes and laboratories held in Room 250 of Westbrook Hall have been moved to Room 102 of Eastbrook Hall. This change will be in effect from October 10 until October 25.

BOOKMARK

www.collegekeyboarding.com
Module 3 Practice Quiz

Create Table

★ **TIPS**

Remember to return to the default font size, font style, and alignment before creating the table.

Select cells before applying formatting commands.

1. Key the main heading in uppercase, bold, 14-point font, centered; tap ENTER.
2. Key the secondary heading in bold, 12-point font, centered; capitalize the first letter of each word. Tap ENTER.
3. Create the table.
4. Select row 1. Bold and center-align column heads.
5. Right-align cells C2–C6.
6. Proofread and check; click Next to continue. (*38-d1*)

MITSUIWA OFFICE PRODUCTS

North American Division

Sales Agent	Territory	Amount of Sale
Stephanie Acosta	Northwest	$1,157,829
Mitzi Fujitsu	Central	$99,016
Joanna B. Breckenridge	Southwest	$6,301,625
Jack M. Harrigan	Midwest	$4,245,073
Lorianna Gonzalez	East	$83,479

Create Table

★ **TIP**

When you need to position a table heading at 2", tap ENTER three times to position the insertion point; then apply the formatting for the table heading.

1. Center the main heading in uppercase, bold, and 14-point font at approximately 2".
2. Key the table using wordwrap. Your columns will be wider, so your text will not wrap at the same position as shown.
3. Bold and center column heads.
4. Proofread and check; click Next to continue. (*38-d2*)

STAGES OF LIFE SPAN DEVELOPMENT

Stage	Biological Development
Infancy and Toddlerhood: Birth to 2 years	The body doubles in height and quadruples in weight.
Childhood: 2 to 12 years	Brain attains 90% of its adult weight by age 5. Physical growth slows; slight height spurts occur between ages 6 and 9. Boys lag behind girls in physical maturation.
Adolescence: 13 to 19 years	Body continues to grow in height and weight. Girls' motor performance peaks; boys' improves.
Adulthood: 20 to 65+ years	Physical functioning peaks at about age 30. Gradual changes in appearance between 40 and 65. Brain becomes smaller and functions slower after 65.

MODULE 4

Memos and Letters

Lesson 32	*Memos*
Lesson 33	*Block Letter Format*
Lesson 34	*Block Letter with Envelope*
Lesson 35	*Modified Block Letter Format*
Lesson 36	*Correspondence Review*
Lesson 37	*Assessment*

LEARNING OUTCOMES

- Lay out interoffice memorandum.
- Lay out block and modified block business letters.
- Create envelopes.
- Work with tabs.
- Improve keying speed and accuracy.

Lesson 32 | *Memos*

New Commands

- Vertical Page Position

KEYBOARDING PRO DELUXE 2

WARMUP

Lessons/32a Warmup

LA   ALL LETTERS

Skill Building

gwam   3'

32b   Timed Writing

1. Key two 1' timed writings, working for speed.
2. Key one 3' timed writing, working for control.

So now you are operating a keyboard and don't you find it   4 | 38
amazing that your fingers, working with very little visual help,   8 | 43
move easily and quickly from one key to the next, helping you to   13 | 47
change words into ideas and sentences. You just decide what you   17 | 51
want to say and the format in which you want to say it, and your   21 | 56
keyboard will carry out your order exactly as you enter it. One   26 | 60
operator said lately that she sometimes wonders just who is most   30 | 64
responsible for the completed product—the person or the machine.   34 | 69

```
1' |  1  |  2  |  3  |  4  |  5  |  6  |  7  |  8  |  9  | 10  | 11  | 12  | 13  |
3' |       1       |            2            |         3         |         4         |
```

1. Center-align and key the main heading in uppercase, bold, 14-point font; tap ENTER.

2. Change the alignment to left, turn off bold, and change to 11-point font. Create a 2-column, 4-row table. Key the table below.

3. Select row 1; then bold the column headings.

4. Turn on Show/Hide. Place the insertion point on the paragraph marker following the main heading. Tap ENTER. Add the following text as the secondary heading; change the font to 12 point.
January – December, 201-

5. Place the insertion point in the last cell and tap TAB to add a row at the bottom of the table.

6. Key the following text in cell A5.
Ms. Clara Lynn Ramirez

7. Key the following text in cell B5.
Vice Chairman and President

8. Proofread and check; click Next to continue. (*38-drill2*)

CALLENTONNI BOARD OF DIRECTORS

Name	Position
Mr. Jason Thomas Carmichael	Chairman of the Board
Ms. Man Jin Callentonni	Chief Executive Officer
Mr. Alexander Paul Fairtlough	Chief Financial Officer

Document Design

FORMATTING TABLES

Formatting can make a table more attractive and easier to read. Even a simple table such as the one you created in Drill 2 can benefit from formatting such as boldface for the table title and the *header row* (the row that contains the column heads).

MITSUIWA OFFICE PRODUCTS ❶

North American Division ❷

Sales Agent	Territory	Amount of Sale
Stephanie Acosta	Northwest	$1,157,829
Mitzi Fujitsu	Central	$99,016
Joanna B. Breckenridge	Southwest	$6,301,625
Jack M. Harrigan	Midwest	$4,245,073
Lorianna Gonzalez	East	$83,479

OXFORD LEARNING SYSTEMS
Computer Forensic Textbooks

Book Title	Publication	Sales	Unit Price
Computer Crimes	2010	478,769.00	49.50
Digital Data Forensics	2010	91,236.00	63.75
Computer Criminology	2011	89,412.50	75.95
Law and Ethics in Computer Crimes	2010	104,511.95	85.99

If your table has a main heading above it ❶, format the heading in a larger font size than that used for the body of the table. A popular option is to set this main heading in all capitals and to center it above the table.

❸ If the table has a secondary heading ❷, the font size should be smaller than the main heading. Secondary headings are not keyed in all caps.

Column heads ❸ in the header row are used to label columns. They are often centered, boldfaced, and shaded.

❹ *Word 2010's* Table Styles feature provides formatting for the entire table. A table style ❹ can emphasize header and total rows and the first or last column. You will use table styles in Lesson 40.

Column widths are usually adjusted to fit the data in the cells; then recenter the table horizontally.

Data file icon
proofread

KEYBOARDING PRO DELUXE 2

*References/Communication
Skills/Proofread*

PROOFREAD AND FINALIZE A DOCUMENT

Data files are extra documents you will need to complete an assignment. When a data file is required, an icon and filename are listed after the drill name. For example, you will use the file *proofread* to complete this activity.

- In *Keyboarding Pro DELUXE 2*, the data file opens automatically when you select the activity.
- Non-*Keyboarding Pro DELUXE 2* users: Download the data files from www.collegekeyboarding.com and save them to your hard drive or flash drive following the instructions on the website. The files are organized by module. For this drill, open *proofread* from the Module 4 folder to begin.

1. Read the text below that outlines the procedures for proofreading and finalizing a document. You will follow these procedures when completing all drills and applications in this book.
2. In the open document, apply steps 1–5 of the proofreading procedures.
3. Proofread and check; click Next to continue. (*32c*)

Before documents are complete, they must be proofread carefully for accuracy. Error-free documents send the message that you are detail oriented and capable. Apply these procedures when processing all documents:

1. Use Spelling and Grammar to check spelling when you have completed the document.
2. Proofread the document on screen to be sure that it makes sense.
3. Preview the document, and check the overall appearance.
4. Save the document, and then print it.
5. Compare the document to the source copy (textbook), and check that text has not been omitted or added. Revise, save, and print if necessary.

New Commands

32d

KEYBOARDING PRO DELUXE 2

*References/Word 2010
Commands/Lesson 32*

⭐ **TIP**

Remember to proofread and preview each document as standard operating procedure (SOP). You will not be reminded to do this.

PAGE POSITION

When formatting a document, the user must decide on the vertical page position. Remember the default top margin for *Word 2010* is 1". To move lower on the page, simply tap ENTER. How do you determine the vertical page position?

Vertical Ruler

The Vertical Ruler is displayed at the far left of the screen. If your Ruler is not displayed, click the View Ruler button at the top of the scroll bars on the top right side of the screen. The blue area at the top of the Ruler is the 1" top margin. The white area (writing area) begins at 0" and extends 9". The blue area at the bottom of the Ruler is the 1" bottom margin. To begin a document at approximately 2", tap ENTER three times until the insertion point is positioned at about the 1" marker on the Vertical Ruler.

Status Line

The vertical page position does not display by default in *Word 2010*. To display it, right-click on the status line located at the bottom of the screen and click Vertical Page Position. The vertical page position now displays at the bottom left on the status line.

Page: 1 of 1   At: 2"

You can also select an entire table, a row, or a column by moving the mouse pointer to different locations on or near the table.

To select	Move the insertion point:
Entire table	Over the table and click the Table Move handle at the upper-left corner of the table. To move the table, drag the Table Move handle to a new location.
Column	To the top of the column until a solid down arrow (↓) appears; click the left mouse button.
Row	To the left area just outside the table until the pointer turns to an open diagonal arrow (↗); then click the left mouse button.

Cells can also be selected by clicking in the cell, holding down the mouse button, and dragging across or down.

DRILL 1   CREATE TABLE USING THE TABLE GRID

1. Create a 3-column, 4-row table using the table grid.
   Home/Paragraph/Show/Hide

2. Turn on Show/Hide and notice the marker at the end of each cell and each row.

3. Position the mouse pointer on the table to display the Table Move handle and the Sizing handle.

4. Drag the Table Move handle down the page. This moves the table. Drag the handle back to the original position.

5. Use the Select button to select column B.

6. Use the Select button to select row 3.

7. Use the Select button to select the entire table.

8. Click in the last cell to position the insertion point.

9. Tap TAB to insert an additional row at the bottom of the table.

10. Proofread and check; click Next to continue. (38-drill1)

USE THE INSERT TABLE COMMAND

The Insert Table dialog box lets you specify the number of columns and rows for the table. This option can be easier to use than dragging over the table grid if you need a large number of rows or columns.

To create a table using the Insert Table command:
Insert/Tables/Table

1. Click the insertion point where the table is to be inserted.

2. Follow the path to display the Insert Table menu.

3. Click Insert Table ❶ to display the Insert Table dialog box.

4. Insert the number of columns by keying the number or using the spin arrows ❷.

5. Insert the number of rows by keying the number or using the spin arrows ❸.

Word automatically creates a table with fixed column widths. You can adjust the column widths in the Insert Table dialog box, or choose an AutoFit option to fit column widths to the longest line or to the current window size.

1. In a new document, display the vertical page position on the status line.

2. Tap ENTER three times to position the insertion point at about 1" on the Vertical Ruler.

3. Key the current date.

4. Print. Verify that the date prints approximately 2" from the top of the page.

5. Proofread and check; click Next to continue. (*32-drill1*)

Document Design

32e

KEYBOARDING PRO DELUXE 2

References/Document Formats/Memo

INTEROFFICE MEMORANDUMS

Informal messages sent to employees within an organization are called memorandums (memos for short). Memos may be keyed on plain paper, on letterhead, in a memo template, or as an e-mail. A common practice is to attach a memo to an e-mail. The e-mail simply transmits the attached memo.

To format a memo:

1. Tap ENTER three times to position the first line of the heading at about 2".

2. Key the memo headings and format them in bold and uppercase. Tap TAB once or twice after each heading to align the information. Generally, courtesy titles (*Mr., Ms., etc.*) are not used; however, if the memo is formal, the receiver's name may include a title.

3. Single-space (1.15 default spacing) the body of the memo. Tap ENTER once after each paragraph.

4. Add reference initials one blank line below the body if the memo is keyed by someone other than the sender. Do not include initials when keying your own memo.

5. Items clipped or stapled to the memo are noted as attachments; items included in an envelope are enclosures. Key these notations one blank line below the reference initials.

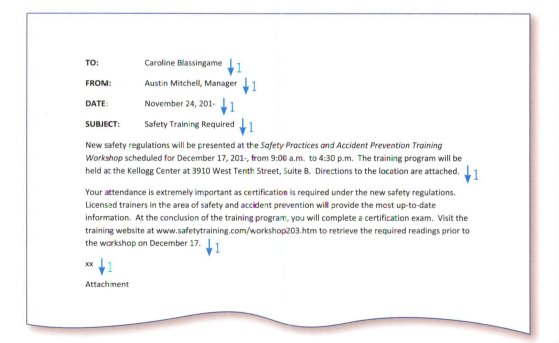

TO: Caroline Blassingame ↓1

FROM: Austin Mitchell, Manager ↓1

DATE: November 24, 201- ↓1

SUBJECT: Safety Training Required ↓1

New safety regulations will be presented at the *Safety Practices and Accident Prevention Training Workshop* scheduled for December 17, 201-, from 9:00 a.m. to 4:30 p.m. The training program will be held at the Kellogg Center at 3910 West Tenth Street, Suite B. Directions to the location are attached. ↓1

Your attendance is extremely important as certification is required under the new safety regulations. Licensed trainers in the area of safety and accident prevention will provide the most up-to-date information. At the conclusion of the training program, you will complete a certification exam. Visit the training website at www.safetytraining.com/workshop203.htm to retrieve the required readings prior to the workshop on December 17. ↓1

xx ↓1

Attachment

To create a table using the table grid:

Insert/Tables/Table

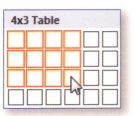

1. Click the insertion point at the position where the table is to be inserted. Follow the path to display the Insert Table menu.

2. Drag on the grid to select the number of columns and rows needed for the table.

3. Click the left mouse button to display the table in the document.

4. Click in the first cell (A1); key your text. The cell widens as you key to accommodate the length of your text. Tap TAB to move to the next cell, and then key the text. Continue to tap TAB and key until all text has been keyed.

MOVE WITHIN A TABLE

The insertion point displays in cell A1 when a table is created. Tap TAB to move to the next cell, or simply use the mouse to click in a cell. Refer to the table below as you learn to key text in a table.

Press or Tap	Movement
TAB	To move to the next cell. If the insertion point is in the last cell, tapping TAB will add a new row.
SHIFT + TAB	To move to the previous cell.
ENTER	To increase the height of the row. If you tap ENTER by mistake, tap BACKSPACE to delete the line.

SELECT PORTIONS OF A TABLE

To apply a format such as bold or a text alignment option to the table text, you must first select the cells to which the format is to be applied. You have two options for selecting portions of a table. You can use the Select command on the Table Tools Layout tab to select parts of the table or the entire table. Or you can use the mouse pointer to make your selections.

To use the Select command to select portions of a table:

Table Tools Layout/Table/Select

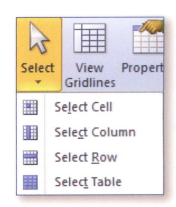

1. Click the insertion point in a table cell; then follow the path to display the Select options.

   a. Choose Select Cell to select only the cell the insertion point is in.

   b. Choose Select Row or Select Column to highlight the entire row or column that contains the cell.

   c. Choose Select Table to highlight the entire table.

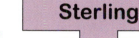

Sterling

1195 Singing Cactus Avenue
Tucson, AZ 85701-0947

TO: Students ↓1

FROM: Madison Pietrzak, Communication Consultant ↓1

DATE: Current date ↓1

SUBJECT: A Business Perspective on Memos ↓1

This memo was requested by your keyboarding instructor for the purpose of describing the changing role of memos and the importance of formatting memos effectively. Sterling uses its logo and company name on the top of its memos. First, you will learn to prepare memos on plain paper. Later you will learn to use templates for them. A template is a stored document format that would contain the company logo and name as well as the memo headings. ↓1

The format does not differ regardless of whether plain paper or a template is used. The headings are positioned about 2" from the top of the paper, and default side margins are used. Headings are keyed in uppercase and bold; tap the ENTER key once after each heading. The body is single-spaced with a blank line between each paragraph. Notations such as reference initials, enclosures, or copies are keyed one blank line below the body. Some companies adopt slightly different styles; however, this style is very commonly used. ↓1

Often a memo is sent electronically. It can either be in the form of an e-mail or as an attachment to an e-mail. Memos were designed to be documents that stayed within a company. However, e-mail is changing the role of memos. E-mails, even though they are formatted as memos, are frequently sent outside of companies. Some companies use e-mail to deliver a document but attach a letter or a memo to it. ↓1

xx ◄——— Student's first and last initials

Memo Format

TABLE FEATURE

The Table feature makes it easy to present data and graphics in a *Word* document. Aligning text, numbers, and graphics in a *Word* document can be tedious if you use only tabs and spaces. A table will help you align columns and rows of text and numbers with ease.

Table: Columns and rows of data—either alphabetic, numeric, or both.

Column: Vertical list of information labeled alphabetically from left to right.

Row: Horizontal list of information labeled numerically from top to bottom.

Cell: An intersection of a column and a row. Each cell has its own address consisting of the column letter and the row number (cell A1).

Use Show/Hide to display end-of-cell markers in each cell and end-of-row markers at the end of each row. End-of-cell and end-of-row markers are useful when editing tables. In Print Layout view, place the mouse pointer on the table to see the Table Move handle at the upper-left corner of the table. Drag the Table Move handle to move the table to a different location in the document. The Sizing handle at the lower-right corner of the table can be used to make the table larger or smaller.

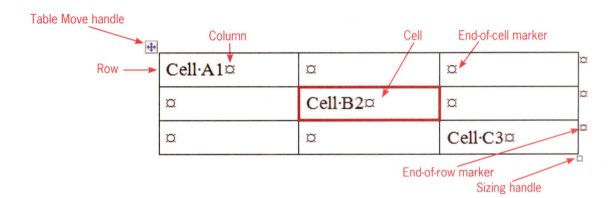

USE THE TABLE GRID

Tables are inserted into existing documents or new documents. Begin creating a table by locating the Tables group on the Insert tab. The Table button contains options for creating various types of tables; you will use two of the options in this module.

Click the Table button to display the Insert Table menu, which provides several methods for creating tables. The table grid ❶ is often used to create tables with a few columns and rows. Larger tables can be created by using the Insert Table command ❷.

32-d1

Memo

DISCOVER

↰ Undo Automatic Capitalization
Stop Auto-capitalizing First Letter of Sentences
✎ Control AutoCorrect Options...

1. Read the memo illustrated on page 111 carefully. Key this memo on plain paper in a new document; do not key the memo letterhead. *Hint:* Select *TO:* and then apply bold. Remember to turn off uppercase. Repeat for remaining heading items.

★2. If the first letter of your reference initials is automatically capitalized, point to the initial until the AutoCorrect Options button appears. Click the button; then choose Undo Automatic Capitalization.

3. Proofread and check; click Next to continue. (*32-d1*)

32-d2

Memo

1. In a new document, key the memo below.

2. Proofread and check; click Next to continue. (*32-d2*)

TO: Caleb Kirkpatrick

FROM: Chloe Wheatley, Chief Learning Officer

DATE: January 5, 201-

SUBJECT: Professional Development Seminars

Hollimon & Associates is pleased to announce a series of enrichment seminars to be offered for its employees in the year ahead. If you have suggestions for seminars that would be beneficial to your team, please let me know.

Our first seminar offering, *First Aid and CPR*, is scheduled for February 10 and 11. The seminar will be offered from 1 p.m. to 5 p.m. in the Staff Lounge. Participants will be awarded CPR Certificates from the American Heart Association upon successful completion of this eight-hour course. If you are interested in taking this seminar, please call me at ext. 702 or send me an e-mail message by January 25.

Please mark your calendar today for this important seminar.

xx

32-d3

Memo

1. Key the memo below to your instructor from you. Key the appropriate information in the memo heading. Use **Keyboarding Progress** as the subject of the memo.

2. Key your name where indicated.

3. Check and close. (*32-d3*)

I have reviewed the timed writings completed during the past week. The progress data and my plan for increasing my skills are shown below:

Name: ←—————————————————— Tap TAB so the contact
information will be aligned.

Highest WPM on 3' Timed Writing:

Fewest Errors on 3' Timed Writing:

Plan for Improvement:

Tables

LEARNING OUTCOMES

- Create tables.
- Change table structure.
- Format tables.
- Incorporate tables within documents.
- Build keying speed and accuracy.

Lesson 38 | *Create Tables*

New Commands
- Create Tables Using the Table Grid
- Create Tables Using the Insert Table Command

KEYBOARDING PRO DELUXE 2

WARMUP

Lessons/38a Warmup

LA | ALL LETTERS

Skill Building

38b Timed Writing

1. Key a 3' timed writing on each paragraph, working for speed.
2. Key a 3' timed writing, working for control.

	gwam	3'
The most important element of a business is its clientele. It is	4	61
for this reason that most organizations adopt the slogan that the	9	65
customer is always right. The saying is not to be taken literally, but	13	70
in spirit.	14	71
Patrons will continuously use your business if you provide a	18	75
quality product and good customer service. The product you sell must	23	79
be high quality and long lasting. The product must perform as you	27	84
claim. The environment and surroundings must be safe and clean.	32	88
Customers expect you to be well groomed and neatly dressed.	36	92
They expect you to know your products and services and to be	40	96
dependable. When you tell a customer you will do something, you must	44	101
perform. Patrons expect you to help them willingly and quickly. Add	49	105
a personal touch by greeting clientele by name, but be cautious about	54	110
conducting business on a first-name basis.	56	113

3' | 1 | 2 | 3 | 4 |

Lesson 33 | Block Letter Format

New Commands

- Date and Time
- Automatic Current Date
- Remove Space After Paragraph

New Commands

33b

KEYBOARDING PRO DELUXE 2

References/Word 2010 Commands/Lesson 33

DATE AND TIME

Date & Time   Most business documents are dated with a variety of formats from which to choose. Many businesses use the month/day/year format for letters, and the numerical format (00/00/0000) for memos and documents with statistics.

To insert the date and/or time:

Insert/Text/Date & Time

1. Click at the point the date is to be inserted.
2. Select the desired date format ❶ (January 29, 2010) or time format ❷ (9:52 AM).

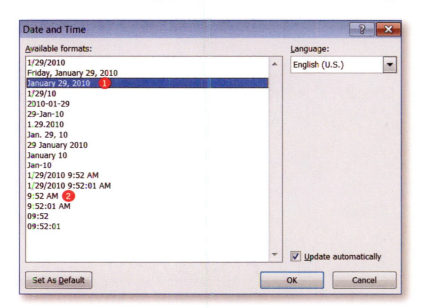

3. Leave Update automatically blank unless you want it to update each time the document is opened. Click OK.

AUTOMATIC CURRENT DATE

To insert the current date:

1. Key the first four characters of the current month. The current month will display.
2. Tap ENTER to accept the date.
3. Tap Space Bar to display the remainder of the current date.

37-d1

Memo

 TIP

Remember to proofread and preview each document for placement before you move to the next one.

1. Key the memo to **Sales Managers**. The memo is from **Miyoko Suno**. The subject line is **E-mail Addresses**. Use the current date.

2. Set a left dot leader tab at 4.25" and a right tab at 6.5" to key the names and e-mail address in paragraph 2. Remove the space below the first two items. Remove the hyperlinks.

3. Continue to the next document. (*37-d1*)

We have received new e-mail addresses from several customers. Please change these addresses in your printed directory. The changes have already been made in our database.   4.25" Leader tab   6.5" Right tab

Remove space →

Jordan, Brenda	....	bjordan@alexander.jones.com
Maillet, Zachary	....	zachary.maillet@twestwood.com
Peterson, Lynn	....	lpeterson@rentswellsupplies.com

New printed directories will be available in about 90 days.

37-d2

Block Letter/Envelope

1. Key the letter below in the block letter style with open punctuation. Add an appropriate salutation. Send a copy of the letter to **Olivia Cavenaugh**.

2. Add an envelope to the document.

3. Continue to the next document. (*37-d2*)

Current date | Mr. John J. Long, Sales Manager | The Record Store | 9822 Trevor Avenue | Anaheim, CA 92805-5885

With your letter came our turn to be perplexed, and we apologize. When we had our refund coupons printed, we had just completed a total redesign program for our product boxes. We had detachable logos put on the outside of the boxes, which could be peeled off and placed on a coupon.

We had not anticipated that our distributors would use back inventories with our promotion. The digital recorders you sold were not packaged in our new boxes; therefore, there were no logos on them.

I'm sorry you or your customers were inconvenienced. In the future, simply ask your customers to send us their sales slips, and we will honor them with refunds until your supply of older containers is depleted.

Sincerely | Bruna Wertz | Sales and Promotions Department | xx

37-d3

Modified Block Letter

1. Key *37-d2* above in the modified block letter format with mixed punctuation.

2. Check the test and close. (*37-d3*)

 BOOKMARK

www.collegekeyboarding.com
Module 4 Practice Quiz

1. In a new document, key your name and right-align it; then tap ENTER.

2. Key the first four characters of the current date, e.g., Octo for October. Tap ENTER and then the Space Bar. The current date displays. Tap ENTER to begin a new line.

3. Insert the date and time in the numerical format 3/15/2011 3:35 PM and tap ENTER.

4. Key the text shown below, inserting the current date and time as shown. Left-align the text.

5. Proofread and check; click Next to continue. (*33-drill1*)

The date inserted above illustrates common business format. The time format also illustrates common business format; however, some businesses prefer to use lowercase (p.m.) for time format. The 3/15/2011 3:35 PM (replace with current date and time) format is often used in tables or with statistical material.

REMOVE SPACE AFTER PARAGRAPH

1 Default Spacing

Michael K. Farrell

Technology Consultant

2 Extra Spacing Removed

Michael K. Farrell
Technology Consultant

By this point, you realize that *Word 2010* automatically adds extra white space after ENTER is tapped. The white space between paragraphs is greater than the white spacing between the lines within the paragraph. The extra white space between paragraphs makes the text easier to read and saves the user time in only tapping ENTER once between paragraphs. However, on some occasions, it is necessary to remove the space added after a paragraph. Remember that your software defines a paragraph when ENTER is tapped. Study the two examples shown at the left.

To remove space after paragraph:

Home/Paragraph/Line and Paragraph Spacing

1. Select the desired lines. Remember you are removing space after a paragraph (or when ENTER is tapped).

2. Click Line and Paragraph Spacing and then Remove Space After Paragraph.

Hint: If necessary, select Add Space After Paragraph to add space back.

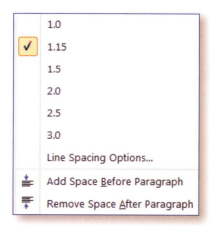

	1.0
✓	1.15
	1.5
	2.0
	2.5
	3.0
	Line Spacing Options...
	Add Space Before Paragraph
	Remove Space After Paragraph

1. Key the following lines; tap TAB to indent each name.

    Distribution:
        Christopher Randall
        Katherine Townsend
        Jessica Hilton
        Kuang-ping Sheng

2. Select the first four lines.

3. Apply the Line Spacing option to remove space after the paragraph.

4. Proofread and check; click Next to continue. (*33-drill2*)

Lesson 37 | Assessment

Skill Building

37b Timed Writing
Key two 3' timed writings.

	gwam	1'	3'

Have simple things such as saying please, may I help you, and | 12 | 4

thank you gone out of style? We begin to wonder when we observe | 25 | 8

front-line workers interact with customers today. Often their bad | 39 | 13

attitudes shout that the customer is a bother and not important. But | 52 | 17

we know there would be no business without the customer. So what | 66 | 22

can be done to prove to customers that they really are king? | 79 | 26

First, require that all your staff train in good customer | 12 | 30

service. Here they must come to realize that their jobs exist for | 25 | 35

the customer. Also, be sure workers feel that they can talk to | 38 | 39

their bosses about any problem. You do not want workers to talk | 51 | 43

about lack of breaks or schedules in front of customers. Clients | 64 | 48

must always feel that they are king and should never be ignored. | 77 | 52

1'	1	2	3	4	5	6	7	8	9	10	11	12	13
3'		1			2			3			4		

Applications

37c

Assessment

 Continue

 Check

When you complete a document, proofread it, check the spelling, and preview for placement. When you are completely satisfied, click the Continue button to move to the next document. Click the Check button when you are ready to error-check the test. Review and/or print the document analysis results.

BUSINESS LETTERS

Business letters are used to communicate with persons outside of the business. Business letters carry two messages: the first one is the tone and content; the second is the appearance of the document. Appearance is important because it creates the critical first impression. Stationery, use of standard letter parts, and placement should convey that the writer is intelligent, informed, and detail minded.

Stationery

Letters should be printed on high-quality (about 24-pound) letterhead stationery. Standard size for letterhead is 8½" × 11". Envelopes should match the letterhead in quality and color.

! WORKPLACE SUCCESS

Organizational Skills

Well-organized employees accomplish daily tasks in a timely manner, avoid stress, and impress their employers and coworkers. Following simple daily time management practices reaps benefits and often even a promotion. How would you rate yourself on the following time management practices?

1. Prioritize tasks to be done each day and the amount of time needed to complete each task. Assign tasks to a specific time on the calendar.
2. Set designated times to answer e-mail and return phone calls.
3. Place calendar/planner on desk in location for easy access to add notes and see priority items.
4. Record notes, phone numbers, addresses in calendar and not on post-it notes.
5. Place phone, notepad, and pen on desk for easy reach.
6. Keep reference books in a designated location—not on the desk.
7. File any materials for which you no longer need immediate access.
8. Prepare folders for pending items, projects, and reading, and file those materials away instead of keeping them piled on the desktop.

36-d5

Document with Tabs

1. Key the agenda below. Begin the title at about 2".
2. Key the two lines of the title in bold, 14 point; center-align. Tap ENTER one time.
3. From the Tabs dialog box, set the following tabs:

0.5	Left tab
5.25	Right tab, Leader #2 (dot)
6.5	Right tab

4. Key through the Announcements line that contains the leader line.
5. Tap ENTER after the Announcements line. Clear the 5.25" and 6.5" tabs; set a left tab at 2.5".
6. Key the remaining document.
7. Proofread and check; click Next to continue. (*36-d5*)

JENSEN BUSINESS CLUB AGENDA

January 18, 201-

Set left tabs here: 0.5" left; 5.25" right dot leader; 6.5" right

Welcome . . . . Brad Tollison

Reports

      Secretary's Report . . . . Jennifer Douglas

      Treasurer's Report . . . . Jeff Cartwright

      Fundraising Committee . . . . Wayne Le

Program . . . . Dr. Watson Phillips

Announcements . . . . Brad Tollison

Clear 5.25" and 6.5" tabs; set left tab at 2.5"

      Community Project Event   Thursday, January 22

      Fundraising Envelopes Due   Friday, February 6

Adjournment

36-d6

Memo

Compose a memo to your instructor using the subject line **Module 4 Quiz**. Key each question shown below and key your response to the question. Do not tap ENTER after the question; just space and key your answer. The first one is done for you. Check and close. (*36-d6*)

1. What are the two letter styles learned in Module 4? **Block and modified block letter styles**
2. What is the tab setting for the modified block letter style?
3. Which letter parts are keyed at the tab you must set when keying a modified block letter?
4. Distinguish between open punctuation and mixed punctuation.
5. If a letter is addressed to a company, what is the appropriate salutation?
6. What four items are included in the heading of a memo?

LETTER PARTS AND BLOCK LETTER FORMAT

Businesspeople expect to see standard letter parts arranged in the proper sequence. Letters consist of three main parts: the opening lines to the receiver (letter address and salutation), the body or message, and the writer's closing lines. Standard letter parts and the required spacing using the defaults of *Word 2010* are explained below and illustrated on the following page.

Block letter style is a typical business letter format in which all letter parts are keyed at the left margin. For most letters, use open punctuation, which requires no punctuation after the salutation or the complimentary closing.

Letterhead: Preprinted stationery that includes the company name, logo, address, and other optional information such as telephone number and fax number.

Dateline: Date the letter is prepared. Position at about 2" (tap ENTER three times). Be sure to begin at least 0.5" below the letterhead.

Letter address: Complete address of the letter recipient. Begin two lines below the date (tap ENTER twice).

Generally includes receiver's name, company name, street address, city, state (one space after state), and ZIP Code. Include a personal title, e.g., Mr., Ms., Dr. Remove the added space between the lines of the letter address.

Salutation (or greeting): Begin one line below the letter address (tap ENTER once). Include courtesy title with person's name, e.g., Dear Mr. Smith.

Body: Begin one line below the salutation.

Use the 1.15 default line spacing; tap ENTER once between paragraphs. Use *Ladies and Gentlemen* when addressing a company.

Complimentary closing: Begin one line below the body. Capitalize only the first letter of the closing.

Writer's name and title: Begin two lines below the complimentary closing (tap ENTER twice). Include a personal title to designate gender only when the writer's name is not gender specific, such as Pat or Chris, or when initials are used, such J. A. Moe.

Key the name and title on either one or two lines, whichever gives better balance. Use a comma to separate name and title if on one line. If two lines are used, remove the added space between the two lines.

Reference initials: Begin one line below the writer's name and title. Key reference initials, e.g., **xx** in lowercase. Replace *xx* with your initials.

Communication Specialists, Inc.

3840 Cedar Mill Parkway
Athens, GA 30606-4384

Current date ↓2

Mr. Marcus Cavenaugh
Pomeroy Financial Services
149 Research Park Road
LaGrange, GA 30240-0140   ← Remove extra space ↓1

Dear Mr. Cavenaugh ↓1

The new user interface introduced in *Word 2007* and enhanced in *Word 2010* as well as the new defaults have been the center of business conversations across the globe. New terminology such as ribbons, galleries, quick access toolbar, mini toolbar, and contextual tabs requires new learning by those who upgrade to *Word 2007* or *2010*. Furthermore, the defaults in line spacing (1.15) and 10 point after a paragraph are only two changes that offer new challenges in document layout. ↓1

Our staff of experts at Communication Specialists, Inc. understands your company's document layout needs as you communicate with your clients, your board of directors, your employees, and other business entities. We also realize that decisions regarding document formats require consideration of four elements: (1) attractiveness of the format, (2) readability of the format, (3) effective use of space on the page, and (4) efficiency in producing the format. Changes provide new opportunities for designing documents that portray the excellent image of your company. ↓1

We encourage you to call our office at 706-555-0138 to set up a meeting with our communication experts to discuss our comprehensive training program. This program is carefully designed to teach efficient use of the software, but most importantly our experts will teach your staff how to create the most attractive and efficient layout for each business document. ↓1

Mr. Cavenaugh, we understand your desire to distribute documents that include the design and appeal of contemporary office technology. We look forward to discussing your design needs with you. ↓1

Sincerely ↓2

Carole Gonzalez   ← Remove extra space
Communication Manager ↓1

xx

Modified Block Letter

1. Format the letter in the modified block format with mixed punctuation. Insert the current date. Remove extra spacing as necessary.

2. Supply the correct salutation, a complimentary closing, and your reference initials. Add an enclosure notation and a copy notation to **Laura Aimes, Sales Representative**. Set a left tab at 0.5" for keying the copy notation.

3. Create an envelope and add it to the letter.

4. Proofread and check; click Next to continue. (*36-d3*)

Ms. Mukta Bhakta
9845 Buckingham Road
Annapolis, MD 21403-0314

Thank you for your recent inquiry about our wireless pet fence. The Hilton Pet Fence was developed to assist many pet owners like you who desire the safety of their pets without the barrier of a traditional fence.

Hilton Pet Fence also provides a customer support service to assist you in training your pet and a technical support team for providing technical assistance. For additional information, please call:

Customer and Technical Support
Telephone: 555-0112
9:00 a.m.-5:00 p.m., Monday-Friday, Eastern Time

Please look over the enclosed brochure. I will call you within the next two weeks to discuss any additional questions you may have.

Alexander Zampich | Marketing Manager

36-d4

Block Letter

1. Key the letter shown below in block letter style with open punctuation. Supply an appropriate salutation. Remove extra spacing as necessary. Use the current date.

2. Send a copy to **Phillip Gilbert** and **Leigh Browning**. Alphabetize by last name.

3. Proofread and check; click Next to continue. (*36-d4*)

AMASTA Company, Inc. | 902 Greenridge Drive | Reno, NV 89505-5552

We sell your digital recorders and have since you introduced them. Several of our customers now tell us they are unable to follow the directions on the coupon. They explain that there is no company logo on the box to return to you as you requested.

What steps should we take? A copy of the coupon is enclosed, as is a digital recorder box. Please read the coupon, examine the box, and then let me know your plans for extricating us from this problem.

Sincerely | John J. Long | Sales Manager | Enclosures

Communication Specialists, Inc.

3840 Cedar Mill Parkway
Athens. GA 30606-4384

2"

Date line   Current date ↓2

Letter address

Mr. Marcus Cavenaugh
Pomeroy Financial Services   ← Remove extra space
149 Research Park Road
LaGrange, GA 30240-0140 ↓1

Salutation   Dear Mr. Cavenaugh ↓1

Body

The new user interface introduced in *Word 2007* and enhanced in *Word 2010* as well as the new defaults have been the center of business conversations across the globe. New terminology such as ribbons, galleries, quick access toolbar, mini toolbar, and contextual tabs requires new learning by those who upgrade to *Word 2007* or *2010*. Furthermore, the defaults in line spacing (1.15) and 10 point after a paragraph are only two changes that offer new challenges in document layout. ↓1

Our staff of experts at Communication Specialists, Inc. understands your company's document layout needs as you communicate with your clients, your board of directors, your employees, and other business entities. We also realize that decisions regarding document formats require consideration of four elements: (1) attractiveness of the format, (2) readability of the format, (3) effective use of space on the page, and (4) efficiency in producing the format. Changes provide new opportunities for designing documents that portray the excellent image of your company. ↓1

We encourage you to call our office at 706-555-0138 to set up a meeting with our communication experts to discuss our comprehensive training program. This program is carefully designed to teach efficient use of the software, but most importantly our experts will teach your staff how to create the most attractive and efficient layout for each business document. ↓1

Mr. Cavenaugh, we understand your desire to distribute documents that include the design and appeal of contemporary office technology. We look forward to discussing your design needs with you. ↓1

Complimentary closing   Sincerely ↓2

Writers name & title

Carole Gonzalez   ← Remove extra space
Communication Manager ↓1

Reference initials   xx

Block Letter with Open Punctuation

Home/Paragraph Dialog Box Launcher/Tabs

1. In the open document, select the body of this table of contents.

2. Set a right dot leader tab (#2) at 5.5"; set a right tab at 6.5".

3. Position the insertion point to the right of the phrase *Letter of transmittal.* Tap TAB twice to position the text at the tab settings.

4. Repeat step 3 to position the remaining lines in the table of contents.

5. Select the body of the table of contents again; move the dot leader tab to 6" to bring the leaders closer to the page number.

6. Proofread and check; click Next to continue. (*36-drill3*)

Applications

36-d1
Edit Letter

1. Open *33-d3*, a block letter keyed in Lesson 33.

2. Select the entire letter and set a tab at the center of the page. Change this letter to a modified block letter with mixed punctuation.

3. Edit the first sentence of paragraph 3 as follows:

   A company brochure with information about our salary, bonus, and retirement plans is enclosed.

4. Add an enclosure notation.

5. Proofread and check; click Next to continue. (*36-d1*)

36-d2
Memo with Tab

1. Key the following memo in correct format.

2. After keying the second paragraph, tap ENTER once. From the Ruler, set a left tab at 2.5", and key the last several lines.

3. Proofread and check; click Next to continue. (*36-d2*)

TO: All Sunwood Employees

FROM: Julie Patel, Human Resources Director

DATE: Current date

SUBJECT: Eric Kershaw Hospitalized

We were notified by Eric Kershaw's family that he was admitted into the hospital this past weekend. They expect that he will be hospitalized for another ten days. Visitations and phone calls are limited, but cards and notes are welcome.

A plant is being sent to Eric from the Sunwood staff. Stop by our office before Wednesday if you wish to sign the card. If you would like to send your own "Get Well Wishes" to Eric, send them to:

Eric Kershaw
County General Hospital
Room 401
P.O. Box 13947
Atlanta, GA 38209-4751

33-d1

Block Letter

1. Key the model letter on page 117 in block format with open punctuation. Assume you are using letterhead stationery.

2. Tap ENTER to position the dateline at about 2". Insert the current date using the Automatic Date feature.

3. Include your reference initials. If the first letter of your initials is automatically capitalized, point to the initial until the AutoCorrect Option button appears, click the button, and then choose Undo Automatic Capitalization.

4. Follow the proofreading procedures outlined in Lesson 32. Use Print Preview to check the placement. Be sure to remove the added space in the letter address and between the writer's name and title.

5. Use Show/Hide ¶ to view paragraph markers to confirm that you have correct spacing between letter parts.

6. Proofread and check; click Next to continue. (*33-d1*)

33-d2

Block Letter

1. Key the letter below in block format with open punctuation. Insert the current date. Add your reference initials in lowercase letters. Remove added space in the letter address and the writer's name and title.

2. Proofread and check; click Next to continue. (*33-d2*)

Current date

Ms. Ramona Vilella
Wicker Hotel and Resort
89 Airport Road
Omaha, NE 68105-0089

Dear Ms. Vilella

Certainly having a web presence is essential, but have you updated your hotel's website recently? Advances in technology and the increased sophistication of your clients are both good reasons for you to meet with our designers at Internet Solutions to discuss advanced hotel web design that will improve your marketing efforts.

Our online reservation system is specifically designed for today's clients; it is easy to navigate and provides many extras such as 360-degree panoramic picture of the hotel lobby, guest rooms, restaurants, spa, and pool as well as maps to your beautiful hotel. Two-way communication is also important today as clients are eager to provide review ratings and valuable comments to others desiring a pleasant hotel experience. Our design offers seamless means of valuable dialog between you and your valued clients.

Call today for a consultation with one of our designers and discuss our many innovative website marketing strategies. Give your clients the best when they are shopping for hotel reservations.

Sincerely

Daniel Jankoski
Marketing Manager
xx

DRILL 1   ADDING/MOVING TAB

1. Open *33-d3*.

2. Select the entire letter by pressing CTRL + A. Alternate method: Point to the left of any text until a right-pointing arrow displays; then triple-click.

3. Set a left tab at 3".

4. Tab the appropriate lines to format this letter in modified block letter format.

5. Select all text again and drag the tab on the Ruler from 3" to 3.25".

6. Proofread and check; click Next to continue. (*36-drill1*)

DRILL 2   MOVING/CLEARING TABS   agenda

1. In the open document, select the three reports—beginning with Treasurer's Report. Move the tab set at 0.25 to 0.5.

2. Tap ENTER after the Announcements line. Drag the 5.25" and 6.5" tabs off the Horizontal Ruler line. Drag the 0.25" tab to 0.5".

3. Tab and key the following announcements:

   Garden Fair, Thursday, May 26, 2 p.m. at the Community Center

   Next meeting, June 20 at 2 p.m.

4. Proofread and check; click Next to continue. (*36-drill2*)

MODIFYING TABS USING THE TABS DIALOG BOX

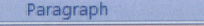

For setting more precise positions not located on the Horizontal Ruler, setting more specific tab types, and clearing all tabs at once, you will need to access the Tabs dialog box.

To set a tab:

<mark>Home/Paragraph Dialog Box Launcher/Tabs</mark>

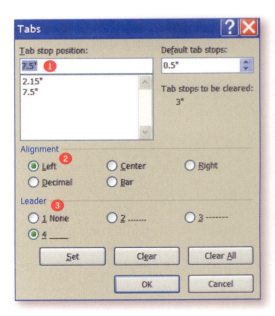

1. Click the Tabs button. The Tabs dialog box displays.

2. In the Tab stop position box, key the desired tab (e.g., 2.15) ❶.

3. Select the alignment of the tab ❷.

4. Select the type of leader tab that is desired ❸.

5. Click Set.

To clear a single tab:

1. From the Tabs dialog box, select the desired tab to be cleared in the Tab stop position box.

2. Click Clear.

To clear all tabs:

From the Tabs dialog box, click Clear All.

DISCOVER

Remove Hyperlink

Insert/Links/Hyperlink

Click the hyperlink and follow the path above. Then click Remove Link.

Shortcut: Right-click and click Remove Hyperlink.

1. Key the following letter in block style with open punctuation. Begin the date at about 2". Remember to remove the extra space in the letter address.

★ 2. Remove the hyperlinks in the third and fourth paragraphs.

3. Check and close. *(33-d3)*

April 4, 201- | Mrs. Rose Shikamuru | 55 Lawrence Street | Topeka, KS 66607-6657 | Dear Mrs. Shikamuru

Thank you for your recent letter asking about employment opportunities with our company. We are happy to inform you that Mr. Edward Ybarra, our recruiting representative, will be on your campus on April 23, 24, 25, and 26 to interview students who are interested in our company.

We suggest that you talk soon with your student placement office, as all appointments with Mr. Ybarra will be made through that office. Please bring with you the application questionnaire the office provides.

Within a few days, we will send you a company brochure with information about our salary, bonus, and retirement plans. You will want to visit our website at www.skylermotors.com to find facts about our company mission and accomplishments as well as learn about the beautiful community in which we are located. We believe a close study of this information will convince you, as it has many others, that our company builds futures as well as small motors.

If there is any way we can help you, please e-mail me at mbragg@skylermotors.com.

Sincerely | Myrtle K. Bragg | Human Services Director | xx

Lesson 36 | *Correspondence Review*

New Commands
- Modifying Tabs Using the Horizontal Ruler
- Modifying Tabs Using the Tabs Dialog Box

Communication

36b

KEYBOARDING PRO DELUXE 2

References/Communication Skills/Spelling

SPELLING

1. Proofread the following signs that were actually posted for the public's eye. Identify the error in each sign.

2. Key the statements correctly.

3. Add at least two examples of incorrect signs you have noticed. If you do not recall any, write two that you think could be confused.

4. Proofread and check; click Next to continue. (*36b*)

   a. Store window sign   Turkeyes' are in the meat department.
   b. Locker room sign   Gentlemens' Locker Room
   c. Door at ballpark   Employees' Only
   d. Store door   Personal Only
   e. Ice cream shop sign   Only cash/checkes excepted

New Commands

36c

KEYBOARDING PRO DELUXE 2

References/Word 2010 Commands/Lesson 36

MODIFYING TABS USING THE HORIZONTAL RULER

Tabs can be added or moved in existing documents. When adding tabs to an existing document, you must first select all portions of the document where the new tab(s) will be applied; then set the additional tab(s). Remember to click the tab selector to select the desired tab and then click on the Ruler to set the tab at the desired location.

Tab selector   Click on Ruler to set tab

To move a tab:

Select all of the text that will be affected and drag the tab to be moved to the new desired location. **Note:** If you do not select all of the text, only the tab that your cursor is on will be moved.

To clear a tab:

Select all of the text that will be affected and drag the tab off the Horizontal Ruler bar.

Lesson 34 | *Block Letter with Envelope*

KEYBOARDING PRO DELUXE 2

WARMUP

Lessons/34a Warmup

LA **ALL LETTERS**

Skill Building

34b Timed Writing

1. Key a 1' timed writing on each paragraph, working for speed.
2. Key one 3' timed writing, working for control.

gwam 3'

Many young people are quite surprised to learn that either	4 | 48
lunch or dinner is included as part of a job interview. Most of	8 | 52
them think of this part of the interview as a friendly gesture from	13 | 56
the organization.	15 | 58
The meal is not provided just to be nice to the person. The	18 | 62
organization expects to use that function to observe the social	22 | 66
skills of the person and to determine if he or she might be effective	27 | 71
doing business in that type of setting.	30 | 73
What does this mean to you if you are preparing for a job	33 | 77
interview? The time spent reading about and learning to use good	38 | 81
social skills pays off not only during the interview but also after	42 | 86
you accept the job.	44 | 87

1' | 1 | 2 | 3 | 4 | 5 | 6 | 7 | 8 | 9 | 10 | 11 | 12 | 13 |
3' | 1 | 2 | 3 | 4 |

Communication

34c letter

SALUTATIONS AND COMPLIMENTARY CLOSINGS

1. In the open document, click in column 3 and key an appropriate salutation for the first letter address found in column 1. Use the comments in column 2 and the information provided below to guide you in the correct choice.
2. Click in column 4 and compose an appropriate complimentary closing.
3. Repeat for the remaining letter addresses.
4. Proofread and check; click Next to continue. (*34c*)

The salutation, or greeting, consists of the individual's personal title (*Mr., Ms.,* or *Mrs.*) or professional title (*Dr., Professor, Senator, Honorable*), and his or her last name. Do not use a first name unless you have a personal relationship. The salutation should agree in number with the addressee. If the letter is addressed to more than one person, the salutation is plural.

	Receiver	**Salutation**
To individuals	Dr. Alexander Gray Dr. and Mrs. Thompson	Dear Dr. Gray Dear Dr. and Mrs. Thompson
To organizations	TMP Electronics, Inc.	Ladies and Gentlemen
Name unknown	Advertising Manager	Dear Advertising Manager

Choose a complimentary closing that reflects the relationship with the receiver. Use *Sincerely* to show a neutral relationship, *Cordially* for a friendly relationship, and *Respectfully* when requesting approval.

35-d1

Modified Block Letter

1. Set a left tab at 3.25".
2. Key the model letter on the previous page in modified block letter format with mixed punctuation.
3. Before keying the enclosure notation, set a left tab at 1". Before keying the copy notation, set a left tab at .5".
4. Add an envelope to the letter. Omit a return address.
5. Proofread and check; click Next to continue. (*35-d1*)

35-d2

Modified Block Letter

1. Key the following letter in modified block letter format with mixed punctuation. Add all required letter parts. Remove the hyperlink in the last paragraph.
2. List the two enclosures in the enclosure notation line.
3. Send a copy of this letter to **Adam Vassel** and **Bethany Corbin**. Alphabetize by last name.
4. Add an envelope to the letter.
5. Check and close. (*35-d2*)

January 14, 201-

Ms. Laura Whittington
35 North Tenth Street
Vicksburg, MS 39183-0035

Please consider this personal invitation to join the National Association of Information Processing Professionals (NAIPP). Membership is offered to the top 25 percent of the graduating class. NAIPP is a nonprofit organization comprised of technical professionals who are striving to stay current in their field. Member benefits include the following:

Career Development Opportunities—Resume preparation services, job search program, 120-day internships in many cities, and access to our online job bulletin board.

Professional Benefits—Industry standard skill testing, discounts on continuing education courses at colleges and universities, recertification programs, publications, medical insurance, financial planning programs, and free international travel services.

Sign on to our website at www.naipp.org to learn about many more benefits. A parking pass and discount coupons for the Multimedia Symposium on February 27 are enclosed.

James Whelan, President
NAIPP Board of Directors

New Commands

34d

ENVELOPES

Envelopes Labels

Create

The Envelopes feature can insert the delivery address automatically if a letter is displayed; postage can even be added if special software is installed. The default is a size 10 envelope (4⅛" by 9½"); other sizes are available by clicking the Options button on the Envelopes tab.

To generate an envelope:

Mailings/Create/Envelopes

1. Select the letter address and then click Envelopes; the mailing address is automatically displayed in the Delivery address box. (To create an envelope without a letter, follow the same steps, but key the address in the Delivery address box.)

2. If you are using business envelopes with a preprinted return address (assume you are), click the Return address Omit box. To include a return address, do not check the Omit box; click in the Return address box and key the return address.

Delivery address box

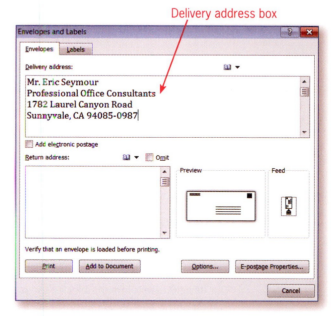

3. Click Print to print the envelope or click Add to Document to add the envelope to the top of the document containing the letter.

DRILL 1 — CREATE ENVELOPE

1. Open *33-d1*.

2. Select the letter address. Create an envelope. Omit the return address.

3. Add the envelope to the document.

4. Proofread and check; click Next to continue. (*34-drill1*)

Note: Your instructor may have you print envelopes on plain paper.

DRILL 2 — CREATE ENVELOPE

1. Go to the Envelopes and Labels dialog box without keying a letter address.

2. Key the following letter address in the Delivery address box.

   Mr. Andrew Callais
   993 North Carpenter Lane
   Shreveport, LA 71106-0993

3. Add the envelope to the document.

4. Proofread and check; click Next to continue. (*34-drill2*)

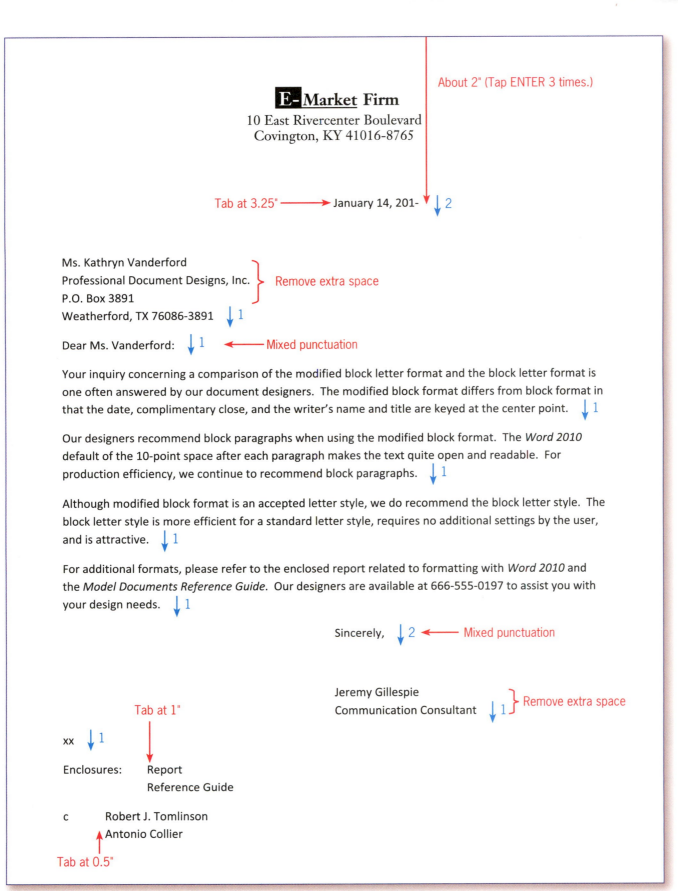

E-Market Firm
10 East Rivercenter Boulevard
Covington, KY 41016-8765

About 2" (Tap ENTER 3 times.)

Tab at 3.25" ⟶ January 14, 201- ↓ 2

Ms. Kathryn Vanderford
Professional Document Designs, Inc. } Remove extra space
P.O. Box 3891
Weatherford, TX 76086-3891 ↓ 1

Dear Ms. Vanderford: ↓ 1 ⟵ Mixed punctuation

Your inquiry concerning a comparison of the modified block letter format and the block letter format is one often answered by our document designers. The modified block format differs from block format in that the date, complimentary close, and the writer's name and title are keyed at the center point. ↓ 1

Our designers recommend block paragraphs when using the modified block format. The *Word 2010* default of the 10-point space after each paragraph makes the text quite open and readable. For production efficiency, we continue to recommend block paragraphs. ↓ 1

Although modified block format is an accepted letter style, we do recommend the block letter style. The block letter style is more efficient for a standard letter style, requires no additional settings by the user, and is attractive. ↓ 1

For additional formats, please refer to the enclosed report related to formatting with *Word 2010* and the *Model Documents Reference Guide*. Our designers are available at 666-555-0197 to assist you with your design needs. ↓ 1

Sincerely, ↓ 2 ⟵ Mixed punctuation

Jeremy Gillespie
Communication Consultant ↓ 1 } Remove extra space

Tab at 1"

xx ↓ 1

Enclosures: Report
                 Reference Guide

c   Robert J. Tomlinson
       Antonio Collier

Tab at 0.5"

Modified Block Letter with Mixed Punctuation

ADDITIONAL LETTER PARTS

In Lesson 33, you learned the standard letter parts. Listed below are optional letter parts. Study the full model illustration on page 126.

Enclosure notation: If an item is included with a letter, key an enclosure notation one blank line below the reference initials. Tap TAB to align the enclosures at 1".

Left tab at 1"

Enclosures: Certificate of Completion
                Receipt

Enclosures: 2

Copy notation: A copy notation (c) indicates that a copy of the document has been sent to the person(s) listed. Key the copy notation one line below the reference initials or enclosure notation (if used). Tap TAB to align the names. If necessary, click Undo Automatic Capitalization after keying the copy notation to lowercase the letter c.

Left tab at C.5"

c   Francine Milam
           Janet Bevill

When two lines are keyed for either the enclosure notation or the copy notation, remove the extra space after the paragraph.

xx

Enclosures: Certificate of Completion
                Receipt

c   Francine Milam
           Janet Bevill

Applications

34-d1

Block Letter/Envelope

1. Key the letter below in block style with open punctuation. Begin the date at about 2". Remember to remove the extra space in the letter address, signature line, and enclosures.

2. Add an envelope to the letter.

3. Proofread and check; click Next to continue. (*34-d1*)

Current date | Mr. Trace L. Brecken | 4487 Ingram Street | Corpus Christi, TX 78409-8907 | Dear Mr. Brecken

We have received the package you sent us in which you returned goods from a recent order you gave us. Your refund check, plus return postage, is enclosed.

We are sorry, of course, that you did not find this merchandise personally satisfactory. It is our goal to please all of our customers, and we are always disappointed if we fail.

Please give us an opportunity to try again. We stand behind our merchandise, and that is our guarantee of good service. Please use the enclosed 20% discount coupon on your next order.

Sincerely | Margret Bredewig, Manager | Customer Service Department | xx | Enclosures: Refund check | Discount coupon

35d

KEYBOARDING PRO DELUXE 2

References/Document Formats/Modified Block Letter

MODIFIED BLOCK LETTER

In the modified block format, the dateline and the closing lines (complimentary close and writer's name and title) begin at the center point of the page. All other guidelines for the block letter style are applied to the modified block letter. Remember to remove the extra spacing between the letter address and other short lines. Review the model modified block letter on the next page.

Dateline:

- Position at about 2".

- Begin at least 0.5" below the letterhead.

- Set a left tab at 3.25". Determine the position of the tab by subtracting the side margin from the center of the paper.

> 4.25" Center of the paper
> –1.00" Margin
> 3.25" Tab setting

Complimentary closing: Begin keying at 3.25".

Writer's name and title: Begin keying at 3.25".

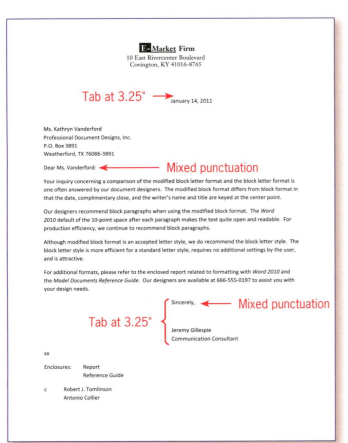

MIXED PUNCTUATION

Although most letters are formatted with open punctuation, some businesses prefer mixed punctuation. To format a letter using mixed punctuation, key a colon after the salutation and a comma after the complimentary close.

34-d2

Rough Draft Letter

1. Key the following letter in block letter style with open punctuation. Begin the date at about 2". Add an appropriate salutation and other missing letter parts.
2. Add a copy notation to **Kristen Sumter** and **Jeremy Portas**.
3. Create an envelope and add it to the letter. Proofread and check; click Next to continue. (*34-d2*)
4. Study the illustration in the *Reference Guide* on folding and inserting letters in an envelope. Fold the letter to insert in the envelope.

Mr. Tan Nguyen

12 Gilbert Ave. *sp*

Baltimore, MD 21218 – *4515*

Thank you for asking about the Tech Training program at Bell college. Whether you are seeking your first job, refreshing your skills or hoping to move to an administrative position, our program will give you the technological skills you need for success.

Many jobs *including non-technical jobs,* also require technological skills. For example, almost every worker must know how to use cell phones and telephones systems with several lines, call forwarding, and voice mail. Fax machines, company intranets, the Internet, and e-mail are part of many jobs.

All 5 occupations that the U.S. Department of Labor predicts will grow fastest from 2011 to 2018 are computer-related. They are computer engineers, computer support specialists, computer system analysts, database administrators, and desktop publishing specialists. Our Tech Training program will prepare you for these high-growth positions.

If you are seeking an administrative position in almost any field, you will need additional technological skills in using accounting, billing, and human resources software. Our *experienced* instructors can help you gain these skills. The enclosed brochure describes the tech training program in full. If I can be of further help please write to me again.

Janie Lopez | Program Coordinator

34-d3

Single Envelope

1. Key a single envelope to the following address. Include your address as the return address.
2. Check and close. (*34-d3*)

Mr. Jacob Gillespie
1783 West Rockhill Road
Bartlett, TN 38133-1783

Lesson 35 | Modified Block Letter Format

New Commands • Tabs

WARMUP

Lessons/35a Warmup

Skill Building

35b Textbook Keying

1. Key each drill, concentrating on using good keying techniques. Tap ENTER twice after each 2-line group.
2. Repeat the drill if time permits.

adjacent reach
1 The people were sad as the poor relish was opened and poured out.
2 Sophia moved west with her new silk dress and poor walking shoes.

direct reach
3 Freddy stated that hurricanes are much greater in number in June.
4 Many juniors decide to work free to add experience to the resume.

balanced hand
5 The eight ducks lay down at the end of right field for cozy naps.
6 Kala is to go to the formal town social with Henry and the girls.

New Commands

35c

KEYBOARDING PRO DELUXE 2

References/Word 2010
Commands/Lesson 35

TABS

Tabs are used to indent paragraphs and to align text vertically. The default tab stops are set at every half-inch position. Take a moment to look at the Horizontal Ruler to identify the small grey lines below each half-inch position. *Hint:* If the Ruler is not displayed, go to View/Show and select Ruler.

Default tab stops

To set a tab:

1. Click the tab selector at the left end of the ruler until it displays the desired tab.
2. Click the Horizontal Ruler where you want to set the tab.

When a new tab stop has been set, all default tabs to the left of the newly set tab are automatically cleared. Therefore, if other tabs are needed, simply choose the desired tab alignment and then click the Horizontal Ruler where the desired tab is to be set.

Tab selector   Left tab at 3.25"

DRILL 1   SET TABS

1. Set a left tab at 3.25". Insert the current date at 3.25" and tap ENTER twice.

2. Set a left tab at 1". Key the following lines and tap ENTER once. Remove the space between the items.

   Enclosures: Promissory Note
   Amortization Schedule

3. Set a left tab at 0.5". Key the following lines. Remove the space between the lines. Undo automatic capitalization in the first line.

   c **Ashley Nobles**
      Ethan Vilella

4. Proofread and check; click Next to continue. (*35-drill1*)

Reference Guide

Capitalize

1. First word of a sentence and of a direct quotation.

   We were tolerating instead of managing diversity. The speaker said, "We must value diversity, not merely recognize it."

2. Names of proper nouns—specific persons, places, or things.

   Common nouns: continent, river, car, street
   Proper nouns: Asia, Mississippi, Buick, State St.

3. Derivatives of proper nouns and geographical names.

   American history   English accent
   German food   Ohio Valley
   Tampa, Florida   Mount Rushmore

4. A personal or professional title when it precedes the name or a title of high distinction without a name.

   Lieutenant Kahn   Mayor Walsh
   Doctor Welby   Mr. Ty Brooks
   Dr. Frank Collins   Miss Tate
   the President of the United States

5. Days of the week, months of the year, holidays, periods of history, and historic events.

   Monday, June 8   Labor Day   Renaissance

6. Specific parts of the country but not compass points that show direction.

   Midwest   the South   northwest of town

7. Family relationships when used with a person's name.

   Aunt Helen   my dad   Uncle John

8. Noun preceding a figure except for common nouns such as *line*, *page*, and *sentence*.

   Unit 1   Section 2   page 2   verse 7   line 2

9. First and main words of side headings, titles of books, and works of art. Do not capitalize words of four or fewer letters that are conjunctions, prepositions, or articles.

   Computers in the News   Raiders of the Lost Ark

10. Names of organizations and specific departments within the writer's organization.

    Girl Scouts   our Sales Department

Number Expression

General guidelines

1. Use **words** for numbers *one* through *ten* unless the numbers are in a category with related larger numbers that are expressed as figures.

   He bought three acres of land. She took two acres. She wrote 12 stories and 2 plays in the last 13 years.

2. Use **words** for approximate numbers or large round numbers that can be expressed as one or two words. Use **numbers** for round numbers in millions or higher with their word modifier.

   We sent out about three hundred invitations. She contributed $3 million dollars.

3. Use **words** for numbers that begin a sentence.

   Six players were cut from the ten-member team.

4. Use **figures** for the larger of two adjacent numbers.

   We shipped six 24-ton engines.

Times and dates

5. Use **words** for numbers that precede o'clock (stated or implied).

   We shall meet from two until five o'clock.

6. Use **figures** for times with *a.m.* or *p.m.* and days when they follow the month.

   Her appointment is for 2:15 p.m. on July 26, 2011.

7. Use **ordinals** for the day when it precedes the month.

   The 10th of October is my anniversary.

Money, percentages, and fractions

8. Use **figures** for money amounts and percentages. Spell out *cents* and *percent* except in statistical copy.

   The 16% discount saved me $145; Bill, 95 cents.

9. Use **words** for fractions unless the fractions appear in combination with whole numbers.

   one-half of her lesson   5 1/2   18 3/4

Addresses

10. Use **words** for street names First through Tenth and **figures** or ordinals for streets above Tenth. Use **figures** for house numbers other than number **one**. (If street name is a number, separate it from house number with a dash.)

    One Lytle Place   Second Ave.   142--53rd St.

Use an apostrophe

1. To make most singular nouns and indefinite pronouns possessive (add **apostrophe** and **s**).

   computer + 's = computer's   Jess + 's = Jess's
   anyone's   one's   somebody's

2. To make a plural noun that does not end in s possessive (add **apostrophe** and **s**).

   women + 's = women's   men + 's = men's
   deer + 's = deer's   children + 's = children's

3. To make a plural noun that ends in s possessive. Add only the **apostrophe**.

   boys + ' = boys'   managers + ' = managers'

4. To make a compound noun possessive or to show joint possession. Add **apostrophe** and **s** to the last part of the hyphenated noun.

   son-in-law's   Rob and Gen's game

5. To form the plural of numbers and letters, add **apostrophe** and **s**. To show omission of letters or figures, add an **apostrophe** in place of the missing items.

   7's   A's   It's   add'l

Use a colon

1. To introduce a listing.

   The candidate's strengths were obvious: experience, community involvement, and forthrightness.

2. To introduce an explanatory statement.

   Then I knew we were in trouble: The item had not been scheduled.

Use a comma

1. After an introductory phrase or dependent clause.

   After much deliberation, the jury reached its decision. If you have good skills, you will find a job.

2. After words or phrases in a series.

   Mike is taking Greek, Latin III, and Chemistry II.

3. To set off nonessential or interrupting elements.

   Troy, the new man in MIS, will install the hard drive. He cannot get to the job, however, until next Friday.

4. To set off the date from the year and the city from the state.

   John, will you please reserve the center in Billings, Montana, for January 10, 2011.

5. To separate two or more parallel adjectives (adjectives could be separated by and instead of a comma).

   The loud, whining guitar could be heard above the rest.

6. Before the conjunction in a compound sentence. The comma may be omitted in a very short sentence.

   You must leave immediately, or you will miss your flight. We tested the software and they loved it.

7. Set off appositives and words of direct address.

   Karen, our team leader, represented us at the conference.
   Paul, have you ordered the DVD-ROM drive?

Use a hyphen

1. To show end-of-line word division.

2. In many compound words—check a dictionary if unsure.

   - Two-word adjectives before a noun:

     two-car family

   - Compound numbers between twenty-one and ninety-nine.

   - Fractions and some proper nouns with prefixes/suffixes.

     two-thirds   ex-Governor   all-American

Use italic or underline

1. With titles of complete literary works.

   College Keyboarding   *Hunt for Red October*

2. To emphasize special words or phrases.

   What does *professional* mean?

Use a semicolon

1. To separate independent clauses in a compound sentence when the conjunction is omitted.

   Please review the information; give me a report by Tuesday.

2. To separate independent clauses when they are joined by conjunctive adverbs (*however, nevertheless, consequently,* etc.).

   The traffic was heavy; consequently, I was late.

3. To separate a series of elements that contain commas.

   The new officers are: Fran Pena, president; Harry Wong, treasurer; and Muriel Williams, secretary.

Use a dash

1. To show an abrupt change of thought.

   Invoice 76A—which is 10 days overdue—is for $670.

2. After a series to indicate a summarizing statement.

   Noisy fuel pump, worn rods, and failing brakes—for all these reasons I'm trading the car.

Use an exclamation point

After emphatic interjections or exclamatory sentences.

Terrific!   Hold it!   You bet!   What a great surprise!

Proofreading Procedures

Proofread documents so that they are free of errors. Error-free documents send the message that you are detail-oriented and a person capable of doing business. Apply these procedures after you key a document.

1. Use Spelling & Grammar to check the document.
2. Proofread the document on screen to be sure that it makes sense. Check for these types of errors:
   - Words, headings, and/or amounts omitted.
   - Extra words or lines not deleted during the editing stage.
   - Incorrect sequence of numbers in a list.
3. Preview the document on screen using the Print Preview feature. Check the vertical placement, presence of headers or footers, page numbers, and overall appearance.
4. Save the document again and print.
5. Check the printed document by comparing it to the source copy (textbook). Check all figures, names, and addresses against the source copy. Check that the document style has been applied consistently throughout.
6. If errors exist on the printed copy, revise the document, save, and print.
7. Verify the corrections and placement of the second printed copy.

Proofreaders' Marks

Mark	Meaning	Mark	Meaning
#	Add horizontal space	/ or *lc*	Lowercase
‖	Align	⌐	Move left
∼	Bold	¬	Move right
Cap or ≡	Capitalize	⌐	Move up
⌒	Close up	⌐	Move down
ℓ	Delete	¶	Paragraph
∧	Insert	*sp*	Spell out
∨ ∨	Insert quotation marks	∼ or *tr*	Transpose
. . . or *stet*	Let it stand; ignore correction	___	Underline or italic

Addressing Procedures

The Envelope feature inserts the delivery address automatically if a letter is displayed. Title case, used in the letter address, is acceptable in the envelope address. An alternative style for envelopes is uppercase with no punctuation.

Business letters are usually mailed in envelopes that have the return address preprinted; return addresses are printed only for personal letters or when letterhead is not available. The default size of *Word* is a size 10 envelope ($4\frac{1}{8}$" by $9\frac{1}{2}$"); other sizes are available using the Options feature.

An address must contain at least three lines; addresses of more than six lines should be avoided. The last line of an address must contain three items of information: (1) the city, (2) the state, and (3) the ZIP Code, preferably a 9-digit code.

Place mailing notations that affect postage (e.g., REGISTERED, CERTIFIED) below the stamp position (about line 1.3"); place other special notations (e.g., CONFIDENTIAL, PERSONAL) below the return address about line 1".

Folding and Inserting Procedures

Large envelopes (No. 10, 9, 7¾)

Step 1   Step 2   Step 3

Step 1: With document face up, fold slightly less than 1/3 of sheet up toward top.

Step 2: Fold down top of sheet to within 1/2" of bottom fold.

Step 3: Insert document into envelope with last crease toward bottom of envelope.

Formatting Decisions

Decisions regarding document formats require consideration of four elements: (1) attractiveness of the format, (2) readability of the format, (3) effective use of space on the page, and (4) efficiency in producing the format. Please note several formatting decisions made in this text regarding defaults in *Word 2010*.

Styles

Word 2010 offers a quick gallery of styles on the Home tab, and a gallery of cover pages. Using these styles results in efficient production of an attractive title page.

Default 1.15 Line Spacing

The default line spacing of 1.15 in *Word 2010* provides readers with a more open and more readable copy.

Space after the Paragraph

The default space after a paragraph in *Word 2010* is 10 point after the paragraph. This automatic spacing saves time and creates an attractive document.

Remove Space after the Paragraph

While enjoying the benefits of efficiency, it is also necessary to the space that is being consumed. For example, extra spacing between the lines of the letter address requires too much space and is not an attractive layout. Note the formats in this book when the extra space is removed by simply clicking on options of the Line Spacing command.

Margins

The default margins for *Word 2010* are 1" top, bottom, left side, and right side. With the side margin default of 1", additional space is needed for the binding of leftbound reports.

Fonts and Document Themes

Microsoft provides true type fonts in *Office 2010* and a number of new document themes that incorporate color and a variety of fonts depending on the theme selected. Color printing has become increasingly popular and more cost effective. Many documents presented in the text are based on the default document theme, *Office*, and use the default heading font, Cambria, and the default body text font, Calibri, 11 point, black text. See the illustration below of the default headings and fonts.

Title (26 pt., Cambria, Color Text 2)

Subtitle (12 pt., Cambria, Italic, Color Accent 1)

Heading 1 (14 pt., Cambria, Bold, Color Accent 1, Darker 25%)

Heading 2 (13 pt., Cambria, Bold, Color Accent 1)

Heading 3 (11 pt., Cambria, Bold, Color Accent 1)

Heading 4 (11 pt., Cambria, Bold, Italic, Color Accent 1)

The default body text is Calibri, 11 pt. Color Automatic (Black).

Default Document Theme: Office:  Office

Letter Parts

Letterhead. Company name and address. May include other data.

Date. Date letter is mailed. Usually in month, day, year order. Military style is an option (day/month/year).

Letter address. Address of the person who will receive the letter. Include personal title (*Mr., Ms., Dr.*), name, professional title, company, and address. Remove the extra spacing in the letter address.

Salutation. Greeting. Corresponds to the first line of the letter address. Usually includes name and courtesy title; use *Ladies and Gentlemen* if letter is addressed to a company name.

Body. Message. Key in default 1.15 line spacing; tap ENTER once between paragraphs.

Complimentary close. Farewell, such as *Sincerely*.

Writer. Name and professional title. If the name and title are keyed on two lines, remove the extra spacing between the lines.

Initials. Identifies person who keyed the document (for example, *tr*). May include identification of writer (*ARB:tri*).

Enclosure. Copy is enclosed with the document. May specify contents. If more than one line is used, align at 1" and remove the extra spacing between the lines.

Copy notation. Indicates that a copy of the letter is being sent to person name. If more than one line is used, align at 0.5" and remove the extra spacing between the lines.

Note: To remove extra spacing between lines, click the down arrow on the Line Spacing command and select Remove Space After Paragraph.

Block Letter (Open Punctuation)

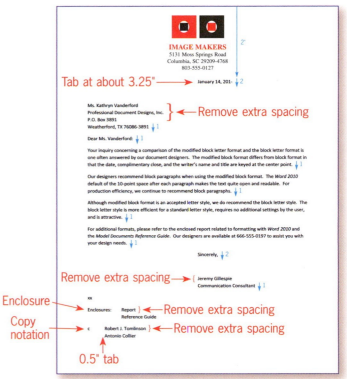

Modified Block Letter (Mixed Punctuation)

Envelope

Academic reports are reports prepared in an academic setting or for scholarly journals.

Margins: Side margins 1" or 1.5" as directed by instructor or manuscript style. Bottom 1".

Report Title: Key at about 2" in upper and lowercase letters, center, and bold.

Spacing: DS paragraphs and indent 0.5". Change spacing after paragraph to 0.

Headings: Bold all side headings.

Page numbers: Number pages at the top right of every page. Include the writer's last name and the page number (LastName   2).

Internal citations: Include footnotes, endnotes, or internal citations to document published material that is quoted or closely paraphrased by the writer.

Footnotes or Endnotes: References cited are often indicated within the text by a superscript number (…story.[1]) and a corresponding footnote or endnote with full information at the bottom of the same page where the reference was cited or at the end of the report.

Bibliography or references: Lists all references in alphabetical order by authors' last names. References may be formatting on the last page of the report if they all fit on the page; it not, list on a separate, numbered page.

Academic Report, Page 1

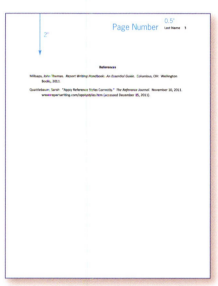

Academic Report Reference Page

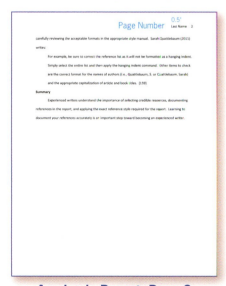

Academic Report, Page 2

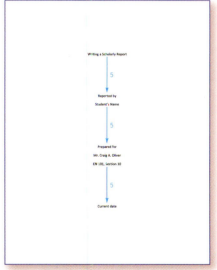

Traditional Title Page

Business Reports

Margins: Tap ENTER three times to begin first page of report and reference page at 2"; default 1" top margin for succeeding pages; default 1" for bottom margin.

Unbound report: Side margins 1"

Leftbound report: Side margins 1.5"

Titles: Title style. Main words capitalized.

Spacing: Default 1.15 line spacing; paragraphs blocked. Tap ENTER once between paragraphs.

Page numbers: Second and subsequent pages are numbered at top right of the page. One blank line follows the page number.

Side headings: Heading 1 style. Main words capitalized.

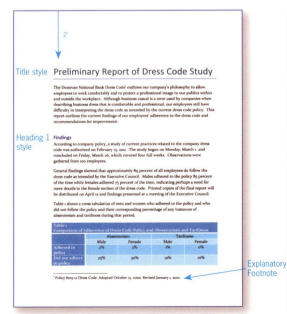

Page 1, Unbound Report

**Page 2, Unbound Report
(Plain Number 3 Style)**

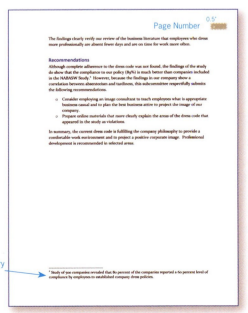

**Page 1, Leftbound Report with
Explanatory Footnote**

**Page 2, Leftbound Report
(Page Number Style)**

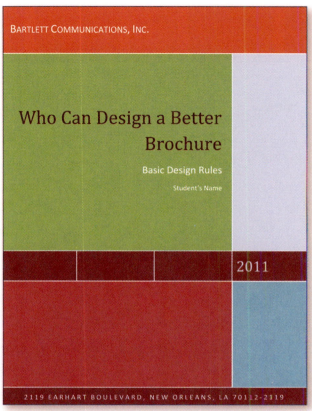

Title Page Using Cover Page Feature

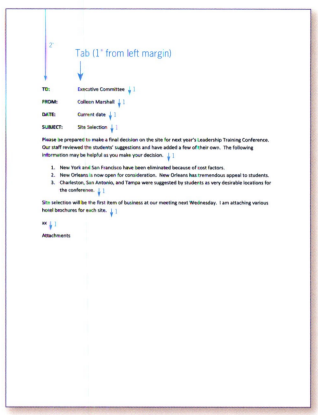

Memo

Personal Business Letter

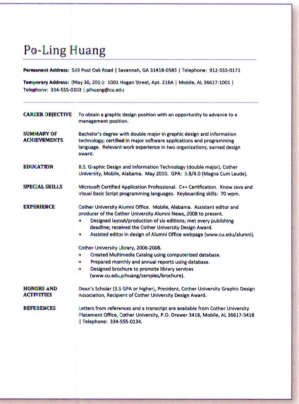

Resume

Command Summary

Lesson	Commands	Lesson	Commands
Module 3 Word 2010 Basics		39	Table Tools Layout: Adjust Column Width, Center Table in Page, Change Cell Size, Text Alignment in Cells, Insert and Delete Columns and Rows, and Merge and Split Cells
26	Format Text: Bold, Italic, Underline, Strikethrough, Subscript, Superscript, Text Effects, Text Highlight Color, Font Color, Font Size, Grow Font, Shrink Font, Change Case, and Clear Formatting	40	Table Tools Design: Apply Shading, Table Borders, Line Style and Weight, and Table Styles
	Mini Toolbar	41	Use Table to Format Resume
	Keyboarding Pro DELUXE 2: Open, Close, New, Print, Exit		Memo with Table
			Letter with Table
27	Start Word	**Module 6 Reports**	
	Save and Save As	43	Styles
	New Folder		Bullets and Numbering
	Close		Cover Page
	Open	44	Custom Margins
	Recent		Go To
	New		Find and Replace
	Print		Document Themes
	Exit	45	Page Numbers
28	Paragraph Formats		Line and Page Breaks
	Alignment: Align Text Left, Center, Align Text Right, Justify		Insert File
	Increase Indent and Decrease Indent	46	Hanging Indent
	Show/Hide		Page Breaks
	Line Spacing		Change Paragraph Spacing
	Quick Access Toolbar, Customize Quick Access Toolbar	47	Footnotes
			Endnotes
29	Scroll Bars		Section Breaks
	View		Show/Hide White Space
	AutoCorrect	**Module 7 Graphics**	
	Spelling and Grammar	49	Insert Shapes
	Thesaurus		Format Shapes
	Translate		Insert Clip Art
	Help		Format Clip Art
30	Clipboard: Cut, Copy, Paste, Format Painter	50	Insert and Format Pictures
	Margins		Picture Tools Format: Size Pictures, Adjust Pictures, and Arrange Pictures
	Orientation		Create, Format, and Modify SmartArt
	Center Page	51	Insert WordArt
Module 4 Memos and Letters			Create Drop Cap
32	Vertical Page Position		Borders and Shading
33	Date and Time		Character Spacing
	Automatic Current Date		Symbols and Special Characters
	Remove Space After Paragraph	52	Equal-Width Columns
34	Envelopes		Balance Columns
35	Tabs		Revise Column Structure
36	Modifying Tabs: Horizontal Ruler/Tabs Dialog Box		Format Banner
Module 5 Tables			Wrap Text Around Graphics
38	Create Tables: Using Table Grid and Insert Table		

AutoCorrect	File/Options/ Proofing/AutoCorrect Options	
Align Text	Home/Paragraph/Click desired alignment (Align Text Left, Center, Align Text Right or Justify)	
Breaks	Page Layout/Page Setup/Breaks	
Bullets and Numbering	Home/Paragraph/Bullets or Numbering	
Center Page	Page Layout/Page Setup/Dialog Box Launcher/ Layout tab/Vertical alignment/Center	
Character Spacing	Home/Font/Dialog Box Launcher/Advanced tab	
Clip Art—Format	Picture Tools/Format	
Clip Art—Insert	Insert/Illustrations/Clip Art	
Close Document	File/Close or Close button at top right of screen	
Columns—Create	Page Layout/Page Setup/Columns	
Cover Page	Insert/Pages/Cover Page	
Cut, Copy, and Paste	Home/Clipboard/Cut, Copy, or Paste	
Date and Time—Insert	Insert/Text/Date & Time	
Document Themes	Page Layout/Themes/Themes	
Drop Cap	Insert/Text/Drop Cap	
Endnotes	References/Footnotes/Insert Endnote	

Envelopes	Mailings/Create/Envelopes	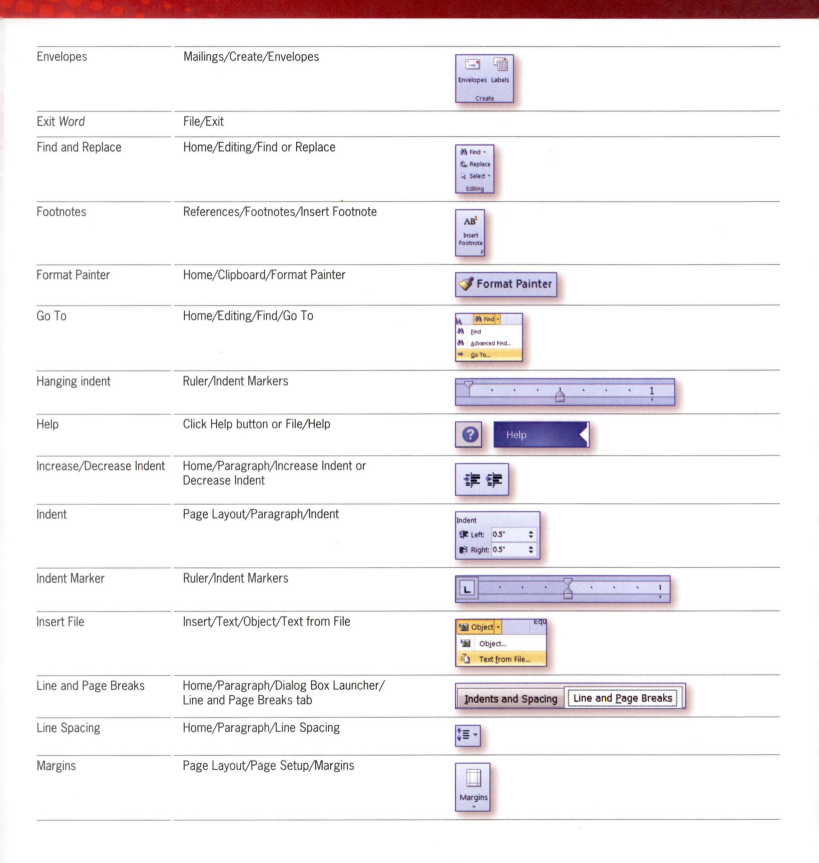
Exit *Word*	File/Exit	
Find and Replace	Home/Editing/Find or Replace	
Footnotes	References/Footnotes/Insert Footnote	
Format Painter	Home/Clipboard/Format Painter	
Go To	Home/Editing/Find/Go To	
Hanging indent	Ruler/Indent Markers	
Help	Click Help button or File/Help	
Increase/Decrease Indent	Home/Paragraph/Increase Indent or Decrease Indent	
Indent	Page Layout/Paragraph/Indent	
Indent Marker	Ruler/Indent Markers	
Insert File	Insert/Text/Object/Text from File	
Line and Page Breaks	Home/Paragraph/Dialog Box Launcher/ Line and Page Breaks tab	
Line Spacing	Home/Paragraph/Line Spacing	
Margins	Page Layout/Page Setup/Margins	

Command	Action	
Mini toolbar	Appears when text is selected	
Open New/Existing Document	File/New or Open; then locate the file	
Orientation	Page Layout/Page Setup/Orientation	
Page Borders	Page Layout/Page Background/Page Borders	
Page Break	Insert/Pages/Page Break	
Page Numbers—Insert	Insert/Header & Footer/Page Number	
Paragraph Borders and Shading	Page Layout/Page Background/ Page Borders/Borders or Shading	
Paste Options button	Home/Clipboard/Paste/Click a Paste Option	
Picture—Format	Drawing Tools/Format	
Picture—Insert	Insert/Illustrations/Picture/Locate and select picture/Insert	
Print	File/Print	
Quick Access Toolbar	Upper-left corner of screen/Use down arrow to customize	
Remove Space After Paragraph	Home/Paragraph/Line and Paragraph Spacing	
Ruler—View	To display: Click View Ruler button Or View/Show/Ruler	

Save and Save As	File/Save or Save As	
Save to Flash Drive (Removable Disk)	File/Save or Save As; click Removable Disk or Flash Drive name and key filename	
Save in New Folder	File/Save or Save As; click New Folder and key name	
Shapes—Add Text to Shapes	Click in the shape and key the text	
Shapes—Format	Drawing Tools/Format	
Shapes—Insert	Insert/Illustrations/Shapes	
Show/Hide	Home/Paragraph/Show/Hide	
Show/Hide White Space	Print Layout View/Position insertion point at top or bottom of page/Click to show or hide white space	
Slider: Zoom in or out	Click Slider/Move left or right to zoom in or out	
SmartArt—Design or Format	SmartArt Tools/Design or Format	
SmartArt–Insert	Insert/Illustrations/SmartArt	
Space After Paragraph	Page Layout/Paragraph/Spacing	
Special Characters	Insert/Symbols/Symbol/More Symbols/Special Characters tab	
Spelling and Grammar	Review/Proofing/Spelling & Grammar	
Status line		

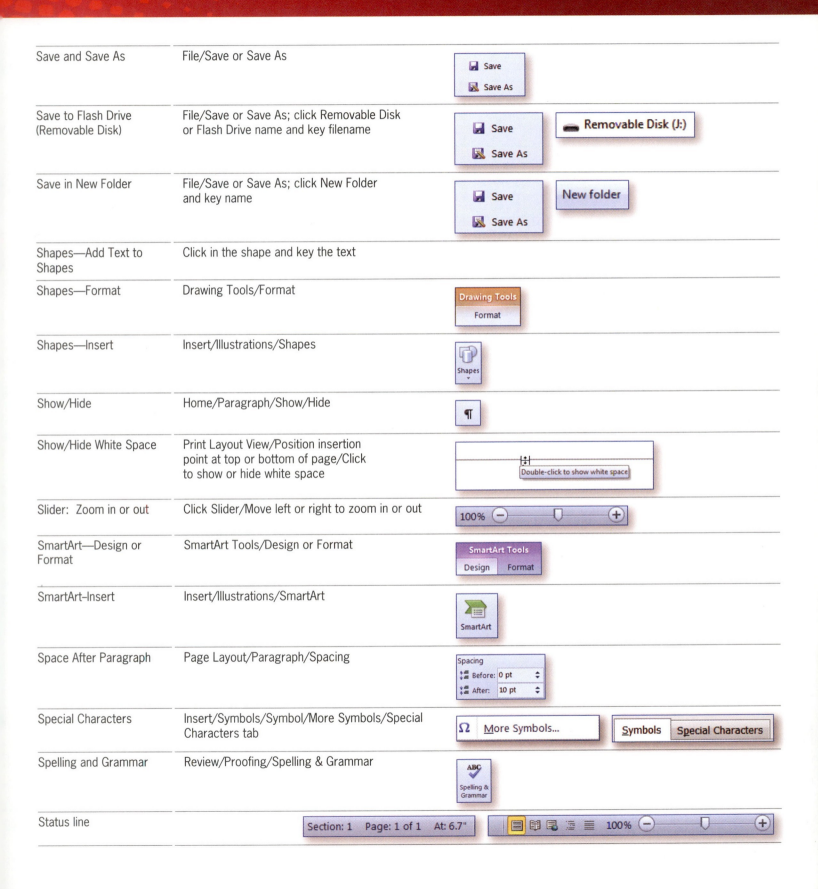

Styles—Change	Home/Styles/Change Styles	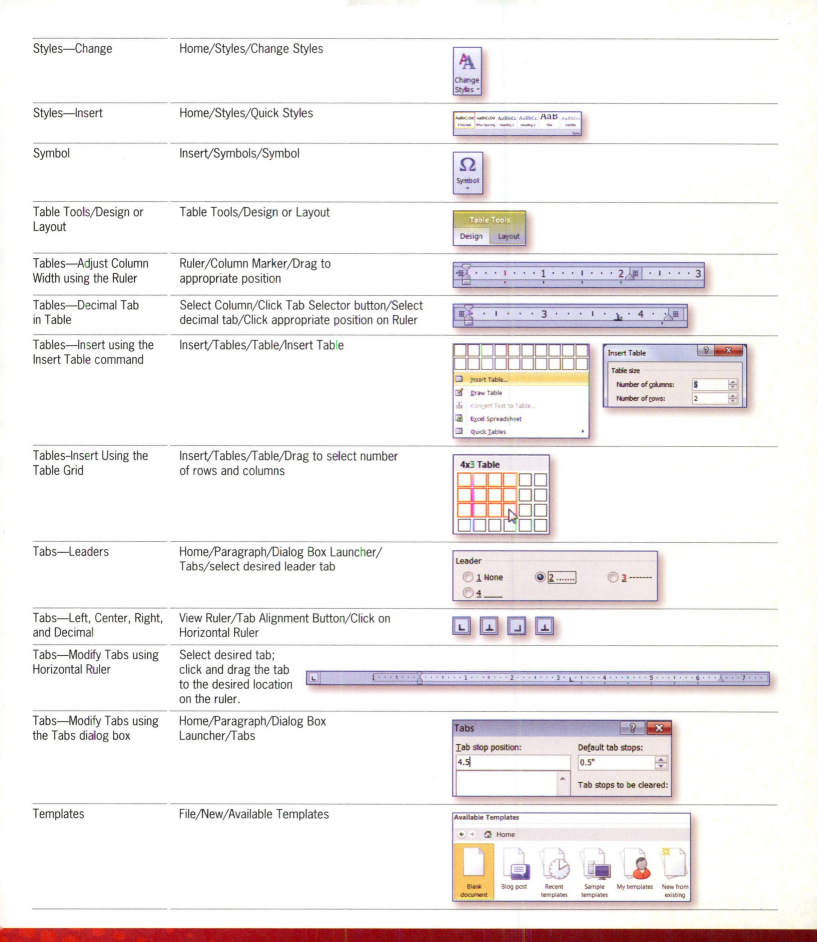
Styles—Insert	Home/Styles/Quick Styles	
Symbol	Insert/Symbols/Symbol	
Table Tools/Design or Layout	Table Tools/Design or Layout	
Tables—Adjust Column Width using the Ruler	Ruler/Column Marker/Drag to appropriate position	
Tables—Decimal Tab in Table	Select Column/Click Tab Selector button/Select decimal tab/Click appropriate position on Ruler	
Tables—Insert using the Insert Table command	Insert/Tables/Table/Insert Table	
Tables–Insert Using the Table Grid	Insert/Tables/Table/Drag to select number of rows and columns	
Tabs—Leaders	Home/Paragraph/Dialog Box Launcher/ Tabs/select desired leader tab	
Tabs—Left, Center, Right, and Decimal	View Ruler/Tab Alignment Button/Click on Horizontal Ruler	
Tabs—Modify Tabs using Horizontal Ruler	Select desired tab; click and drag the tab to the desired location on the ruler.	
Tabs—Modify Tabs using the Tabs dialog box	Home/Paragraph/Dialog Box Launcher/Tabs	
Templates	File/New/Available Templates	

Text Formats —	Home/Font/Click desired text format command (Font, Font Size, Grow Font, Shrink Font, Change Case, Clear Formatting, Bold, Italic, Underline, Strikethrough, Subscript, Superscript, Text Effects, Text Highlight Color, Font Color)	
Thesaurus	Review/Proofing/Thesaurus	
Translate	Review/Language/Translate/Choose Translation Language/Select word to translate and Bilingual Dictionary displays	
Vertical Page Position	To turn on: Right-click status bar/Click Vertical Page Position	
Views—Document	View/Document Views/Select view	
Views—View Buttons	Select view buttons on status bar	
Word Options	File/Options	
Word-Art—Format	Drawing Tools/Format	
WordArt—Insert	Insert/Text/WordArt	
Wrap Text	Select graphic/Format/Arrange/Wrap Text	

Windows 7

WINDOWS DESKTOP

Windows 7 is the newest operating system software released by Microsoft. The operating system software controls the operations of the computer and works with the application software. *Windows* 7 works with *Word* in opening, printing, deleting, and saving files. It also allows you to work with photos and pictures, play music, and access the Internet.

When you turn on your computer, *Windows* displays a login screen followed by a password screen. See your instructor for login and password information. The *Windows* 7 desktop displays after you have logged in.

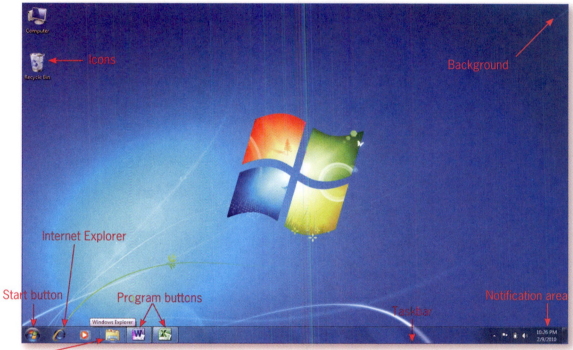

Desktop Elements

The illustration above shows the default *Windows* 7 Aero desktop. The Aero theme has a semitransparent glass design that gives objects a three-dimensional appearance. In order to see the graphical enhancements of the Aero theme, your computer hardware and version of *Windows* 7 must support it.

The components of the *Windows* 7 desktop are described below and on the next page. Read about each component and then point to the object on the desktop to view the ScreenTip that displays identifying each element.

- *Taskbar.* The taskbar displays across the bottom of the window. Use the mouse to point to each of the items in the taskbar. Look for the ScreenTip that displays identifying each element.

- *Start button.* Click the Start button to display the Start menu. The Start menu provides access to programs and files on your computer.

- *Program and file buttons.* Buttons display for the programs that are open or pinned to the taskbar and allow you to switch between them easily. The illustration shows that both the *Word* and *Excel* programs are either open or pinned to the taskbar. The *Internet Explorer* icon is displayed to provide quick access to the Internet. Click the *Windows Explorer* icon to display the libraries that provide easy access to your files.

- *Notification area.* The notification area provides helpful information, such as the date and time and the status of the computer. When you plug in a USB drive, *Windows* displays an icon in the notification area letting you know that the hardware is connected.

- *Icons and Shortcuts.* Icons, small pictures representing certain items, may be displayed on the desktop. The Recycle Bin, which represents a wastepaper basket, displays when Windows is installed. Other icons and shortcuts may be added.

- *Background.* The default background is the *Windows* logo on a blue background. The background can be changed or customized to include a personal picture or a company logo.

START MENU

The Start menu is the launching point for all programs on your computer. Click the Start button to display the Start menu. Your menu may not look exactly like the illustration.

You can access all programs, documents, and other computer resources from the Start menu. The Start menu consists of a left pane and a right pane. The left pane lists the programs that you recently used. Click the All Programs command ❶, located toward the bottom of the left pane, to display a list of all the programs loaded on your computer. The Search programs and files box ❷, located below the All Programs command, will help you quickly find items stored on the computer. Key the search criteria in the search box, then *Windows* 7 will search everything stored on your computer including documents, programs, and pictures and display the search results.

The right pane contains links to files and resources on your computer. The link to *Windows* 7 Help and Support ❸ is located toward the bottom of the right pane. The Shut down button ❹ is located at the bottom of the right pane.

WINDOWS 7 HELP AND SUPPORT

On-screen help is available for the *Windows 7* operating system by clicking the Start button and then clicking Help and Support on the Start menu. If your computer is connected to the Internet, you will be able to access the help files on both the hard drive of your computer and those stored on the Microsoft website.

The fastest way to get help is to key a word or phrase in the Search Help box and tap ENTER; all the Help pages that contain the word or phrase will display. You can also click the Browse Help topics link and then click an item in the contents listing of subject headings that appear. Some subject headings contain Help topics within a subject heading. Click the Help topic to open it, and click the subheading to narrow your search.

DRILL 1	USE WINDOWS 7 HELP

1. Display the *Windows 7* desktop.

2. Click the Start button and select Help and Support.

3. Click Learn about Windows Basics. Then choose Using your mouse. Read the information on the screen.

4. Click in the Search Help box at the top of the window and key **Close Window Button**. Tap ENTER.

5. Click the first option, Working with windows. Read the information.

6. Click the Close button ▬✕▬ in the upper-right corner of the window.

COMPUTER FOLDER

You will be working with auxiliary drives, including CD/DVD and universal serial bus (USB) flash drives. USB flash drives vary in size and shape and can hold gigabytes of information. They are also called thumb drives, memory keys, pen drives, and key drives. The USB drive needs to be plugged into a USB port in order for the computer to read the drive. Your computer may have several USB ports; the Computer folder will show you which port you are using.

To access drives on your computer:

1. Click the Start button to display the Start menu.

2. Click Computer in the right pane to view the drives and storage devices connected to your computer.

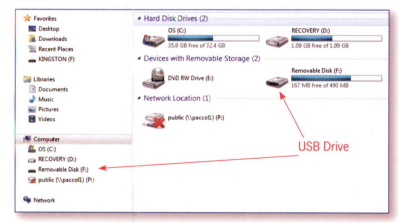

A logical filing system needs to be created so that a file is saved and can be quickly and easily retrieved. This is true for both paper and electronic documents. A paper document is placed in a file folder, which is then placed in a particular file drawer in a designated file cabinet. The computer has several drives in which files can be saved. The drives are labeled with letters followed by a colon (C:, D:, E:). The hard drive, which stores the software, is usually labeled as drive OS (C:). If you are using a USB drive to save your files, the USB drive is often designated as drive E: or F:. Click the Start menu; then click Computer in the right pane to see the drives on your computer.

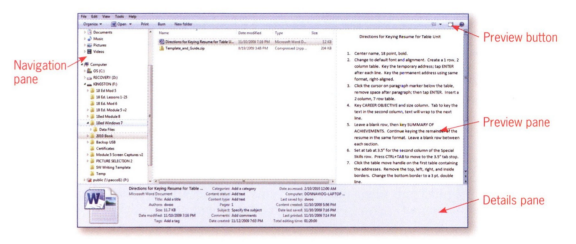

Windows Explorer is divided into sections, called *panes*. The left pane is the Navigation pane, which shows the drives on the computer and the files stored on each drive. If an expand icon ▷ displays to the left of the folder or drive, that means that the folder or drive contains subfolders. You can expand the list to view the subfolders by clicking the ▷ button. Once the list is expanded, the expand icon changes to a collapse icon; clicking the collapse icon ◢ will hide the subfolders.

The Navigation pane displays your computer drives and the hierarchy of the files stored on each drive. This helps you identify your current location in relation to other files on the computer. When you copy, move, or delete files and folders, you can see how it affects the organization of the computer.

The right pane in *Windows Explorer* lists the contents of the folders. Click on a folder in the Navigation pane to display the contents of the folder in the right pane. If you want to get a preview of what a file looks like, you can click the Preview button in the upper right to display an additional pane that will show a preview of your file.

A details pane displays across the bottom of the window. This pane contains information about the file.

WINDOWS 7 LIBRARIES

When you open *Windows Explorer*, it displays four default libraries—Documents, Music, Pictures, and Videos. The libraries display similar types of files regardless of the drive they are stored on. For example, the Pictures Library will list all the pictures stored on the C: drive as well as any that you may have on a USB drive or other external drives that are plugged into the computer. The Documents Library lists all the documents (*Word, Excel, Access*, etc.) that are stored on drives connected to the computer. This differs from the way the Navigation pane displays the folders, in that the Navigation pane displays according to the contents of each drive.

Documents, by default, save in the My Documents folder. To view the My Documents folder, move the mouse over Documents in the left pane; then click the expand icon. Click the expand icon to the left of the My Documents folder to display its contents.

DRILL 2   USE WINDOWS LIBRARIES

1. Click the *Windows Explorer* icon. The libraries display in the right pane.

2. Move the mouse in the left pane over Documents. An expand icon displays to the left of Documents.

3. Click the expand icon to display the My Documents subfolder.

4. Click the My Documents expand icon. Scroll down and click the Pictures expand icon.

5. Click the Public Pictures expand icon to display the Sample Pictures folder.

6. Click the Sample Pictures folder to display the pictures in the right pane.

QUICK ✔

The left pane should show the Public Pictures folder expanded. The pictures should be displayed in the right pane.

FILE ADDRESSES

The address bar, located at the top of the *Windows Explorer* window, shows the location or address of the file. Each level of the file hierarchy is separated with a ▶ symbol; the highest level display at the left of the address bar. The ▶ symbol indicates the next lower level. If this address displays in the address bar:

Computer ▶ E: ▶ CIS 101 ▶ Homework
DRIVE   FOLDER   SUBFOLDER

it tells you that the file resides in a subfolder called Homework, which is located in the CIS 101 folder and saved on the E: drive.

You can move up the hierarchy by clicking on the higher level in the address bar or by clicking on a higher level in the Navigation pane. In the above address, you can display the contents of the CIS 101 folder by clicking on CIS 101 in the address bar. Likewise, you can display the folders on the E drive by clicking the E: in the address bar.

WORK WITH FILES AND FOLDERS

Folders are extremely important in organizing files. You will create and manage folders and the files within them so that you can easily locate them. A folder can store files, or it may contain subfolders that store files. The use of folders and subfolders helps to reduce clutter so that you can find, navigate, and manage your files, folders, and drives with greater speed. File folders can be created using *Windows Explorer* or by accessing the Computer folder on the Start menu.

NAMING FILES

Good file organization begins with giving your folders and files names that are logical and easy to understand. A filename should be meaningful and reflect the contents of the file. Filenames can be up to 255 characters long (but in practice you won't use filenames that long). In addition, the following symbols cannot be used in a filename: \ / : * ? " , . The descriptive name is followed by a period (.), which is used to separate the descriptive name from the file extension. The file extension is three or four letters that follow the period. When renaming a file, do not delete or change file extensions as this may cause problems opening the file.

To create a file folder:

1. In the left pane of *Windows Explorer* or the Computer folder, click the drive that is to contain the new folder.
2. Click the New folder button located below the menu bar. A yellow folder icon displays at the bottom of the right pane with the words *New folder* highlighted.
3. Key the new folder name and tap ENTER.

Rename Files or Folders

Occasionally, you may want to rename a file or folder.

To rename a file or folder:

1. Access *Windows Explorer* and display the contents of your removable storage drive (or the location where you have been instructed to save your document files or folders).
2. Click the file or folder icon to be renamed.
3. Choose Organize on the toolbar.
4. Select Rename.
5. Key the new name and tap ENTER.

TIP

You can also right-click a file or folder icon, and then left-click Rename from the Shortcut menu. Key the new name, and tap ENTER.

Copy, Move, or Delete Files or Folders

Copy a file to leave it in its current location and make a duplicate of it in another location. The new location can be a network location, USB, CD, the desktop, or other storage location. *Cut* a file when you want to move it. This lets you paste the copy to a new location and automatically remove it from the original location. The pasted copy may be placed on the original storage drive or network location or on a separate location. *Delete* a file to remove it from the location where it is stored. If that location is your hard disk, the file is moved to the Recycle Bin. If the location is a USB drive, CD, or another auxiliary drive, the file is permanently removed.

To copy a file or folder, highlight the file or folder icon in the *Explorer* window, choose Organize from the toolbar, and then select Copy. Navigate to the desired location, choose Organize from the toolbar, and select Paste. Moving a file or folder is similar to copying, except after you highlight the file or folder icon in the *Explorer* window, you choose Organize from the toolbar and select Cut. Click on the desired location, choose Organize, and select Paste.

To delete a file or folder, highlight the file icon in the *Explorer* window, choose Organize from the toolbar, and select Delete. A dialog box will display asking you to confirm the deletion. Choose Yes, and the file is deleted. When you delete a file or folder from the hard drive, it is not removed from the storage immediately. It moves to the Recycle Bin and remains there until the Recycle Bin is emptied. This gives you the opportunity to restore the file to its original location if you discover that it should not have been deleted.

Note: You can also access the Cut, Copy, and Delete commands by selecting the filename in *Windows Explorer*; then right-click and choose the desired command from the menu.

To empty the Recycle Bin:

1. Double-click the Recycle Bin icon on the desktop.
2. Click Empty the Recycle Bin from the toolbar.
3. Click Yes to confirm that you want to delete the item(s) permanently.

★ **TIP**

To delete a file or folder permanently from your computer without first sending it to the Recycle Bin, click the filename and press SHIFT + DELETE.

DRILL 3 | **COPY FOLDER TO A DIFFERENT DRIVE** file management

1. Insert your USB drive or other storage device.
2. Access the Computer folder to display the drives on your computer.
3. Click the USB drive icon.
4. Click the File Management folder to select it.
5. Click Organize in the toolbar and select Copy.
6. Click the Documents folder.
7. Click Organize on the toolbar and then select Paste. The folder contents remain on the USB and have also been copied to the new location. You should see the File Management folder on your USB drive.
8. Leave the Computer folder open if you are continuing with Drill 4.

DRILL 4

MOVE/RENAME/DELETE FILES

 file management

1. Open the Computer folder and navigate to the USB drive.

2. Expand the File Management folder.

3. Click once in the Files and Folders pane (right side) to select the file named *john doe*. Click Organize on the toolbar and choose Rename. Key **new john doe** and tap ENTER.

4. In the Files and Folders pane, click the *new john doe* file icon once. Choose Organize from the toolbar, and then select Delete. Confirm the deletion of this file from your storage device.

5. Expand the File Management folder. Highlight the *assignment 1* file icon. Choose Organize from the toolbar, and select Cut. Access the Assignments folder on your storage drive. Choose Organize and then select Paste.

6. Use the procedures just described to move the file *term paper 1* to the Term Papers folder on your storage drive.

7. In the File Management folder, create a new folder and name it **Keyboarding**.

8. Move the file *keyboarding homework* to the Keyboarding folder on your storage drive.

9. Rename the File Management folder **Practice**.

10. Delete the Assignments folder and all its contents.

★ **TIP**

You can also drag and drop files or folders to a new location when you are copying or moving.

WORKING WITH MORE THAN ONE WINDOW

When more than one file is open, an icon displays in the taskbar identifying the software that was used to create each file. Move the mouse over the software icon to display a thumbnail of the file. Click on each icon to display the open file on the screen. If your computer supports the Areo theme, you can use the Windows Flip feature to switch between windows. To perform the Windows Flip, press ALT + TAB. You can also display the windows as a three-dimensional image by holding down the Windows key (⊞) and then pressing the TAB key. As you continue to hold down the WINDOWS + TAB keys, you will see the windows rotating in order. Release the keys when the file you want to work with displays in front.

To display multiple windows side by side, right-click on a blank area of the taskbar and select Show windows side by side from the menu.

DRILL 5

WORKING WITH MULTIPLE WINDOWS

 practice

1. Open *Windows Explorer* and find the file *word document* located in the Practice folder. Double-click the filename to open the file in *Microsoft Word*.

2. Click the *Windows Explorer* icon on the taskbar. Open the file *lighthouse logo* located in the Practice folder.

3. Use Windows Flip to switch between windows.

4. Hold down the WINDOWS + TAB keys to display the files as 3-D images.

5. Display the two windows side by side.

6. Close both files and log off, if necessary.

The *Word* document should display next to the lighthouse logo. It does not matter which displays on the left or right.

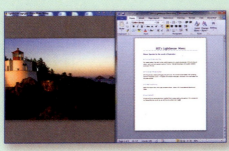

Index